essential

SONGWRITING

essential

SONGWRITING

Everything You Need to Compose,
Perform, and Sell Great Songs

C.J. Watson

D&C
David and Charles

A DAVID & CHARLES BOOK
Amendments copyright © David & Charles Limited 2007
Copyright © 2006 F+W Publications

David & Charles is an F+W Publications Inc. company
4700 East Galbraith Road
Cincinnati, OH 45236

First published in the UK in 2007
First published in the USA as *Essential: Songwriting* by Adams Media in 2006

A catalogue record for this book is available from the British Library.

ISBN-13: 978-0-7153-2731-9
ISBN-10: 0-7153-2731-3

Printed in Singapore by KHL
for David & Charles
Brunel House, Newton Abbot, Devon

Visit our website at www.davidandcharles.co.uk

David & Charles books are available from all good bookshops; alternatively you
can contact our Orderline on 0870 9908222 or write to us at FREEPOST EX2
110, D&C Direct, Newton Abbot, TQ12 4ZZ (no stamp required UK only); US
customers call 800-289-0963 and Canadian customers call 800-840-5220.

Essential: Songwriting is intended as a reference book only. While author and
publisher have made every attempt to offer accurate and reliable information to
the best of their knowledge and belief, it is presented without any guarantee.
The author and publisher therefore disclaim any liability incurred in connection
with the information contained in this book.

Contents

Acknowledgments

This book wouldn't have happened without Eric Hall (Editorius Rex), Julie Gutin, Carol Smith (interviews), Al DeTrolio (research), Elizabeth Marlowe (legal), Candy Paull, Jacky Sach, Scott Gunter, Don Wayne, Steve Fox, Jimmy Payne, and Bart Herbison.

Top Ten Characteristics
of a Great Song

1. An idea that has an original element; if it's been done, it's not great.

2. A common thread, musical and/or lyrical, that people react to on a gut level; if they don't relate, it's not great.

3. A killer hook. You need one line that sums it all up and concentrates the message and the emotion into one climactic moment; if there's no payoff, it's not great.

4. A well-reinforced hook. The story should create a tension that peaks or resolves itself in the hook. Also, people have to be able to remember what your song is called when they go to the record store to buy it or call up the radio station to request it; if there's no build and release, it's not great.

5. A great story, even if it's a simple emotional snapshot, needs to have something interesting to draw the listener in; if it's boring, it's not great.

6. Real feelings; if it's fake, it's not great.

7. Well-crafted lyrics that get the story and the feelings across in a clear, accessible manner; if nobody understands it, it's not great.

8. A catchy melody, one that is not only memorable, but also has prosody to complement the lyrics; if it doesn't "sing," it's not great.

9. A performance and production that captures the essence of the song; even "Stardust" sounds like a bad song when some tone-deaf tequila chugger tries it at karaoke night; if it sounds awful, it can't be great.

10. A great publisher or plugger to get it cut; a song isn't great until it's out there doing its job, touching lives, and earning money.

Introduction

▶ SONGS ARE A MULTIBILLION-DOLLAR BUSINESS. Unfortunately, only one in every several thousand songwriters will see any significant income for his or her efforts. Why is this? In part, it may be because there are several million songwriters on the planet competing for a couple thousand jobs. Lack of true desire also plays a role; songwriting is a great hobby, but few want to put in the amount of effort it requires to become a professional tunesmith.

Of those who have the talent and desire, the main reason for failure is lack of information. Songwriting as a profession encompasses multiple disciplines and areas of expertise. It's not enough to know how to write a great song; you must also be able to shape and develop the song to reach the intended audience and make sure that it gets properly demo-ed, heard by the right people, marketed, cut, produced, and marketed some more. Competition within the songwriting world is friendly but fierce, and a weakness or lack of knowledge in just one area has been the downfall of countless "good" writers.

Yes, there are people whose job it is to record, produce, and do all the other things that help a song on its way to the top, but they don't always know what they're doing and they're not always on your side. The best way to ensure success is to know how these jobs are supposed to be done and how the result can affect your song. With that thought in mind, this book is designed to be a comprehensive overview of as many elements of songwriting and the songwriting business as possible.

You may notice that, at times, this book moves frequently between the "nuts and bolts," technical part of songwriting (known as the "craft" side) and the ephemeral, spiritual, sometimes mystical "art" side, with occasional forays into the nasty, convoluted maze of the business side. This is because being a professional songwriter means living in a state of flux between these three worlds. In order to find a balance between expressing yourself as an artist and reaching other people with your art, or between making good music and making a good living, it's necessary to learn to juggle these seemingly disparate elements.

While some music history is included in the text of this book, it is by no stretch of the imagination a comprehensive history of music. It's merely a basic overview with special attention given to events, inventions, people, and things that affected songwriting and songwriters. For the serious or advanced writer, further study of music history may prove helpful in understanding the ways in which market trends develop and what kinds of songs are more immune to market change than others. To put it another way, knowing where songwriting has been will help you figure out why it is where it is—and where it's going to go next.

If you simply can't wait to start writing a song, feel free to skip the historical bits and come back to them later. There won't be a quiz, you won't flunk or get detention. Of course, you might miss the part about the secret handshake, developed by sixteenth-century songwriting monks, the one that can *still* get you into a publisher's office today, but you didn't want to know that anyway, did you? Seriously, while no book can give you a guaranteed recipe for success in this or any other business, this book can give you the ingredients for that recipe and teach you how to combine them in a way that, hopefully, will have listeners asking for seconds. So, are you hungry yet? Well, then let's get cookin'.

Chapter 1

History of Songwriting

To understand the history of songwriting, it's necessary to understand the history of music. Factors like cultural change and the invention of new instruments or technologies influence the way in which songs are written. And when a new kind of music comes around, composers or songwriters are mostly responsible, so the history of music *is* the history of songwriting.

Origins of Music

No one knows where the first song came from. Did Neolithic men sing around the first campfire? Did Adam croon a tune to Eve in the Garden of Eden? We may never know. Many believe that rhythmic chanting with percussive accompaniment from weapons may have been the first form of song. Prehistoric Rap? Well, sort of. . . .

At some point, ancient people discovered that blowing across a hollow tube, like an animal bone or reed, produced a pleasing tone and that a string under tension (like a hunting bow) sounded pretty cool. An archeological dig in the Ukraine has uncovered 20,000-year-old flutes made of wooly mammoth bones—you won't find *those* at your local music store!

Roman writers, Cicero among them, were perhaps the first to leave a written record of the use of music for purely entertainment or artistic purposes. Ancient Roman manuscripts give us the first known descriptions of events where music was made simply for the sake of making music, separate from educational, work-related, or ceremonial uses.

The First Song, the First Songwriter

Most songs and songwriters of the pre-Renaissance world have been forever obscured by time. Even after the development of musical notation, songs were mostly passed down through the generations by rote and modified to suit the changing times without reference or regard to the original songwriter.

We have no idea where the first song originated, who wrote it, what instrument was used, if there were lyrics, or what culture fostered its conception. What we *can* be sure of is that whoever wrote the first song probably had no idea of the importance of what was occurring, only that something wonderful was happening. That feeling is common to all songwriters, whether they are professionals or amateurs, rock stars, classical composers, Music Row hit-makers, or any other lucky soul who writes songs for fun or profit.

Tribal Music

Some of the first music happened in a tribal setting. Early tribes used drums and horns to communicate across long distances. Setting music in the context of a language and encouraging the development of a musical vocabulary probably hastened music development. Ancient people also used music for religious rites, festivals, and as a form of oral history.

Work songs, Chanties, Marching Songs

One of the earliest song forms, worksongs, were sung to relieve the boredom of repetitive labor and provided a rhythm to keep a work crew in synch. One of the basic forms of the work song is the field holler, sung by farmers, serfs, and slaves while tending crops.

FACT

Work songs were usually written by the ordinary working people who used them. From these humble beginnings have sprung a wealth of past and present musical forms; work songs influenced most later musical forms. Today, historians find work songs a rich resource of information about the people and times from which they originate.

Another work song variant, the "chanty" was a favorite of sailors. To prepare a large vessel to sail, steer, drop anchor for the night, or make the ship safe from an oncoming storm requires large crews of people to work together in precise coordination. The sea chanty provided a rhythm to keep things running smoothly at times when a mistake could mean disaster for the whole crew.

You could say that marching songs are a subset of work songs. By establishing a beat, marching songs helped people walk as an organized group, thus moving more quickly and at a uniform speed. By setting a pace, marching songs allowed for precise timing in processions and parades. One of the most famous marching songs is undoubtedly *Yankee Doodle*, sung by American soldiers during the Revolutionary War. In many cultures, work songs are still a part of everyday life.

Ancient Music

Knowledge on ancient music is fragmentary and information on ancient songwriters even more so. Some ideas, like the invention of string instruments, seem to have developed independently in different parts of the world. Others, like Pythagoras's discovery of the mathematical relationships of musical intervals, appear to have originated in one place and spread from there. The picture we have of musical history is still changing, as new information is unearthed and old information re-examined in light of new facts and theories. The little we do know suggests that creators of music in the ancient world were often highly regarded, at times revered, and in some cases, possibly even paid.

Perhaps the earliest known polyphonic music (music with different notes being played at the same time) is recorded on a set of clay tablets found in Syria and believed to be almost 3,500 years old. The tablets contain lyrics and music for a song, including accompaniment, vocal melody and harmony, and even tuning instructions for the harp. Until the discovery of these tablets, most historians believed that all music composed before about A.D. 400 was monophonic (having only one melodic line with no harmony or counterpoint).

In the World of the Ancient Greeks

One of first cultures known to have developed a system of music theory is that of ancient Greece. Somewhere around 500 B.C., the Greeks started classifying musical scales and modes. Many of the musical modes used today (Lydian, Dorian, Aeolian, and so on) take their names from the Greek system.

Greek notation was not developed enough to communicate ideas precisely, so we don't really know what their music sounded like. But we do know that the Greeks were possibly the first people to study the effects of music on the mood. Ancient Greek writings discuss how different modes and instruments affect the mental and emotional state of the listener. Impressed with this seemingly magical power, they believed music capable of moving physical objects and influencing the will of the gods.

In Hebrew Culture

Music also played an important part in ancient Hebrew culture. The book of Psalms in the Old Testament contains song lyrics, and some versions have notation marks that are similar to those later used to illustrate melodies in Christian Plainchants.

Since only copies exist, it's not known if the notation found in these books is part of the original manuscript. We do know, however, that the Hebrew King David was a well-regarded musician and songwriter.

FACT

According to Norse mythology, the sounding of a magical horn will signal the world-ending battle of Ragnarok (something like Armageddon). In the Judeo-Christian story of Jericho, a trumpet blast toppled the city walls. Among the mythological deities directly linked to certain instruments are Apollo (kithara), Hermes (lyre), Dionysus (aulos), and Pan (pipes).

Evensongs and Plainsongs

Greek and Hebrew music were the main influences in the development of Plainsong, from which most modern music is descended. Also called plainchant, chant, or Gregorian chant, plainsong originated as a form of worship music in the early Christian Church.

Plainsongs were monophonic, which led historians to mistakenly believe that all music predating the plainsong must have been as well. For several centuries, plainsong was the only formally composed music in most of the Western world.

Bards and Minstrels

We're not sure exactly when singers, musicians, and songwriters started getting paid (or how many seconds after that first "paid gig" they quit their day jobs). Myths and historical accounts from thousands of years ago mention musicians performing for the pleasure of kings and gods alike. In various times and places, they have been called bards, minstrels, jongleurs, minnesingers, and a lot of other things. Some traveled; others found steady employment and stayed in one place. In many ways, the modern singer-songwriter has more in common with these performers than with the composers of formal court music who were the better-known songwriters of early times.

Middle Ages and the Renaissance

During the Middle Ages in Europe, it became fashionable among royalty to have groups of musicians play to entertain the court of lesser nobles, visiting dignitaries, and various hangers-on surrounding them. As these performing ensembles became larger and more organized, the nobility began retaining conductors and composers, the same person often filling both roles, to direct the players and provide new music. The fortunate outcome of this was that songwriters were subsidized to devote significant amounts of time to composing.

The lute, a guitar-like instrument, was one of the most popular instruments of the Renaissance period. Too quiet for large-ensemble music, the lute was often used by singers to accompany themselves in cozier settings, often to impress members of the opposite sex. Evidently, some things never change.

The Age of Rebirth

More musical changes would come with the dawn of the Renaissance, a word that means "rebirth", because of the revival of older artistic styles in music as well as in other arts and sciences, which had been largely stagnant since the fall of the Roman Empire.

The Renaissance began in Italy in the fourteenth century and lasted until the sixteenth century. This period brought about an enormous shift in the fortunes of composers. As independence and creativity gained value, composers ventured beyond the restrictive forms of medieval music and developed more individual styles. The introduction of the moveable-type printing press to Europe was another big change. Printed sheet music became relatively inexpensive and could be shipped to more places than a composer could possibly hope to travel. Taken together, these changes meant that, for the first time, it was possible for composers of music to become world renowned in their own lifetimes.

Ballet

Ballet was a Renaissance innovation that combined court music with dance. Balthasar de Beaujoyeulx staged what many consider to be the first ballet in 1581. Originally, ballet used sung or spoken interludes to fill in the plot. As the art form developed, composers used music and dance to tell the story and stopped using lyrics. The earliest ballet dancers were French nobility, including King Louis XIV.

Opera

Another musical innovation of the Renaissance, the opera originated in Italy in the late-sixteenth century. The 1597 opera *Dafne*, by Italian composer Jacopo Peri, is considered by many to have been the first true opera. While no copies of *Dafne* exist, two complete operas from the year 1600—one of them by Peri—have survived intact. Part of opera's importance is that it put emphasis on individual singers.

Baroque Music

The Baroque Age followed the Renaissance, lasting until the mid-eighteenth century. This period was witness to large-scale changes in the way music was written and performed.

The patrons who financed Baroque composers considered music a disposable commodity to be listened to and thrown away, usually without being published. Of more than a thousand surviving pieces by Bach, only eight were published in his lifetime.

Previously, music was mostly used to complement lyrics. But Baroque composers found a different approach—they used music directly, to express emotions and tell stories. While Renaissance music stressed polyphony (several competing melodic lines), Baroque music used homophony (chords played under a single melody). Moreover, musicians of the Baroque period were expected to embellish and improvise upon the written parts.

Classical and Romantic Music

The late-eighteenth century witnessed the birth of both the classical and Romantic forms of music. Many composers of the time wrote in both styles, or even combined them. During the Classico-Romantic period, the way in which lyrics were written changed significantly. Up to this point, most lyrics for formal music were written in Italian, French, or Latin. Composers in this period began writing in their native languages, which helped increase the popularity of Classico-Romantic music in England and Germany.

Symphonic Music

The symphony, perhaps the best known of all classical forms, had its immediate predecessor in the work of Johann Stamitz, a mid-eighteenth-century German composer. Basing his work on a form of Baroque opera music called "sinfonia," Stamitz added dynamic and tempo changes, chords played in unison (as opposed to counterpoint), and notation that was explicitly written out instead of being somewhat open to interpretation. Stamitz's work also contributed greatly to the development of the sonata and string quartet forms.

Many classical and Romantic composers got melodic ideas from folk songs and work songs. Improvised music and the study of other people's compositions were also areas of inspiration. Ideas for subject matter often came from religion, myth, or literature.

The Birth of American Music

As the Industrial Revolution gave rise to a larger and more affluent middle class, music became an affordable hobby for more people. Music was becoming a business, and a brisk trade evolved in the selling of printed sheet music for popular songs. This meant that the writers of those songs could actually *make money* for licensing their work to be reproduced.

Some of the first known contracts between a songwriter and a publisher were for the songs of Stephen Foster, the most popular songwriter of his time and arguably the first modern songwriter. Foster received only a tiny fraction of what his songs would have earned today, and he was often the victim of piracy by publishers and performers alike. At age thirty-seven, he died with the clothes on his back and thirty-eight cents in his pocket.

But the American music industry continued to change and grow. The twentieth century saw the most dramatic changes in songwriting of any period in history. The invention of affordable devices that could record, duplicate, broadcast, and amplify music completely changed the industry, as the average person gained more access to music.

FACT

The first national anthem of record is that of Great Britain, "God save the King" (or "Queen"), which dates back to at least 1745. The idea quickly spread throughout Europe and the rest of the world. These days, nearly every country, state, province and, in some cases, city, has an official song.

Birth of the Blues

The blues was born of work songs that combined African rhythms and melodies with those of American and European folk and sacred music. The blues first appeared around the time of the Civil War and became a recognized style around 1900. Early blues writers seldom received credit for their work—publishers, record executives, and recording artists often falsely claimed authorship of songs. The importance of the blues in American music is undeniable; it influenced the development of rock, R&B, country, jazz, and many other forms of music.

Ragtime and Jazz

Ragtime, a mixture of classical music with blues and folk idioms, emerged just before the turn of the twentieth century with the works of composer Scott Joplin. Ragtime's bouncy rhythms and fresh, new sound quickly made it popular in the United States and abroad. "Tin Pan Alley" songwriters soon picked up on the popularity of the new form; Irving Berlin's "Alexander's Ragtime Band" became a huge hit and propelled ragtime to the forefront of popular music.

An offshoot of ragtime, jazz took a sophisticated compositional approach and applied it to other emerging forms of American music. This allowed jazz to capture the ear of the upscale crowd, while its raucous, improvisational nature also made it a natural fit for the wild times of prohibition. Though it was later overshadowed by more mainstream styles, jazz evolved with the times and has retained a steady share of the music market over the years and into the new millennium.

Expansion of Music Media

Sound recording was invented in the early 1800s. Unfortunately, no one could figure out how to play back recorded sounds until Thomas Edison invented the phonograph over seventy years later. Even after Edison's marvelous discovery, it took the innovations of many more inventors to find affordable ways to copy recorded material. As recordings became more affordable, the market grew and the record business became a moneymaker for publishers and songwriters.

The Radio

The next important step was the invention of the radio, and it's still debated as to who invented it. Certainly, Tesla, Marconi, De Forest, and several others all deserve some credit. The first commercial radio stations began to spring up around 1920. Within a few years, radio had become an important part of the music business, presenting the opportunity for a single performance of a song, live or recorded, to reach millions of people.

Radio also spawned a new and profitable genre, the jingle, a short song that advertises a product. Jingles are good for songwriters in two ways: Songwriters make money for writing jingles, and revenues from airing jingles and other commercial advertisements are the main source of income for radio stations, which pay performance royalties collected by songwriters.

FACT

Affordable audio copies and broadcast performances suddenly made songwriting a potentially profitable profession. The Copyright Act of 1909 gave songwriters a whopping "two cents per copy" royalty to split with publishers. Soon thereafter, the American Society of Authors, Composers, and Publishers (ASCAP) began collecting performance royalties from radio stations and live venues.

Movie Soundtracks

With the advent of movies, a new chapter in music history was born. Early movies didn't have sound, but some theatre owners began having organists or pianists play along with movies to spice things up. Eventually, moviemakers started commissioning scores to be written for their films, recording them onto disks, which were then played on a separate machine. When movies with sound were invented, some songwriters made whole careers of writing songs and soundtracks for movies.

The Hit Parade Era

In the mid-twentieth century, a popular form of radio show emerged, the "hit parade" or "countdown." These shows were novel in that they played the most popular songs and didn't stick to any genre. In addition to pop singers of the day, you might hear a swing band, a country-western singer, or any number of other styles of music. This musical cross-pollination was a preview of things to come.

Swing and Big Band

Swing music, also called "big band," was a union of jazz and blues traditions with compositional elements, ensemble size, and instrumentation more akin to symphonic music than to the small ensembles and loose arrangements of the former genres. In the swing orchestra, bandleaders worked out elaborate structures and precise arrangements for melody-driven tunes.

Country Music

Country music has roots in the songs of Appalachia, which were based on the folk traditions of Scotland, Ireland, and England. Cowboy songs (a form of work song), post-Reformation hymns, and the blues were also seminal influences in the development of country music. Originally called "old time music" or "hillbilly music," country evolved rapidly when WSM-AM 650 began broadcasting the Grand Ole Opry in 1925. Today, Nashville, Tennessee, the hub city of country music, is home to the largest songwriting community on earth.

Doo-Wop and R&B

In the late 1930s, vocal groups began exploring an a cappella–based style of music that became known as "doo-wop." Originally an urban form of street music, doo-wop used voices to fill roles usually reserved for instruments. After years as a marginal genre, doo-wop exploded in 1953, then merged with rock and roll. Doo-wop contributed greatly to the development of rock-n-roll and R&B and even influenced country music via vocal groups like the Jordanaires.

What is R&B?
R&B is short for rhythm and blues and this music style is just what it sounds like, a combination of blues with rhythms from other styles of music.

Jump (a form of blues), boogie-woogie, jazz, swing, and gospel were the initial influences leading up to the birth of R&B in the late 1940s. R&B gave rise to soul music and was a big influence on rock-n-roll and other styles.

Rock and Roll

Rock and roll music, also called rock-n-roll or simply rock, was possibly the most important musical influence, both artistically and commercially, of the late-twentieth century. Rock's roots in blues, doo-wop, country, R&B, jazz, pop, and folk gave it a broad appeal, and the ability of rock-n-roll songwriters to draw influence from nearly all other styles made Rock adaptable to virtually any musical taste. Rock not only influenced other art forms, but also language, fashion, and politics. Rock and roll firmly established the young working class as the major music market. A number of different technological and social factors combined to make this possible:

- Commercial advertising revenues made radio a profitable industry, causing thousands of radio stations to spring up all over the world.
- The growing reach and affordability of radio made it possible for almost anyone to have access to musical broadcasts on a regular basis.
- Inexpensive record players allowed working class people to have recorded copies of their favorite songs and performing artists right in the home.
- Electric instruments and public address systems let rock musicians perform live concerts for huge audiences.
- The small size and relative portability of a rock band made it much more potentially profitable than a symphony or swing band.
- Rock's demographic, the post-WWII "baby boom" generation, was the largest potential market in history.

Rock broke down racial barriers—the racial diversity of rock's performers and its roots in country and blues made it accessible, yet new and exciting, to teens of different backgrounds. This brought together different markets and gave rock-n-roll an even bigger slice of the demographic pie.

Rock-n-Roll Family Tree

Rock-n-roll may be the most diverse musical genre the world has ever known. A partial list of some of the better-known rock-n-roll sub-genres would include the following:

- Rockabilly
- Surf music
- Folk rock
- Blues rock
- Psychedelic rock
- Pop rock
- Acid rock
- Country rock
- Hard rock
- Southern rock
- Soft rock
- Swamp rock
- AOR
- Prog-rock
- Jazz rock
- Symphonic rock
- Heavy metal
- Punk

- New wave
- Speed metal
- Jam
- Thrash
- Death metal
- Hardcore
- Grunge
- Alternative
- Melodicore
- Emo
- Goth rock
- Nu-Metal
- Rap metal
- Indie rock
- College rock
- Arena rock
- Roots rock

FACT

Just as composers of the eighteenth and nineteenth centuries often wrote both classical and Romantic music, late-twentieth-century songwriters often wrote more than one style. A professional songwriter of the rock-n-roll age could have hits in the rock, soul, and country genres, sometimes with the same song.

And this is just to name a few! Rock-n-roll has also influenced nearly every other form of music. As radio markets became less segregated, record labels began using professional songwriters to write radio-friendly hits for R&B acts. These songwriters infused R&B with rock-n-roll's teen appeal and pop's approach to songcraft. The result was called soul. Many regions had their own brands of soul. One in particular, Detroit's "Motown" style, became so popular that it is considered by many to be a separate genre. Soul music was instrumental in the rise of funk, disco, hip-hop, rap, modern R&B, and nu-soul, and influenced rock, pop, and country.

Songwriting Empires

A few times in recent history, enough talented songwriters have gathered in one place and had sufficient success with a particular set of techniques to become famous as a group or school of writing. Here's a quick look at the "big three": Tin Pan Alley, Brill Building, and Music Row.

Tin Pan Alley

In the late 1800s, the Tin Pan Alley area of New York City became the songwriting capital of the world, and it held on to that status for nearly seventy years. In the early days, publishing revenues mostly came from the sale of sheet music. Traveling performers exposed the public to new songs and people then bought sheet music for the song, so they could play it at home. Most of these touring acts were based in or booked out of New York, making it the perfect place to start a publishing business. Eventually, royalties from record sales outstripped those from sheet music, and the more record-oriented Brill Building empire eclipsed the sales from Tin Pan Alley.

Brill Building

The second New York City based songwriting empire centered around the Brill Building on Broadway. As record sales outstripped sheet music and rock and soul became the dominant genres, a new generation of songwriters rose to prominence. By applying Tin Pan Alley's successful strategies to newer forms of music, Brill Building songwriters ruled the charts for many years.

Music Row

Music Row became a major player in the music business in the 1950s. RCA Records, in need of a regional office in the Southeast, set up shop near downtown Nashville. Already in the process of becoming a music hub, Nashville quickly blossomed as other record companies and music publishers from both coasts followed suit. Today, Music Row is home to hundreds of publishers and record labels, the nearby Berry Hill district boasts hundreds of recording studios, and Nashville is home to more than 20,000 songwriters by some estimates.

The Music of Today

Today, music draws influences from an increasingly diverse genre pool. Songwriters such as David Byrne and Paul Simon combine pop with African and world music. Nashville songwriters like Anthony Smith and Chris Wallin add elements of modern rock, funk, and alt (alternative) to country, while continuing to develop its rich storytelling tradition. Rock keeps changing, fusing with newer styles like hip-hop and recombining with its own sub-genres. The critics who said rock-n-roll wouldn't last have grown silent, while their successors say the same about rap and hip-hop.

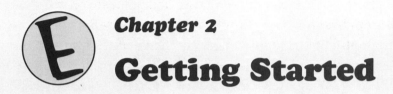

Chapter 2

Getting Started

Many people think that songwriters just sit down and *voilà!*—a beautiful, perfect song magically starts pouring out within seconds. While this does happen sometimes, it's the exception and not the rule. It takes hard work and some preparation, and there are lots of tricks and tools used by professionals that can help get you off on the right track.

The Most Important Points

What do you need to know in order to write a song? Many people, including professional musicians and singers, feel that there are a number of important things they absolutely *must* know even before they can begin. The problem is, they have no idea what these things *are* or where they can be learned. But in reality, the only crucial element you absolutely must know before you can write your first song is, simply, that you can do it.

So the good news is, you don't need any special knowledge to write a song. You can go and write one now. But it doesn't mean it's going to be a *great* song. With a few extremely rare exceptions, songwriters usually spend several years learning how to make a good song great.

The First Rule of Songwriting

The one unchangeable rule of songwriting is this: All rules are subject to change. If you walk into a publisher's office with a song that's a surefire hit for 1987, you will probably walk out with a disappointed look on your face three and a half minutes later. But that could change next year: Eighties revival music could be the next big thing. Of course, it could be Bolivian folk music or polka—you just never know. A few years ago, salsa and Christian contemporary formats weren't even listed on major music charts. These days, you can make serious money writing for these genres.

FACT

A study of the hits of the last few decades will reveal patterns useful to the enterprising songwriter. Demographic trends and world events may influence the subject, style, groove, and other factors of popular songs at a given time. Be aware of these factors when you write or make selections from your catalog for pitching.

Most rules of songwriting have changed at one time or another. Think lyrics are a must for a pop hit? Look up Floyd Cramer's "Last Date" or Vangelis's "Chariots of Fire"—the melody may be the most crucial element. On the other hand, most rap songs replace melodies (as they are recognizable to people brought up listening to the twelve-note scale, used in most popular music) with music samples. The point is this: Pay attention to what's going on *right now* and try to figure out what will happen next. Trends in popular music can change quickly and dramatically. It's not unheard of for a publisher to fire half of the songwriting staff after a market change. The rules change from time to time. If you know them, you'll be prepared for the changes and able to deal with them.

It's Up to You

You need to pay attention to the trends if your goal is to make money and earn artistic kudos with songwriting. Otherwise, you can write songs any way you please and no one can stop you. There are, however, guidelines that can help make your songs enjoyable to more people, yourself included.

The Songwriter's Toolbox

The first order of business for a beginning songwriter is to assemble the tools needed for the job. Which tools you need is your decision. The important thing is to assemble them in one place and keep them there when not in use. Otherwise, you may find that your significant other has written a grocery list on your new song or your dog has made a chew toy of your "lucky lyric" pen.

ALERT!

Different toolboxes and sets of tools suit different needs: You might not need reference books for a half-hour lunch break at work but you might want a couple of favorites for a long trip. Use a desk drawer or a toolbox at home, a satchel at work, and a backpack to take to the park.

A desk drawer makes a good songwriter's toolbox. Backpacks, briefcases, tackle boxes, and book bags have the advantage of being portable. Some writers even pack the bare essentials into their guitar cases. Things you might want in your toolbox are simple—something with which to write (like a pen), something on which to write (like paper), some reference books, and a small, portable recording device.

Pens, Pencils, Chalkboards, and Word Processors

Some songwriters can write on anything or with anything. As rumor has it, a popular Rolling Stones song was written with an eyeliner pencil on the back of a hotel room ironing board. Other songwriters are particular, even superstitious, about what they use. The most popular combination is probably a #2 pencil and a yellow legal pad. Some songwriters prefer ballpoint pens and unlined paper. Others prefer a mechanical pencil, a gum eraser, and "eleven-line" paper (which allows for the melody to be written above the chords in standard notation and the bottom line for lyrics). Some even use large chalkboards. Many songwriters find that a computer gives them the option of creating multiple versions of a song, cutting and pasting words or lines to different places, and having "ready to print" lyric sheets when finished. Try all of these options and find the one that works best for you.

You'll need to acquire serious verbal skills to compete with pro writers. How? By doing what *they* do! Many pro songwriters do crossword puzzles and play games that focus on vocabulary and language skills. Reading is a double whammy: It helps develop language skills and is also a great source for song ideas.

Whatever you use, make at least two copies as soon as the song is finished. Put one in your toolbox and put one in a safe place other than your home. Why? If your computer crashes, your house burns down, or your significant other goes insane and starts merrily feeding your songs into the shredder, you'll be very glad that you have extra copies stashed away.

You'll also want a recording device to capture the melody and groove of your song. Portable recorders with built-in microphones are available in a number of recording formats and are perfect for your toolbox. Make sure the recorder you buy has either removable media (something you can take out of the machine and copy, like a cassette) or a "line out" so you can transfer the recording to another medium.

Reference Books Every Songwriter Should Own

Somewhere, you'll want to keep a stash of books to be used as part of the songwriting process, and you may want paperback versions if you travel frequently. Here's a list to get you started:

- A new dictionary that includes slang terms
- A rhyming dictionary
- A thesaurus and/or synonym finder
- At least one book of popular quotations
- A set of encyclopedias
- Recent newspapers or periodicals (for song ideas)

Also consider reference books that list homonyms, homophones, antonyms, phrases, sayings, quotes, puns, and so forth—anything that helps you think about words. Many of these reference materials can be found in software or online versions.

A Good Writing Environment

Where do you plan to write? Finding a place, or several, where you feel comfortable can boost the creative process. Many songwriters talk of hot spots, places, or rooms where they write well. Some successful writers have getaways in the mountains or by the ocean where the peace and beauty of the surroundings brings out their best work. Some find they do their best writing in the car, on a walk, in a coffee shop, or on a city bus. Find out what works for you.

Caffeine and Snacks

Coffee and other caffeinated beverages can be a songwriter's best friend—or worst enemy. Caffeine makes the brain work *faster,* effectively raising the IQ. Some songwriters find that ideas flow more quickly after a cup of coffee, tea, or other caffeinated beverage. However, some people get jittery and have trouble focusing. If you have high blood pressure, heart problems, or any condition that might be affected by caffeine, drinking coffee may not be the best thing for you.

Blood sugar also affects the mental process. What you eat before and during a writing session can influence your creativity and productivity. A low blood sugar level, as you might have after a heavy meal or several hours without eating, can make you feel tired. An especially high blood sugar level, like you get after your fifth candy bar in a session, can make you feel euphoric, fidgety, or even sick. Many songwriters are compulsive snackers who work with a pen in one hand and a bowl of goodies in the other. Healthy snacks like fruit will boost the blood sugar without the burnout factor of processed sugars. Veggie snacks like carrot sticks and celery are perfect for the songwriter who just needs something to chew on—and you'll still be able to fit into your tux when the Grammy people call.

Consider the Lighting

Light level and type can affect the mood. Many songwriters find that diffuse light—like that from lamps, track lights, and upward-facing halogen lamp—is better than bright overhead lights.

As a general rule, try not to use older-style fluorescent lights in your writing environment. Many writers report a drop in creativity when working in settings with this kind of light. Regular light bulbs, halogen bulbs, and the new "natural" fluorescent lamps all get high marks from most writers.

ALERT!

Finding out what conditions put you in a creative mood can be a big boost to your songwriting, but don't let concern over these factors keep you from writing when things aren't perfect. Sometimes you'll write a great song when conditions are absolutely wrong for it.

You will also want to find out what time of day works for you. Some people are at their creative best in the morning, some in the afternoon or evening, and some late at night. You may find that you have one peak time, that you have two or three spots that work well, or that any time is a good time to write a song.

The Pitter Patter of Little Feet

Here's a common complaint: "I had this great idea going and I was just starting to write it down when . . ." A ringing phone, a knock at the door, a barking dog, or a child attempting to set the dog on fire can all interrupt the creative process.

What can you do about it? Usually, a little planning and some help from a spouse, family member, or friend can prevent these problems before they occur. If there's someone in the house who can screen calls, watch the kids, and answer the door, ask them, beg them, *pay* them if you have to. It'll make your writing time much more productive.

Otherwise, turn off the phone, put a note on the door, put the dog out, and send the kids to the movies before you get started. Distractions don't just cost the time they take up, but also the time spent regaining focus and finding the groove to get the feel of that song again. If you can't remove distractions, do your best to ignore them. Getting mad will only make things worse. Interruptions happen. Sometimes you just have to grin and bear it.

Where Do I Begin?

For many songwriters, getting started is the absolute hardest part of writing a song. Some write down the first thing they think of, knowing that they can rewrite or make changes later. Others use techniques like brainstorming or word palettes to get the creative juices flowing. Many start with music and worry about lyrics once a "mood" has been established through composing. In short, there are many ways to begin a song. It doesn't matter where you start. What matters is that you *do*.

Starting with an Idea

Starting with an idea is good if there's something going on that inspires or moves you. Current news, neighborhood gossip, books, movies, and relationships provide a never-ending source of new ideas for songs. Learn to look and listen with a writer's eyes and ears; you'll be amazed how much there is to write about.

Where do great song ideas originate?
Just about anywhere. Jackson Browne's hit song "Doctor My Eyes," in which the eyes are a metaphor for the self, was inspired out of a real eye problem Browne was having at the time. Use what you have, be creative and open minded with it, and see what happens.

Starting with Words

The different meanings of a word, the rhythm of a particular phrase, the sound of a rhyme, or the flow of a sentence can all be good jumping-off points to a writing session. Don't be afraid to "doodle" or play with words as if they are building blocks or puzzle pieces. If you find a word or phrase you like, look for other words and phrases that go with it and find rhymes for all of them. Try twisting or reversing the meanings of things.

Countless songs have been written with a common phrase as the starting point. Even if you start with an idea, you may want to look for a short phrase that sums it up nicely. A short phrase used as a central theme is called a "hook." Many professionals prefer to start with a hook and build a song around it.

Starting with Music

A bit of melody, a chord sequence, or an instrumental lick have inspired countless songs. Some writers prefer to create within the confines of the imagination, whereas others may hum, whistle, or plink around on the guitar or piano, looking for the little something special that gets things moving.

Many songs use identical chord patterns but, if the words and melodies are different, people don't usually notice. A good exercise is to take the chords from a favorite song and write your own song over them.

Try putting familiar chord patterns to a different groove or arranging the chords in a different order.

For those with home studios, an increasingly common way of coming up with musical grooves is to sample an existing recording, build a loop from a small piece of it, add tracks around the loop, then delete the loop, change the tempo or other elements of the new tracks, and see what it sounds like.

Starting with a Beat or Groove

Starting with a beat or groove is a great way to write a specific kind of song. Left to their own devices, most songwriters write ballads (slow songs) nine out of ten times. Publishers and recording artists, however, are usually looking for fast songs (up-tempos). See a problem? A good way to overcome the natural inclination toward ballads is to write to a beat or groove from a drum machine.

Realistic Expectations

Don't expect your first song, or your first hundred, to be hits. It took years or decades for most successful songwriters to start writing cuttable songs. More importantly, it usually takes writing lots of bad, mediocre, and good songs to work up to writing great ones. Give yourself time to grow artistically without the pressure of coming up with a hit song right away. Remember, writing a bad song is more fun than not writing at all. Even hit writers come up with a stinker every now and then. As you learn and develop, your percentages will improve.

There's no preset number of songs you must write before you get a winner. Some songwriters write thousands of songs and never get a break. On the other hand, Laura Nyro and Holly Tashian each had cuts (commercial recordings) with their very first songs. For most songwriters, it takes a few dozen songs to get to the first good one and several times more to start writing cuttable songs. Just remember, if you go see a publisher with three pretty good songs, you probably won't be invited back. Give yourself time to learn what you're doing. After your hundredth song, you will probably look back at that first masterpiece and laugh, cringe, or both.

Many songwriters start with simple songs for and about their children, families, and friends. This has the advantages of being a topic you know well and a built-in market—who wouldn't be tickled to have a song written for them? As with all writing, start with what you know, keep it real, and worry about the fine points later. Above all, have fun and enjoy the opportunity to express yourself in music.

Writing a lot of songs can help you become a good songwriter but it's also important to give each song a good effort instead of hurriedly writing a million songs. It's the habits you develop and lessons you learn in writing many songs, not the sheer number of songs you write, that makes the difference.

When Is a Song Finished?

That's your decision to make, and of course you may change your mind later. Market changes and artistic growth can lead you to change a song that was finished years ago. A better question may be, "Is it complete?" Or, "Is it done, for now?" Here's a handy checklist to help you determine if a song is complete:

- Does it say everything it needs to say?
- Is everything said in the best possible way?
- Does each line say something?
- Is there any unnecessary information that doesn't add to the song?
- Are the tenses and viewpoints consistent and easy to follow?
- Are the parts of the story in the best possible order?
- Do the words of one section connect well to the next?
- Do the melodic elements flow and connect from section to section?
- Is the song's length approximately where you want it to be?
- Does it *feel* done?

Editing and Rewrites

A change often made in completed songs is "editing down" for time. Radio stations want songs in the two-and-a-half to four-minute range. While it's true that many songs outside these parameters have become hits, it's much easier to get airplay for a three-minute song than for a five-minute song. Solutions may be as simple as speeding up the song a little (be careful not to push the tempo to a pace that rushes the singer or ruins the feel of the song) or removing or shortening intro sections and instrumental passages that aren't adding anything important to the song. Cutting out entire verses is an option; advanced options include condensing two verses into one, cutting a verse in half, or using an implied chorus—a severely shortened chorus (usually just the first line) that leads directly to the bridge or to a fadeout.

FACT

A song may sometimes end up being rewritten after it's a hit. Charlie Daniels' rewrite of "Uneasy Rider" provided him with another hit years after his original version.

You may also find it prudent, from time to time, to edit for content and market. Certain words, topics, situations, or portrayals of racial or ethnic stereotypes may hinder a song's chances of being recorded or played. It's not only what you say, but how you say it: A rap song can get plenty of airplay with a line like, "Keep gettin' hassled by the cops. Fo' a playa, the heat never stops." But a line that goes: "Metro cop Nazis got me in stitches. / Get me an Uzi they'll be dead sons of . . ." probably won't get played. Neither of these examples would be appropriate language for a country song—they just aren't consistent with this particular genre. Keep in mind the intended audience for a song and adjust the language to get the story or message across to that group.

As you become a better writer, go back over your catalog of songs every so often to fix problems that you couldn't solve (or didn't see) back in your newbie days. You may also want to regularly check the language, situations, and musical content of your songs to see if they are relevant in the current market.

Chapter 3

Thinking Like a Songwriter

Language and music skills play key roles in songwriting success, but the most important, overlooked, and easily learned talent is the ability to think like a writer. Ideas are the most valuable commodity in any form of art. If you learn how to originate and develop ideas, the battle is half won.

Where Good Ideas Come From

Where do songwriters get their ideas? The answer is simple; hit songwriters get ideas from their own lives and the world around them. Perhaps the most important thing you can do in the idea department is to simply be aware of the world around and within you from a writer's perspective. At first, this will be a very self-conscious process. Listening to your own conversations and examining your life for ideas will make the world seem a little unreal until you get used to it.

FACT

Sometimes a great idea will get stuck in a song that even a rewrite can't save. There's no rule that says you can't recycle your own ideas. Some songwriters will write several versions of the same song idea to get to the right one.

Always have a recording device, pen, and paper within easy reach to save a catchy phrase, a situation, or a concept. Taken to excess, this can drive your friends and family nuts, so try not to be too obvious. With practice, this process becomes second nature and you'll no longer be conscious of it—your writer's alarm will simply alert you when a song idea presents itself.

Priming the Pump

Ideas may come to you in the strangest settings or in the most mundane of circumstances. Some writers have special places or activities that seem to get them going. For Tony Lane, Neil Young, and many others, driving around does the trick. Van Dyke Parks and Carlos Santana get ideas in the shower. Among the places, situations, and activities that have proved fertile ground for songwriters are vacuuming, golfing, "doodling" on an instrument, walking, contact juggling, sitting in a Laundromat, and grocery shopping. On the opposite end of the spectrum, some writers require quiet or solitude to get the ideas flowing. For them, sitting in the woods, engaging in prayer or meditation, watching the ocean, and lying in bed before falling asleep are the situations that work best.

Once you get rolling, you'll come up with plenty of ideas. The key is to organize your ideas and not lose track of them. Write down your ideas as soon as you get them and keep them in a file in your toolbox for when you need them.

Write What You Know

When you write a song, you create a world for the listener. To draw someone into that world, it must be convincing enough to make him or her want to believe that it's real. This is why many writers peak in their forties and fifties; people who have lived more can convincingly portray more situations.

This doesn't mean that young writers can't write great songs. If a young writer is careful to write from an authentic perspective, he or she may have advantages in some areas. A song about first love from a fifty-year-old writer will tend to be a fond remembrance, while a song on the same topic from a fifteen-year-old may more accurately capture the urgency, magic, and uncertainty of the situation.

Writing what you know can mean different things, depending on your level of songwriting experience. For the beginner, it means sticking with places, situations, and emotions you have actually encountered. As your writing progresses, you'll be more able to extrapolate and project your own feelings and experiences into semi-fictional or even totally made-up situations.

Brainstorming

Brainstorming is the act of defining what you will write. This includes idea and hook generation, picking topics, experimenting with melodies and grooves, playing with rhyme schemes and meter configurations, and anything else that gets you going. Brainstorming should be part of your scheduled activities. If something clicks, stop brainstorming and start songwriting.

Some suggestions to get your brainstorming session started:

• Make a list of your favorite songs. Look at each song and ask yourself where the idea might have originated.
• Think about current events in your life and in the world. Is there anything you feel moved to write about today?
• Are there any new musical trends with which you've had the desire to experiment?

Watch and listen to the world around you. A song idea could come from something as simple as watching pigeons in the park or seeing two people on a first date. Don't spy or pry, just be alert and let your imagination provide the rest.

Be aware of your own thoughts and feelings, too. Most things we feel are similar to feelings that all people have had at one time or another. Finding a way to relate these common feelings is one of the most important parts of a songwriters work.

Ideas from Literature, Movies, and TV

Characters, places, and situations from history, myth, and mass media can provide an almost limitless source of song ideas. Here are some examples:

• **Plays:** *Romeo and Juliet* resulted in "Fire" by Bruce Springsteen
• **Books:** *Tom Sawyer* inspired Rush's "Tom Sawyer"
• **Movies:** *Key Largo* led to "Key Largo" by Bertie Higgins
• **Cartoons:** Roadrunner served as inspiration to "Wylie Coyote" by Great Divide
• **TV:** Late-night Westerns inspired "Roy Rogers" by Sir Elton John
• **Mythology:** "God of Thunder" by Kiss is a song about Zeus
• **Historic places:** "Waterloo" by Abba refers to the scene of the Battle of Waterloo

Sometimes these characters or places will provide the hook or central idea; other times, they can help set a scene or provide a rich metaphor to spice up your song. Mentioning a well-known character or place can often conjure up whole volumes in the listener's imagination.

FACT

Even couch-potato time can be productive for a songwriter. When you're watching a movie or TV show, look for characters and situations to use in songs. Current movies and TV shows are also good places to find the latest catch phrases.

Relationship Mining

When writing about a relationship or emotional situation, reflect on similar experiences you've had from several different perspectives: Compare how you feel about the situation now and how you felt at the time. Imagine how the other people involved might have felt. This will give you a choice of viewpoints and degrees of objectivity or subjectivity, and also the benefit of being able to write a heartbreak song without having to get your heart broken all over again.

The next best thing to writing from personal experience is writing from situations you have seen or heard about. In some cases, writing from direct observation may have a small advantage over writing from personal experience: You may see some situations more objectively. Writing from observation can also give you the opportunity to better understand situations, places, and feelings you might not be personally familiar with, like giving birth or fighting in a war. This is where friends and family come in. Be a good listener when Uncle Ralph wants to tell war stories. Ask questions, too: How did it feel? What did you eat? Who were your friends? Turn on your "write brain" and see through someone else's eyes.

A Few Words of Warning

You must be very careful about how you use the information gained by observing and talking to others. Uncle Ralph may not want the world to know he got a tattoo of a hyena on his left calf while on shore leave in Singapore. Likewise, your best buddy, Sue, might not want her secret childhood crush on your brother made public knowledge. One option is to change things around a bit: "My cousin (uncle) Charlie (Ralph) got a tattoo of a dingo (hyena) while on vacation (shore leave) in Sydney (Singapore)." Another way is to simply ask permission. It might make Uncle Ralph's day to be in a song. Either way, from a legal standpoint, it's better to change the names of anyone involved.

Developing Your Idea

Let's say you've got a great new hook idea, "Love in the Jungle." You're not sure if the song is about love in an actual jungle or if the jungle is a metaphor for the city or the modern world. In fact, other than the hook and a vague idea of the groove, you have no idea what the song is about. What do you do now? Define the set of possibilities at your command and pick the ones that you think will work best for the song. Don't worry, you can always change your mind later and go back as many steps as you want.

Word Palettes

Making a word palette can help get the ideas flowing. Look at the idea: What's happening? Love! Where? The jungle! Hmmm . . . What are some words that would paint a picture of where the song (at least metaphorically) takes place?

- Make a list of words that mean jungle: Congo, Amazon, veldt, forest.
- Make a list of things and creatures you might find in the jungle: vine, tiger, lion, gazelle, trees, monkeys, parrots, toucans, waterfall, blue lagoon, elephant, snake, idol, coconut, man-eating plants, drums, volcano.
- Make a list of sensations and conditions in the jungle: hot, humid, steamy, rainy, dark, the taste of coconut milk, the smell of tropical flowers, the sound of drums in the distance.

- List words that describe feelings about the jungle: scary, wild, savage, primitive, dangerous, sexy.
- List the characters, real or fictional, you might encounter in the jungle: witch doctor, Tarzan and Jane, native tribes, headhunters, Amazons, Dr. Livingstone, King Kong.

For more options, get a thesaurus or synonym finder and look up the words you have written down.

Now you have a list of images, feelings, sensations, and characters to add life and dimension to your song. Even if the jungle in the song ends up being a metaphor, these things, properly applied, can help to connect the rest of the song to the central idea. Look for phrases based on the words in your palette: monkey around, king of the jungle, swingin' through the trees. Find wordplays based on your palette selections: only toucan (two can) play, I'm not lion (lying). You can worry about what's too silly or too obscure when you actually start putting the song together. For now, just let your mind roam freely and see what happens.

Remember, the purpose of brainstorming exercises is to inspire you. Don't worry about finishing an exercise before you start actually writing the song. If the feeling hits you, go for it. That word palette isn't going to disappear while you're working, but your inspired idea might if you don't strike while the iron is hot.

Rhyme Palettes

Instead of having a primary focus on meaning or context, the rhyme palette's main purpose is to find words that rhyme with the song's hook or with things on the word palette. You can search for rhymes in one of three ways:

1. With the aid of a rhyming dictionary or similar software application.
2. By mentally running through the alphabet (at, bat, cat, fat, gat, hat, and so forth).
3. By trying really hard to think of rhymes.

Options one and two may yield more rhymes. Option three is better for finding near rhymes that are a bit more interesting and also helps warm up the creative part of the brain.

ALERT!

Keep an eye on where your story is headed. Setting out with a clear vision of what you want to say gives you a much better chance of ending up with a song that bears up to repeated listening. Many songwriters do a brief outline, detailing the points they hope to cover, before beginning the lyric.

Getting the Story Across

Remember that the listeners only know what you tell them. You can do this through direct information: "I was a poor kid from a small town in Louisiana." Or you can provide information to be inferred: "I grew up on the wrong side of the tracks in a one-horse Bayou town." Melody, groove, and chord structure can also convey emotional information (minor keys tend to sound sad) or help set the scene (a chord pattern of C/Am/F/G over a medium cha-cha groove conjures up the 1950s).

Continuity

Make sure that your storyline is clear and easy to follow. If you lose a listener's attention, you probably won't get it back. The events in your song should all connect to the hook in some way. Verses don't have to relate to each other, but elements within a verse should all work together and support the central theme. The event flow of your songs doesn't have to be linear. Flashbacks and foreshadowing can be useful, but make sure the storyline can be followed and to develop the idea or plot at a pace that doesn't bore the listener.

It's easy to fool yourself into thinking your storyline is clear. After all, *you* know the whole story. Test your story's clarity by getting outside feedback. Remember not to tell your test audience what the song is about before you play it. Instead, ask questions about the story after you play the song for someone.

Songs in the Moment

Tense, to put it simply, is when the action in your song takes place. Tense can be a tricky business, especially when changing tense within a song. This must be done carefully, so as not to confuse the listener. Be careful and consistent.

Present tense is often best for love songs, statement-of-self songs, heartbreak songs, or any song in which you want to express vivid emotions. The power of these songs is in helping the listener become the singer in his or her imagination. Since the listener is hearing the song now, putting the song's action in the present can help someone connect more directly to your song.

If you need to give past information in a present tense song, do it from a view point that sets up a contrast to the present: If you say, "I was lonely," you are frontloading to be able to say, "Now, I'm not." If you say, "I've been working up my nerve," it's easy to move ahead to, "Now the moment is here." To flash back from a present moment, a phrase like, "I remember the time" gives a connection from the *now* to the *then*.

Telling a Story

For story songs, past tense usually works well. As long as the story events are told in the order in which they happened, it's relatively easy to jump forward along a timeline to different story scenes without confusing the listener. Usually, a story song will use the first verse to set the time and the scene, the second verse to give more specific or more personal information, and the chorus to reinforce the central theme or idea. The bridge or third verse may give the climax of the story or detail present situations or emotions that were affected by the events in the story. "Strawberry Wine" is a beautiful example of this form.

"The Devil Went Down to Georgia" is a story song in past tense. The story takes place in the past. However, the song makes good use of present tense quotes from the two characters in the story. In Anthony

Smith's "Impossible to Do," the verses list a series of seemingly impossible things the singer plans to do in the future and contrasts them against a chorus focusing on past events that, while easily accomplished, can't be undone.

Choosing the Tense

There are usually several possible ways to set the tense of a song or song section. You'll have to decide what's best on a case-by-case basis. During the writing of your first few hundred songs, you'll develop an instinct for dealing with tense.

> **Can different tenses be used in the same verse or line?**
> Clarity is the real issue with matters of tense. You can do anything as long as the information gets through clearly. For an example, look at this line from "Amazing Grace": "I once *was* lost, but *now* I'm found."

Meanwhile, the best way to learn tense sense is by doing. Try the following exercises:

- Write a story song in past tense. Use the first half of the first verse to connect present to past. Stay in past tense through the rest of the verses and the chorus. Use a bridge after the second chorus to connect the past back to the present.
- Write a "wish list" song. Use present tense in the verses to talk about things you already have. Use future tense in the chorus for your wish list.
- Write a story song about an historical event. Create two characters, one who lived at the time and the other a present-day descendant who finds a letter from the ancestor detailing a story, real or made up, relating to the historical event. Write the whole song in past tense. The challenge is to make the jumps from "long ago" past tense to recent past tense in a clear and easy-to-follow manner.

- Write a "life cycle" song with a verse-chorus-verse-chorus-bridge-chorus structure. Use past tense in the first verse, present tense in the second verse, and future tense in the bridge. Write one chorus that works without changing it.

- Write a song in present tense with no reference to things in the past or future. Apply this to other tenses, too. If you try it, you'll see that this may seem simple, but it's really tough.

The Art of Saying Without Saying

Simplicity and directness are some of the prime virtues of songwriting, but sometimes just saying something outright sounds drab. What to do? A simple but indirect description can liven up an otherwise boring lyric. Instead of saying: "She was happily married but life was tough / She worked too much but at least she had love . . . " try something more like: "Days at the fact'ry were hard and too long, / But the ring on her finger helped her keep keepin' on."

Instead of narrating your song like a wildlife documentary or a tennis match, use objects, places, actions, and expressions to color your story. This involves the minds of listeners in two ways; it makes them visualize the object, place, action, or expression and it also gets the deductive part of the brain working. ("Watson, by the ring on her finger, I deduce that she is *married!*" "Amazing Holmes, how *do* you do it?")

Don't make the listener work *too* hard to figure things out. Pointing out that a character walks with a limp will not tell everyone that he was shot in the leg during an argument over a poker game in pre–Civil War New Orleans. When the song is complete, check through and make sure that the average person will be able to figure out your story.

Painting a Picture

Sometimes it's the little things that make a story seem real. When you look at a famous painting, the small details are what usually make its impact so big. Take the Mona Lisa, for example, it's not the background or the woman's clothes or the fact that she is smiling that make the painting so poignant. It's the precise degree of the smile that has delighted art enthusiasts for hundreds of years.

Take the same care with your story. Visualize the details of your characters—not just how they look, but how they feel and move and react. If you have a clear picture in your mind, it will be much easier to give a clear picture to the listener.

Details are great, but don't focus on unimportant details that distract from your story. Pick out the ones that are relevant, and use them to make your song more realistic.

Making a Movie

The techniques used in moviemaking can also help you write a better song. Notice how a movie scene will often begin with a general setting to put the story in context? A town square, a breakfast table, a busy street, the middle of a battle, or a table for two are all places that stir up subconscious impressions and help people tune in to a story. Once you've established the scene, you can zoom in on the details and take the listener with you.

Alternately, scenes may start with an extreme close up of something—a wine glass, a ring, a phone, or someone's eyes. This technique provides a clue that action is about to occur; the glass will be picked up, the ring will be taken off, the phone will ring, the voice behind the eyes will speak.

The storytelling approaches of various movie styles can apply to songwriting. Try writing an abbreviated version of a Western, a comedy, a three-hankie chick flick, or an historical drama. As an alternate idea, try using techniques from plays, radio and TV shows, and music videos.

Dealing with Writer's Block

Sometimes no matter what you do, nothing comes—at least nothing that's any good. You can't get warmed up at the start of a session, you're in the middle of a new song and your brain locks up, or everything's great right up to the last line of the song and, all of a sudden, the muse has left the building. You keep trying, but nothing happens. You start to panic. "What if this feeling never goes away?"

Welcome to the club. Writer's block has been around as long as writing, and it happens to the best writers in the world. It's not fatal or permanent, though it usually feels that way. No need to panic, it usually passes quickly on its own.

Breaking the Block

If you don't feel like waiting, there are several time-tested cures. Here are a few favorites for jump-starting a stalled song:

- **Take a break.** Sometimes your brain overloads and needs to cool down. Go get something to drink, have a snack, take a walk. Don't even think about the song while you're taking a break. That's why it's called a break!
- **Look for corners.** Have you painted yourself into a corner? Killing off your hero halfway through can make things anticlimactic. Maybe he should die in the last verse. This cure works especially well after taking a break first.
- **Switch gears.** Stuck on lyrics? Work on the melody. Can't get the beat right? Get back to the lyrics.
- **Make a move.** Work on a different part of the song. Chorus trouble? Skip down to the bridge. Can't get the second line of the verse quite right? Write the third line, then come back. If you have several trouble spots, try working on each one for ten minutes and then switching to a different part when time's up.
- **Mix it up.** Rearrange the words in the line you're trying to write or rearrange the lines in that particular section of the song. You may even want to try switching the order of the verses, starting with the

chorus or moving the bridge to a different spot. If it doesn't work out, you can always put things back where they were.

ALERT!

If you have a problem with the rhymes, look for other options. Ending a line with "orange" makes it awfully difficult to rhyme. Maybe "banana" would work better. Sometimes even a good rhyme word that fits into the song isn't the right word to use. Looking for some other options certainly won't hurt and might just solve your problem.

Whatever approach you take, keep in mind that the writer's block will pass, and you are just going to have to keep going until you get back into the flow of things.

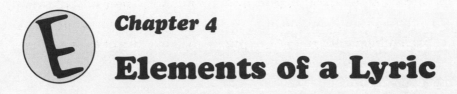

Chapter 4

Elements of a Lyric

In a recent survey of publishers, the number-one most important factor in hiring a new staff writer was the strength of the writer's lyrics. Becoming a better and more versatile lyricist is top priority when it comes to writing cuttable songs. A lot of lyric samples will appear in this chapter. Unless noted, they aren't from real songs and serve only to illustrate the lesson.

Different Lyrical Styles

Different kinds of songs require different lyrical styles to complement them. Your background, age, experiences, or education may give you a head start in some styles, but don't let that stop you from becoming adept at lyric genres with which you have had limited experience. Just as an actor can learn an accent or develop a character for a movie part, you can learn a new lyrical style and expand the kinds of songs you are capable of writing.

Pop Lyrics

Modern pop lyrics are usually either trendy or timeless. Last year's slang will do you as much good as a pair of parachute pants. If you don't know what parachute pants are, they were a form of clothing that was extremely popular for about a year (or fifteen minutes, depending on where you lived) and then, quite suddenly, no one would be caught dead in them.

> **Is "pop" really a genre?**
> Pop is short for "popular." What's popular changes from time to time. Pop lyrics and music tend to be highly accessible versions of whatever the popular genres are at a given time. A rock, hip-hop, or country song can be a pop song, if enough people get it.

Trendy lyrics aim at the teen market (which buys the most CDs and has the newest, coolest slang terms). Examples of trendy lyrics include the Avril Lavigne song "Sk8er Boi" or, for its time, The Beach Boys classic "I Get Around."

Lyrics in the timeless style must not only transcend barriers of time, but also economic status, ethnicity, and geography. Tough? Yes! Worth it? You bet! A timeless song can keep royalty checks coming for the rest of your life and beyond. A list of timeless lyrics might include "Unforgettable," "Evergreen," "Crazy," and "Freebird." Simple elegance and natural flow define the timeless lyric.

Pop lyrics can be about most subjects, but love and relationships are the all-time big sellers. A pop lyric should be accessible to a large market so, aside from the newest "teenspeak," try to avoid language that's regionally or demographically specific.

Rock and Alt

A good rock lyric is emotionally charged, dynamic, and forceful. Rock is about energy, so think powerful, think active, think passionate, and rock on! General rock topics include feeling boxed in, rebellion, wanting to have fun, passion, comeuppance, and angst or depression. Most rock lyrics have a tight, rhythmic meter and are easy to follow. This doesn't mean writing for third graders, it means getting to the point.

Alt songs may be deeper, moodier, or more meditative and cover a broader range of subjects in addition to the general rock topics. In rock or alt, an uptempo danceable song or a love ballad that isn't too wimpy will usually be where the money is.

ALERT!

Be careful with lyrics that deal with rebellion, angst, or depression. You wouldn't want your song to be unfairly blamed for a riot or a suicide. When dealing with these subjects and emotions, use an approach that let's the listener know he or she is not alone in feeling a certain way.

Country Music

Country songwriting has expanded to include other musical forms. It's the level of lyric writing and storytelling that sets country apart. Many great country songs have been based on stories the songwriter heard as a child from family or friends. Established country songwriters also recommend reading short stories and watching movies, sitcoms, talk shows, or news stories to get story ideas.

Modern country lyrics cover many topics, so there's no need to start writing stories about cows and whiskey and cheating spouses; Nashville has more than enough of those already. Hallmarks of a modern country lyric are a conversational tone, a sense of humor, and reinforcement of basic values like hard work, faith, and honesty.

Jazz and Rap

While numerous and wonderful exceptions occur, jazz is usually more about the melody and the sound of the words than the actual lyric. Not that you can't have a great lyric in a jazz song, but make the melody and meter top priority. Pay careful attention to vowel sounds in a jazz lyric. Jazz treats the voice like an instrument and vowels influence the tone of the voice.

Because of its droning, nonstandard melodic forms, rap requires very close attention to meter and rhyme. The *rhythm* of the lyric carries the song along. Instead of melodic/lyric prosody, try finding metric/lyric prosody. In rap, the lyric *is* the song, so make it tight and interesting and be extremely careful in your word choices. If you're serious about writing rap, you may wish to study the different lyric styles of the East and West coast rappers as well as other sub-genres.

Write understandably, but never "dummy down" a song. If you feel the lyric is beneath you, your writing will reflect that and hurt the song. A better way is to see the challenge in learning how to write simple lyrics that can communicate complex ideas.

Targeting Your Market

When writing for a specific market, whether it's country, pop, or Bolivian folk music, the choices you make in word usage, syntax, and grammar can affect your success as much as your storytelling and melodic skills. Paying attention to every line, every word of your song, as well as the overall flow and style, can bring rich rewards. Ignoring these things can assure you a permanent place as the best songwriter in the whole produce department, maybe even the whole grocery store.

Vocabulary Choices

An important choice faced frequently by songwriters is picking exactly the right word to fill a spot. Colorful words can help a lyric stand out and make a song more vivid, but make sure to use words that are understandable to your target market and are appropriate to the song. For instance, some publishers tend to shy away from songs with words like "cogitate," "fuchsia," and "Australopithecus." Instead, try "think," "pink," and "missing link." Use words that are natural to the kind of person who would sing or listen to your song.

If you're not sure the listener will understand a certain word, the way in which you use it may help explain it. Many people didn't know the true meaning of the word "ironic" when Alanis Morissette's song of the same title came out. In the song "Ironic," Morissette writes about situations with the question of whether they were ironic, and further reinforces the explanation by the use of simile (it's like . . .) and metaphor (it's a . . .) in the "B" section.

Colloquialisms and Vernacular

Colloquialisms are common sayings with an informal tone. Vernacular is an informal mode of speech. Both are used frequently and successfully in songs. "I Fall to Pieces," "God Only Knows," and "Somethin' in the Water" are all song hooks made from colloquialisms. Vernacular speech is particularly useful in a song where a conversational feel is needed.

FACT

Colloquialisms and vernacular speech patterns are often regional in nature and may confuse people who are unfamiliar with a particular saying or type of speech: To a British person, the word "Yankee" means "American"; to a Southerner it means someone from North of the Mason-Dixon line. Make sure to use the right kind of language for the style and market of the song you are writing.

Syntax and Grammar

Used well, "bad English" can make for a great song. You may come under fire from your mother or the English teacher/amateur songwriter down at the local songwriter's association, who insists that, "Proper grammar and syntax are the building blocks of any good song." Thank them for their advice and politely ignore it. Look at the following line: "Although I have made repeated attempts, I cannot obtain any gratification whatsoever."

Technically correct? Yes. Does it read like a hit lyric? No! It just sits there. It feels stuffy and old. However, if the line is made more conversational with a double negative, and some redundancy is added for dramatic effect, the results are golden—you get the hook to "Satisfaction" by Mick Jagger and Keith Richards.

Now, take the line "We shall not retire until the sun rises." It just doesn't have the punch of the Garth Brooks classic "Ain't Goin' Down 'til the Sun Comes Up." Though there are errors made in grammar (ain't), diction (goin'), and it ends with (gasp!) a preposition, the line has a conversational tone that's appropriate to the song, a catchy rhythm, and a great contrast between "up" and "down."

What matters is that your song is authentic to its genre, that the language feels natural, and that you get your point across to the listener as precisely as possible. Use bad English if, and only if, it makes your song better. If it does, use it without guilt or remorse. Remember, the primary object of a lyric is to communicate to the listener. Whatever does that best for a particular song is the right way.

Writing Rhymes

Songs haven't always rhymed. Ancient Hebrew songwriters rhymed ideas instead of sounds—they stated an idea or concept and then restated it in different words. Even now a song occasionally hits the charts that doesn't rhyme. Billy Vera's "At This Moment" is a prime example. However, it's much, *much* easier to market a song that rhymes. What makes for a great rhyme? That depends on what year it is and what style you're writing.

Listen to the radio and to your favorite CDs, and compare where the rhymes are and what kind of rhymes are used. You'll be amazed at all the options you find.

The Rhyme Scheme

"Rhyme scheme" is the term used to describe where rhymes are placed in the song. Within a given section (verse, chorus, or bridge) the rhymes are designated, in order of appearance, by letters of the alphabet. AA rhyme scheme has two lines that rhyme:

He reached into his **pocket**
And found a silver **locket**

An ABAB rhyme alternates the rhyming lines, as follows:

He reached in his **pocket**
And what should he *find*
But the fine silver **locket**
Of the girl on his *mind*

Inner Rhymes

Rhymes can work at the end of the lines as well inside them. Rhymes occurring inside a line are called, you guessed it, "inner rhymes." These are one of a songwriter's secret weapons: Consciously or unconsciously, we expect to hear rhymes at the ends of lines. Inner rhymes come as a surprise to the ear. This helps keep a listener's attention. Where you choose to place inner rhymes can give different effects:

- **Back-to-back**: " I went *down***town** and watched the girls walk by."
- **Very close together**: "I went *around* the **town**, calling out your name."
- **Further apart**: "I went *down* to the bad side of **town** to see a girl I used to know."
- **In two different lines**: " I get so *down* when I come home to visit / Is it this **town** or knowin' you're in it."

You can also put more than one set or internal rhymes into a line or set of lines. The following couplet contains a complex set of inner rhymes:

I'm in a U-*haul* **packed** wall to *wall* headin' **back** to TenneSEE
Good-*bye* to the **smog** and the *high* stress **job** yeah what I NEED

(From "Hometown Girl," Copyright 2002, C.J. Watson, Kevin Ball; used by permission.)

As you can see, the A and D rhymes are in italics, the B and E rhymes in bold, and the C rhymes in all caps. The rhyme scheme is ABABC/DEDEC. Play with different schemes; see what you can do with ABCABC or ABCA/DBCD. Make up your own patterns and see if you can write a set of lines that fit.

An important trick many pros use is to make sure that the rhyme scheme in the verses is different from that of the chorus. This, along with melodic shifts and changes in the meter and dynamics, makes the chorus stand out and helps your song to keep a listener's attention.

Imperfect Rhymes

In the previous lines, you might notice that the words "U-Haul" and "wall" rhyme perfectly, which is to say that the final vowel and consonant sounds are the same. Likewise the words "goodbye" and "high" are nearly perfect rhymes because they end in the same vowel sound.

But some rhymes are imperfect. "Packed" and "back" are pretty close; they both have a short "a" sound, like in the word "at," followed by a "k" sound. However, "packed" has an additional "t" sound at the end, so this pair doesn't rhyme perfectly. "Tennessee" and "need" each have a hard "E" as the last vowel, but one ends in a consonant, "D," while the other ends with the vowel. "Smog" and "job" end in different consonants, but have the same vowel sound.

In the past, much importance had been placed on perfect rhyme. In some cases, it's still the way to go. For the more formal-sounding songs in the timeless pop style, perfect rhyme often works best. But in today's more conversational songs, an imperfect rhyme can be a fresh alternative. When people hear "heart" at the end of a line, they usually expect to hear "start" or "apart" for the rhyme. If you surprise them by using "car," they might listen more closely to see what comes next.

Don't Force It!

Never accept an awkwardly phrased or stilted-sounding line just because it ends with a perfect rhyme. Forced rhymes sound amateurish and make a listener think about the rhyme instead of the story or the melody. If you don't find a perfect rhyme that floors you, look for an imperfect rhyme that *does*. If you can't find an imperfect rhyme, try a different word in the rhyme spot.

Some songwriters use "made" rhymes that rely on regional or genre-specific diction styles. For example, John Fogerty's diction allows him to rhyme words like "door" and "slow" perfectly. With most singers, these two words would be a fairly weak rhyme. However, made rhymes may limit a song's marketability to a few artists.

FACT

On rare occasions, a rhyme may be made by distorting a word in a previously unheard-of way. A classic example is Roger Miller's "Dang Me," in which he rhymes "purple" with "maple surple" for humorous effect. This is extremely difficult to pull off and is almost exclusively used in novelty songs, but you may wish to try it anyway.

Pay Attention to Meter

"Meter" is the term used to describe the number of syllables in each line of a section of a song and which syllables are emphasized. Volumes have been written about types and uses of meter in songwriting as well as in poetry. For a modern songwriter, simply studying the rhythm and stresses of popular songs will probably be more help than reading about spondee and iambic pentameter. Meter in today's songs often tries to mimic the rhythms of natural conversation rather than force lyrics into rigid poetic forms. That being said, studying meter in songs or poetry can be valuable to a songwriter and there are some things that should be covered here.

Sense of Symmetry

With meter, as with rhyme, a certain sense of symmetry is necessary for a song to have a cohesive feel. If you use an 8/6/8/5 meter (each number represents the number of syllables in a line) and an ABCB/ABCB rhyme scheme in the first verse, the second verse should follow suit. Not that you can't occasionally wedge in an extra word, but make sure that the verses feel alike and are easily identifiable as verses. This helps to provide a sense of place within the song, like chapters in a book or scenes in a movie.

Stretching Vowels

Sometimes you may need more syllables in a line than you have words to fill them. An alternative to adding unnecessary words is to stretch the vowels in some words to cover multiple syllables. A perfect example of this is found in the Frankie Valli and the Four Seasons song "Big Girls Don't Cry," in which the words of the hook only make up four syllables but are sung as eight.

Decide on the right syllable stretching technique on a case-by-case basis and be careful not to overuse it: Too much and it can start to sound cheesy, or, in the case of "letting it ride," it can distort the meter.

Some vowels, like the "eye" sound in "cry" and the "oo" sound in "blue," lend themselves to stretching by being sung as trills or yodels and simply changing notes wherever the melody normally requires it. In "Big Girls Don't Cry," for instance, this is done by sliding between two notes in the word "big." The other stretched words repeat certain sounds, but "big" adds a syllable by changing notes. Sometimes you can just let one note ride for several beats.

Prosody, Alliteration, and Clichés

"The Good, the Bad, and the Ugly" might be an apt title for these tricks of the trade. Prosody is good. Alliteration can be a nice piece of ear candy or an ugly distraction. Clichés are usually bad unless used *before* they become clichés. Maybe one of your lines will be a cliché someday. But let's hope it's not a cliché just yet.

Prosody

Simply put, prosody means that something sounds like what it is. If you have a slow, sad-sounding piece of music and write a lyric over it that describes how much fun you have skateboarding, it might confuse the listener. Likewise, a bouncy, uptempo number about losing your mom in a car crash doesn't seem appropriate. When writing lyrics to a melody, listen carefully to see that the melody evokes the right kind of mood.

Alliteration

When different words within a line or stanza of a song begin with the same sound, it's called "alliteration." Think of it as rhyme in reverse. With alliteration, the words can be adjoining, like "Manic Monday," or separate, as with "Wind in the Willows." Although it can be used effectively in almost any kind of song, alliteration is especially good for songs with a light or silly tone. Who can forget the all-time classic, "Great Green Globs of Greasy Grimy Gopher Guts"?

Overused Words and Phrases

There's at least one big publisher in Nashville who doesn't want to hear the words "love" or "heart" in another song as long as he lives.

Why? He listens to *hundreds* of songs every week, and guess which words he hears the most?

Emotions are the real underpinnings of any good song. You want to get the listener to feel what you feel, but using emotional words like love and heart is not the best way to get that feeling across. While there's no argument that love songs, anti-love songs, lost-love songs, or love-gone-bad songs are big moneymakers, people get tired of hearing the same words in every song. Look for alternatives. Describe your love instead of just stating its existence and location. When you do use words like love and heart, make sure that they mean something.

When a colloquialism or other phrase gets overused, it becomes a cliché. Most beginning writers imitate the lyrics of songs they grew up with. Unfortunately, sayings that were fresh and trendy a few years ago get overused and begin to seem tired or generic to a listener's ears.

There are thousands of cliché phrases to be avoided, but a top-ten list might look something like this:

1. We'll never part.
2. It's really true.
3. I can't live without you.
4. That's the way it goes.
5. We can make it if we try.
6. How can I make you see.
7. Got to make him (or her) mine.
8. Soft as a dove.
9. Please don't go.
10. Then you'll understand.

Unnecessary Words

Anyone who's written more than a few songs knows that some words are perfect for those times when you need to fill a hole in a line. "Just," "really," "very," "well," "baby," and many others can come in handy, but it's easy to become dependent on filler words and to overuse them. A common practice of professional songwriters is to look over a completed song and see if it needs a "just-ectomy," which is to say "Are there any unnecessary words that can be replaced by better ones?" The following two lines show the results of a quadruple bypass just-ectomy:

Before: "I said well now *baby* that's *just really very* sad."
After: "I said well now sweet pea that'd make a statue cry."

Sometimes there's only one word that works in a given spot. As long as it works naturally, without sounding forced, and doesn't bring the song down or appear too often in the same lyric, it might be just the thing you need in a particular spot.

Visual Writing

A song is made of sound and words and can only get across conversation and other things expressed by sound and words, right? Wrong! A song is made of *sound* and *words* and both, especially words, can be used to make sensations real in the imagination. Writing to evoke the senses of the listener is called "visual writing." Since there are five senses, this is an incomplete term, but it's the one most publishers use, so we're stuck with it for now.

Impressionism

A great lyric device is to give an impression of something that gets the listener to fill in details from his or her own imagination. You could say, "He didn't seem trustworthy. I got the impression he was hiding something." That gets the information across, but doesn't involve the listener. If you say, "His shifty eyes looked away and he changed the subject," a number of things happen. You give a partial visual—shifty eyes—which begs the imagination to complete it (by supplying the rest of the face) and gives some information about the character. Some action (looking away) gives further clues. By the time you get to "he changed the subject," the listener has enough information for it to mean something—that the person, who doesn't look trustworthy, is hiding something. You'll have the listener's full attention as he or she waits for the next story clue. What conclusions would you draw from the following lines?

- "The waiter brought champagne and I thought /
  'bout the ring in my pocket that three months pay bought."
- "He sits in the bleachers, watching them play /
  and dreams of his own younger days."

Specificity

Sometimes it's better to spell your information out in CAPITAL LETTERS than to give an impression that may not get your point across. If you're writing a song about falling in love with a classic truck, you could say, "Shining like a cherry in the late September sun, the automotive relic of a time and place long gone" or "She was a cherried-out, half-ton, fire engine red, 1950 Studebaker flatbed."

ALERT!

Being specific can be a good thing, but being overly specific or technical can limit your potential audience. Focus on important details and use terms that your target market can understand. Tell your listener that the transmission was shot, but not that it was a problem in the rear differential caused by viscosity breakdown!

Which of these lines packs a more *complete* story? Which line has its visual focus on the subject? Most importantly, which line will appeal to people who are likely to be interested in a song about a truck? While both of these lines *might* work in the song, the second line has more pertinent information and less dispensable information. Using the first line would mean having to use at least one more line just to establish that it's a truck. Since you can't fit an infinite number of lines in a three-minute song, this could mean having to leave out other information.

Finishing Touches

When your lyric is nearly done, read it aloud several times. If you have a melody, sing it, too. Look for spots that don't feel right. If you keep telling yourself that a particular line is good enough, it's probably not. Here's a lyric checklist to help you out. Remember that a lyric can be technically perfect and still be a bomb.

1. The story is clear and easy to follow.
2. The lyric style works well with the musical style.
3. The lyric matches the mood of the music.
4. The rhyme scheme is consistent and rhymes are unforced.
5. The meter is interesting and fairly symmetrical within sections of the song.
6. The style and vocabulary choices are appropriate to the target market.
7. The syntax and grammar of the song feel natural.
8. Any unnecessary words and clichés have been removed or replaced.
9. The song makes the listener see the story.
10. It feels done.

Thinking Outside the Box

Once you've got a firm grip on the fundamentals of lyric writing, bend the rules, break them, make new ones, and try them out. The songwriters who make the biggest splash are the ones who find new ways of saying something or, if they're really lucky, a thing that no one has ever said.

Look for great songs that break the rules and figure out why they work: There may be a new rule hiding in there somewhere. Songwriting rules are really guidelines to help you avoid trouble spots. Most times, it's easier to color inside the lines, follow the rules, and do what you know will work. Sometimes, though, it's fun to try something different. Whether it works or not depends on how you do it and whether or not it's a good day. (E)

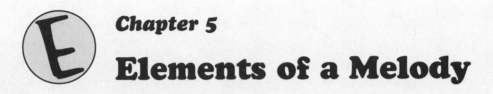

Chapter 5

Elements of a Melody

I n the days of classical music, melody was king. Today, that still holds true for some genres. In any musical style, with the exception of rap, melody is at least the second most important part of a great song. After all, a song without melody is a poem, but a melody without lyrics can still be considered a song.

Melodic Styles

As with lyrical styles, the lines separating different melodic styles have blurred considerably in the last fifty years. These days, it's not uncommon to hear Dolly Parton covering Collective Soul, Dave Matthews doing a tune made popular by Johnny Cash, or Johnny Cash singing a song by U2 or Soundgarden. While different genres are sometimes known for particular melodic elements, these elements can be used effectively to flavor most other styles of music.

Another way to look at melody writing might be to ask yourself, "What elements do great songs from all these styles have in common?" You'll find that most great songs have a melody that works with the lyric, either to magnify, add to, emphasize, modify, or in some cases, purposefully contradict the words. Melody affects the listener on a sub-conscious level. An effective melody is memorable, hummable, and elicits a gut-level, emotional response. A melody must *move* the listener in one of two ways, emotionally or physically. If you can make listeners laugh, cry, or smile, it's a good sign. If you can make them dance, you're on to something. If you can do both, you will be smiling as you dance into the bank.

FACT

One of the cheapest and easiest ways to study the rhythmic components of different melodic styles is by tapping out familiar melodies with a pencil. Using the eraser end, tap the melody on a pad of paper. After a while, you can see where the stresses are by where you tap harder.

Pop Melodies

Pop is more of a treatment given to other genres than a true style unto itself. Almost any kind of song can be a pop song if it's successful enough. Frank Sinatra, Madonna, Gloria Estefan, and Prince can all be considered pop artists. Pop melodies draw from most other styles of music: Sinatra's brand of pop was influenced by jazz and swing,

Madonna's by club and world music, Estefan's by Latin and disco, and Prince's by rock, R&B, and soul.

The trick to using other genres as influences in pop melody writing is to distill them down to their basic elements, define what makes those elements likeable to the general listening audience, and then craft a simple catchy melody from them.

Rock and Alt

Rock has subdivided into dozens of micro-genres. From a basic viewpoint, rock melody is about power and rhythm, like the blues and R&B music that influenced early rock-n-roll. To give a rock melody full impact, pay close attention to its rhythms. A rock or alt melody should be rhythmically catchy with a high degree of symmetry in the meter. If a line has extra syllables that break the flow of the intended meter, consider rewriting the line to match the meter or finding a rhythmic pattern that has a close mathematical relationship to the original meter.

The Melodies of Country

Country's traditional melodic roots are in Appalachian folk, Southern gospel, cowboy songs, and the blues. Over the years, influences including rock-n-roll, modern folk, and even some jazz have made themselves a place in Nashville. Alt-tinged melodies and hip-hop groove and meter have taken country in some exciting new directions lately. On the other side of the coin, a strong resurgence in bluegrass and the rise of the Americana and roots movements have shown that country's traditional roots aren't tapped out yet.

Other Styles

The use of syncopation, unusual intervals, exotic modes and scales, and notes outside the scale are common in jazz. With jazz, melody often reigns supreme. A good rule of thumb for jazz composition is to write a melody line that will sound equally as good in an instrumental version as it will with a vocal rendition.

While some purists insist that rap has no discernible melody, pitch variations are just as important to rap music as to many other genres. The hallmark of a rap "melody" is that the pitches change, usually up but occasionally down, with the stresses of the meter. These modulations are as closely related to pitch variations common in speaking as to those used in traditional melodic composition.

Hip-hop combines melodic elements of soul, rap, R&B, rock, jazz, funk, and may also have ska, dub, and reggae influences. It's common for hip-hop songs to switch back and forth between singing and rapping.

Writing Effective Melodies

There are countless tools, tricks, and schools of thought regarding melody writing. Let's look at a couple that have proven themselves time and again—through history, on the charts, and in the marketplace—to be fundamental to an effective melody.

Patterns Within Patterns

One of the keys of melodic success is in being able to create variations on a theme. In this way, you can start with a bit of melody and expand it to fit the section. If you happen on a combination of notes you like, try the same intervals a third higher, try stretching the same notes over twice the amount of time. Try them backwards and see what happens. Don't be afraid to experiment with any possibility for variation that crosses your mind. The advantage of using several variations on one melodic figure is that it can give the melody of the whole section a sense of cohesiveness.

While it may be okay to have the melodic elements of a section based around a single bit of melody, be careful not to do it too much from one section to the next. Otherwise, the chorus could end up sounding too much like the verse, and vice versa.

Differentiating Sections of a Song

Sometimes the hardest part of melody writing is coming up with a second melodic figure that complements the first but that still sounds different enough to signal a new section. You can emphasize a slight variation in the melodic structure by changes in the chord pattern, groove, meter, and sometimes key of a new section. Differentiating sections of a song keeps the song from becoming boring.

Melodic Hooks

Melodic hooks are the ear candy that will make a song stick in someone's head. Quick, what song do you hate the most? You can probably hum the melodic hooks in your sleep. Now, what's your favorite song? Same deal, right?

As with great lyric lines, there may be more than one melodic hook in a song. The most important place to have a melodic hook is underlying the lyric hook, but ends of verses, intros, solos, and anywhere in the chorus are all good places for melodic hooks.

The melodic hook underlying the lyrical hook is called the "motive," and it is one of the most often overlooked secrets of songwriting. In theory, that sounds pretty simple—all you have to do is make sure that the melody and meter that go with the hook complement and magnify that hook. When perfectly matched, a motive and a hook add up to far more than the sum of their parts.

Many successful songwriters either start with a motive and look for a hook, or vice versa, and then base the rest of the song around the result. Most motives are simple and contain just a few syllables and a few notes.

Prosody, the Sequel

Take as much time as you need to establish prosody between the motive and the lyric hook: Let the motive express in a musical way what the hook says with words. This is the most crucial place in your song for the prosody to be right on target. Strong motive prosody is one reason that songs like "Somewhere Over the Rainbow," "Yesterday," and "When a Man Loves a Woman" are still popular so many years after their initial release.

When writing a melody to a lyric, prosody is often used to reinforce the existing message in a direct manner, but it may also be used to add a different shade of meaning than the words alone convey. In the Lee Ann Womack song "I Hope You Dance," the melodic motive gives the listener a sense of the deep metaphor beneath the simple lyric hook. In Linda Ronstadt's "Poor, Pitiful Me," the slight playfulness of the melody contrasts with the lyric just enough to add a touch of ironic humor to the song's hook.

Ups and Downs

One of the easiest ways to incorporate prosody into your writing is by moving the melody upward or downward in response to an emotional or visual movement in the lyric. With a "sad" lyric, moving the melody down at the end of a line can help emphasize the emotional impact of pain or loss expressed in the words. A perfect example of this is the last line of the Willie Nelson/Patsy Cline song "Crazy," which ends a whole octave lower than it begins. Even in a relatively happy song like "When a Man Loves a Woman," the up to down melodic movement adds an aching, desperate quality to the lyric, giving the listener the feeling that the singer doesn't just love this woman, he loves her so much it *hurts*. With physical or visual lyric elements, this kind of prosody can bring a word or line to life. Take a listen to Bette Midler's recording of "Wind Beneath My Wings." Notice that when she sings the word "fly," the melody makes a long, slow climb that gives a distinct impression of someone soaring to great heights.

Tonal Palettes

The notes you use for the melody of your songs can sometimes be just as important as the words you choose for the lyric. At least as far back as Ancient Greece, songwriters have known the power of certain scales or modes to bring out a particular emotion. A Phrygian mode conjures up images of Spain, a minor pentatonic mode can establish a rock or blues feeling, and a harmonic minor scale can sound like a band of Hungarian gypsies or a traditional Hebrew dance.

As a general rule, minor scales and modes sound sad and major scales and modes sound happy, but this doesn't mean that sad songs always have to have minor key melodies and chords. How the note choices work in combination with the lyric and the chords can influence and even contradict the expected emotional impact of a mode or scale. A good example of how tonal palette choices can alter the vibe of a song is the George Jones hit "He Stopped Loving Her Today." The lyric, a tale of lost love, would be unbearably sad and bordering on melodramatic, if set to a minor key melody. Instead, the simple arrangement of major chords and a stately, major scale melody make the song a sadly sweet tribute to a man hopelessly in love.

Can I change modes in a song?
Many songs stick with the same scale or mode all the way through, but there's no reason you can't try changing modes from section to section. Doing this can produce shifts in the mood or feel of a song and help differentiate sections.

Vowel Choices

Pay special attention to your choice of vowels in places where a note is to be held for any amount of time. You can't sing a "T" or a "K" sound for any longer than they would normally be sounded in conversation and even soft consonants like "N," "M," and "R" will often sound odd if held out. It's almost always vowels that get stretched, held, trilled, and yodeled.

Make sure that the words you choose for these spots have vowels that sound right for your song. Also, pay attention to the consonants that end these words. Some consonants get lost or don't sound good after a long hold on a vowel. Often, the best choice for a word that is to be held out is one that ends on a vowel. If a word sounds clumsy when held, the solution can be as easy as finding a different word or rearranging the line so that a better sounding word falls in that spot.

Meter (Again!)

The duration and timing of notes makes a big difference in how well those notes work together. Generally speaking, the verse can have a busier meter with more syllables or notes and the chorus should be a bit simpler to let the important information of the central theme stand out more clearly. Meter can affect prosody: Listen to Commander Cody and the Lost Planet Airmen do "Hot Rod Lincoln" and notice how the fast-paced, staccato meter accentuates the lyric's subject of racing down the highway. The spaces you leave open can be important, too: Notice that in the Billy Joel/Garth Brooks song "Shameless," space left after the hook makes it stand out.

Melodic Range

Melodic range is, to put it simply, the distance between the lowest and highest notes in a melody. If you read standard notation, a quick glance through the sheet music is all it takes to find the highest and lowest notes in a melody. You can also measure melodic range by picking out the melody on an instrument.

Don't confuse the melodic range with actual range in the written key. If you're a baritone, don't worry that your melody is too low for Celine Dion. As long as the melodic range of the song is within the singer's melodic range, the song can easily be transposed to the right key for that singer.

Artist-Specific Limitations

If you are writing with a specific artist in mind, you will want to pay special attention to that artist's vocal range and style of singing. Mariah

Carey might not be interested in a song that has a driving rock-n-roll melody and Mick Jagger will probably pass on a power ballad that requires a four-octave range, intense yodeling, and the lung capacity of a small whale.

To determine the melodic range, tonal palettes, vowel sounds, trills, glides, and intervals that the artist or group favors, simply listen to previous releases. Not only will it help you make your song more appealing to a particular artist, it will also help you decide if any of your existing songs might be appropriate to pitch to that artist. In addition, you'll discover that some kinds of melodies can be pitched to multiple artists. For instance, a song that is well suited to Reba McIntyre might also be good for Dolly Parton or Aretha Franklin; a song that's just right for Bob Seger might work just as well for Travis Tritt or James Otto.

Exploding the Chorus

The chorus usually contains the title, the motive, and the central theme of the song. More than any other part, the chorus should stand out and be memorable. For this reason, professional songwriters often raise melody, simplify meter, use dynamic shifts, and add instruments or harmonies to explode the chorus. Reserving the upper part of the melodic range for chorus is a good idea.

Looking for Memorable Melodies

Where do great melodies come from? This may be one of the biggest riddles of songwriting. We all use the same twelve notes, but the order and duration of those notes makes for an infinite number of possible melodies. Great melodic ideas can result from a number of different writing approaches.

Inspiration

Sometimes you get lucky; divine providence gives you a hint, the subconscious takes over, or the muse speaks through you. However you choose to look at it, there are times when it just *happens*. While you can't make it happen, you can learn how to let it happen. Whenever you get an inspired melody, write for as long as the feeling lasts, then look for any factors that might have put you in the right frame of mind. Was it a hot bath? Knowing you have the day off tomorrow? Learning a new chord? Were you just whistling and—poof!—a brilliant melody appeared? Find out what gets your muse working and set aside time for those activities.

Invention

If you put a hundred monkeys plunking away at a hundred pianos for an unlimited amount of time, eventually one of them would come up with a perfect melody. Of course, the monkey's publisher would want a rewrite and the other monkeys would immediately come up with curiously similar melodies, but that's not the point. Whether you sing, whistle, or play an instrument, just goofing around and making mistakes will often yield surprising results. When you find something, try variations of the original idea or play around some more in the same mode. Hopefully, at some point, inspiration will take over.

FACT

Music is closely related to math, but don't let that scare you. Many successful melodies have been written by applying mathematical formulas. Pick a scale, play a note. Now go up two notes, then back down one, then repeat the process. Try going up three spots and down two, and see what happens.

Innovation

You can't use someone else's melody for your song, but you *can* use it as a starting point for experimentation. Existing songs can be a rich source of melodic ideas. Listen to your favorite songs or to the radio, notice how different songs approach and develop melodic ideas and how they use various modes, meter configurations, and other elements. One great exercise, used by Paul Simon, is to play a harmony to an existing melody, then change and develop it until it becomes a totally different song.

Keeping Up with Current Trends

Different kinds of melodic figures and methods of melodic development fall in and out of vogue on a regular basis. In order to sustain a career as a professional songwriter, it helps to learn to adapt to these trends as quickly as possible. This requires the ability to identify an emerging trend, figure out what makes it different, and master the new style before it falls out of fashion.

The cheapest way to keep up on what's going on is to listen to the weekly top-forty countdown on the radio. *Billboard* magazine can give you a more in-depth look at the charts and also a view into several different markets. Music video channels feature weekly countdowns that, though not as accurate, may be slightly ahead of radio charts as sales indicators.

Analyzing Melodic Elements

If you study music trends, you'll notice that production styles change more often than melodic approach. If you hum a "modern" melody, you may hear similarities to melodies from other styles and periods of time. Focus on the melodic elements first and worry about production when it's time to make a demo.

When you analyze current melodies, look at how they move from section to section, the kinds of meter that give a particular feel, and the types of intervallic shifts that identify a style. You may notice that a new style is a variation of an old one: The quick, wide intervals found in the alt songs of Alanis Morissette and Jewel are very similar to those found in the cowboy songs of Roy Rogers and in Swiss yodeling.

Keeping abreast of current trends requires more than just checking out the top forty. Most of the music you hear on the radio today was written at least two years ago. Familiarity with past styles and close observation of developing markets and trends in music hubs can help you react quickly when things change.

Getting Out of a Rut

A common struggle faced by most songwriters is developing a recognizable style without becoming redundant. There's not much difference between a groove and a rut. Every songwriter has probably felt that his or her last few songs sound too much alike. What should you do when this happens? If your last few songs were big hits, keep writing until someone complains. If not, there are several ways to expand your horizons and cover some new musical territory.

Identify What You Do

Take some time to analyze your own melodic structures. Figure out what scales, modes, keys, intervals, time signatures, and chord movements are in your songs. If all your songs are waltzes in the key of "C" that use major scales for their melodic basis and I, IV, V chord patterns, you might have found the problem.

Do all your songs sound like something from Willie Nelson's third album? If so, it might be time to listen to his first, second, and fourth album or try listening to some Waylon Jennings for a change.

Trying Something Different

Just being aware that you want to write a different kind of melody may be enough to get you headed in the right direction. If not, here are some options for expanding your melodic possibilities:

- Learn an unfamiliar mode or scale and write a melody with it.
- Learn some new chords or new voicing for the old ones.
- Arrange chords in a different order than you usually do.
- Write a melody in a musical style you've never tried before.
- If you normally write with an instrument, try writing without one, or vice versa.
- Experiment with a computer program that lets you write melodies in standard musical notation and then plays them back for you.

What If I Can't Sing?

Many great songwriters can't sing well. Some can't sing at all. This shouldn't stop you from writing a melody. If you're one of those people who can't even sing in the shower, there's still hope.

The first order of business is to determine the severity of your problem. Examine your singing, and be realistic with your assessment. An important point to consider is your experience. No matter how good you are, or think you are, performing experience will absolutely make you a better songwriter.

If you come to the conclusion that you're far from being a good singer, your biggest worry will be whether or not to use your own voice on a demo. If you think there's a possibility for improvement, take some vocal lessons when you have time and money.

Solutions for the "Tonally Challenged"

Call up a friend that everyone says is a good singer. Get a guitar or a keyboard, it doesn't matter if you can play or not. Pick a note. (On a keyboard, just play a note right in the middle. On a guitar, pluck one of the two middle strings.) Try to make the note that you hear from the instrument with your voice. If it seems too low or high, find one that's better suited to your voice. When you feel that you have matched the note you heard from the instrument, ask your friend if it was on pitch.

If the answer is yes, try a few other notes and see how you do. If you match several correctly, then your sense of pitch is good and you just need some singing lessons and lots of practice. Remember, the voice is an instrument and instruments require practice for control. Singing requires a different type of muscle control than talking. Frequent singing, under the supervision of a qualified instructor, will get your voice in shape in a few months. Think of a vocal teacher as a personal trainer for voice muscles.

If you can't match the notes perfectly, but you get close, you need to train your ears a little. Practice matching notes and singing with the radio or CDs for a few weeks and test yourself for signs of improvement. Get vocal lessons from a patient teacher.

Help! I'm Awful

If your friend says you're not even in the ballpark and it all sounds the same to you, don't despair just yet. You may have never developed the part of the brain that recognizes pitch. Have your friend play two different notes. Do they *sound* different? If so, guess which ones are lower and higher. Try this with several different combinations of notes. If you can do it consistently, then the pitch sense in your brain is working at least partly and the signals may be getting lost between there and your vocal cords.

Sign up for piano or guitar lessons and learn to play some melodies. Build up to picking out favorite melodies by ear and having your teacher check the results. As you progress, your sense of pitch will slowly get better. Try singing along as you play. This will forge a connection between your brain and your vocal muscles. As soon as you can sing the notes you play, add vocal lessons to your learning regimen.

What if you can't even *hear* the difference between two notes? Don't give up just yet. Some people who were nearly tone-deaf have trained their ears through patience and practice. Buy a cheap, used keyboard or guitar. Spend twenty minutes a day just making notes and listening to them. If they start sounding different after a few months, get some lessons and build your way up through the other steps. Some very famous songwriters started out right where you are.

If, after several months of work, you still can't hear a difference between two notes, consider focusing on lyrics. If you can't do that either, congratulations, you are now qualified to be a publisher or a record company president, but keep trying!

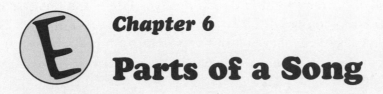

Chapter 6

Parts of a Song

Each song is made up of a series of smaller sections or parts, like verses and choruses, as well as many other song parts that can work with these sections to augment and emphasize the main body of your song. While some successful songs have had only one section that is repeated several times, most hit songs these days have at least a verse and a chorus. Ask yourself what parts your song needs to be the best it can be.

The Sum of All Parts

Each part of a song imparts a different kind of information. There are no unbreakable laws as to what kind of information must be contained in a given section, but knowing the names, traditional forms, and functions of the different parts of a song can help you to write more effectively and make it easier to communicate with publishers, producers, studio musicians, and other songwriters.

By giving a different kind of musical information in each part of the song, you lessen the chances of a listener becoming bored. By repeating this musical information each time a section comes back around, you give a blueprint of sorts that helps guide the listener through the song without becoming lost or confused.

Although some sections of a song may give new lyrical information each time they occur, the way in which the information is presented, as well as the rhyme scheme, meter, and type of information, is the same every time the section repeats.

If your song had no recognizable form to the melody, meter, rhyme scheme, or lyric structure, it would be hard to follow and nearly impossible to sing along with. Even if you're one of those songwriters who delights in breaking the rules, it helps to know them first, so you can make sure that you're breaking, bending, or twisting a given rule in exactly the right way to make your publisher have a seizure. Read on: There might be rules you didn't know about, waiting to be broken.

First Up, the Intro

The intro is usually a short instrumental section to warm up the listeners and alert them to be ready for the song's lyrics. If an intro gets the listener's attention, he or she might then listen to your song.

Not all songs have intros. Some start off cold with a verse or chorus (e.g., "American Pie" by Don McLean). Others have an intro that is based on the motive or another melodic hook from the main body of the song (e.g., "Centerfold" by J. Geils Band). Still others are stand-alone sections, written especially for the job (e.g., "Freebird," by Lynyrd Skynyrd). While most intros contain a melodic hook of some kind, some are nothing more than a brief chord sequence with no melody at all (e.g., "Pinball Wizard" by The Who) or a bass and drum groove (e.g., "Another One Bites the Dust" by Queen). Sometimes a single chord is all you need (e.g., "A Hard Days Night" by The Beatles). For now, it's up to you to decide if your song needs an intro and, if so, what kind.

FACT

The order and function of different song parts have changed somewhat over time. In the early and middle parts of the twentieth century, it was common practice to have a spoken or sung introduction to a song that set up the story. Intros these days tend to be instrumental.

Recurring Intros

Often, the intro is repeated at various points in the song. This frequently occurs between the first chorus and second verse. In this capacity, the intro acts as a break that lets a listener soak in the information he or she has received and get ready for the next round. Examples of songs with recurring intros include "Careless Whisper" (George Michael), "Light My Fire" (The Doors), "I Can't Tell You Why" (The Eagles), and "Rocky Top" (various artists).

Signature Licks

A signature lick is a short instrumental phrase that acts as a melodic hook separate and independent from the lyric. Signature licks don't have to be reserved for intros, but a signature lick in the intro can be a great way to make your song stand out.

Nowhere was the importance of an intro signature lick more important than in the heyday of classic rock. Rock songs like "Play That Funky Music" (Wild Cherry) and "Honky Tonk Women" (The Rolling

Stones) are instantly recognized by listeners within a second or two after the song starts. Signature licks also liven up country songs ("Margarita-ville" by Jimmy Buffet), pop songs ("A Fool Believes" by The Doobie Brothers), alt songs ("Longview" by Green Day), and virtually every other popular genre.

When writing a signature lick, think of it as a melodic hook without words over it. It's not a blindingly fast, complex solo but rather something to make people hum along or play air guitar to and get them into the song before the lyric starts. Think of it as a tag that says, "Hi, my name is [title]" and to let people know what song is about to start.

A great signature lick is one that can make a listener's ears perk up in the first two seconds. This gives him or her the chance to say, "Hey, listen. This is that song I was talking about" before the lyric actually starts. That way, the listener (and the listener's friends) can hear your whole song. Sweet, huh?

The "Seven Second" Rule

Although intros may run in excess of twenty seconds on the radio, you should keep your demo intros to seven seconds or less. Publishers don't have time to listen to long intros. They sometimes listen to hundreds of songs on a given day. A fabulous intro doesn't mean anything to a publisher if the hook doesn't sizzle, the chorus doesn't explode, and the overall song isn't what's needed on a given day. If you want, you can go ahead and write a longer intro, play it live, record it for your own listening pleasure, and put it on your CD. Just make sure the version you play for publishers and other music business professionals keeps to the seven-second rule.

Unless you have a clear, strong vision for the intro of your song, don't worry too much about making it stand out. In many cases, producers and studio musicians will change or add an intro when an artist or group records your song. From a songwriter's standpoint, short and simple is usually your best bet.

Writing the Verses

Lyric information in the verse sets the scene and fills in the details so that the chorus information, which is usually more general, has a firm foundation on which to place the central statements of the song. Since the verse often contains the first lyrical information a listener hears, it's a perfect spot for details and visuals that help make your song real in the mind of the listener.

Think of a verse as being like the props and set for a movie. If you went to see a movie about King Arthur and the actors stood around in blue jeans in front of a crayon drawing of a castle, no amount of great acting could make you imagine that it was real. On the other hand, period costumes and a set that looked like a real castle would help you suspend disbelief enough to stop worrying about what's real and what's not. That's what a verse should do for your song: give the imagination "permission" to get into a story as if it were happening.

ALERT!

Just because the verse needs to carry a lot of the descriptive information doesn't mean that you should allow it to become overly long in order to make everything fit. Try to keep verses to a maximum of thirty seconds long. If you need more room, try a faster meter with more syllables per line.

In a story song, verses often act as a prologue, carry the bulk of the plot, and sometimes give an epilogue to the story. In a life cycle song, the verses will usually each cover a period of time or scene of importance. In a love song, the verses often give evidence to support the central theme. If your chorus is built around the hook "your love feels like home," then a verse that says, "You're comfy as my old easy chair and warm as mama's kitchen on Thanksgiving" adds depth and meaning to the statement made by the hook. In a humorous or novelty song, the verses may set up the chorus to be a punch line or they may contain a series of jokes or funny situations about which the chorus makes a general statement that ties them all together.

What about the Hook?

For the professional songwriter, the hook is perhaps the single most important part of the song. Usually the title, or contained within the title, the hook is the essence and embodiment of the song's central theme or message. Sometimes the hook is a common phrase; other times a phrase is twisted into a play on words, like "Not on Your *Love*" or "Lifestyles of the *Not so* Rich and Famous."

Hooks cannot be copyrighted. Any songwriter can take any hook and use it. Still, using a recent hit for your hook is usually a bad idea: It's unoriginal and may confuse listeners. A hook from thirty years ago might be a great start for a new song, especially in a different genre. Some hit songs that share the same hook are "I'm Sorry" (Brenda Lee, 1960; John Denver, 1975), "My Love" (Petula Clark, 1966; Paul McCartney, 1973), and "Venus" (Frankie Avalon, 1959; The Shocking Blue, 1970; and Bananarama, 1986).

A scan through the charts will reveal that there are dozens of different kinds of hooks. However, some kinds seem to have better luck than others. Here's a list of some of the types of hooks that reappear in hit songs decade after decade. Included are a few examples of each kind and the years they charted:

- **Common phrases:** It's Now or Never (1960), Tossin' and Turnin' (1961), I Heard It Through the Grapevine (1968), That's What Friends Are For (1986), Miss You Much (1989).
- **Names:** Tammy (1957), Big Bad John (1962), Hey Jude (1968), My Sharona (1979), Jack and Diane (1982).
- **One-word hooks:** Don't (1958), Yesterday (1965), Escape (1979), Jump (1984), Faith (1987).
- **Dances:** The Twist (1960), The Hustle (1975), The Safety Dance (1982), The Electric Slide (1991), Watermelon Crawl (1995).

Mini-trends like "the" songs ("The Letter," "The Chair," and "The Ride") and "un" songs ("Unforgettable," "Unbreakable," and "Unbelievable") pop up often enough to make them potential hook-hunting ground.

A quick look at the fifty all-time top singles in *Billboard* magazine shows that well over half of all hit hooks revolve around a central theme of love (first love, passion, love lost, and other variations), but a hook can be about anything. Don't believe it? Also in the top-fifty singles are songs about dancing in jail, racial harmony, cold-blooded killers, poverty, a famous battle, the plight of the working man, and astrology, just to name a few.

FACT

Keeping your hook short and sweet makes it easy to remember, talk about, and ask for, not just for listeners and people who buy music, but also for DJs, program directors, publishers, artists, reviewers, and other music business professionals. Over half of all hit songs have a hook/title of three words or less.

The Chorus Section

The hook is generally included in the chorus section, because it directly addresses the hook's information with each line. Sometimes the chorus simply restates the message presented in the hook. At other times, the chorus may be a list of ideas that culminates in the hook.

The chorus usually appears two or three times during the song and contains the most important information, so it needs to be even tighter and catchier than the other parts. The most wonderful verse you've ever written would probably get boring if you used it three times in the same song. The chorus needs to be absolutely bulletproof to make a listener want to hear it again and again.

Lyrically, chorus information is sometimes more abstract than verse information and is often a philosophical statement or moral of the story supported by the verses. It's usually presented in a leaner and more compact style than that of the verses. A simpler meter with longer notes and less syllables can help keep this density from bogging down the chorus or making it too heavy. If the other parts of the song have done their jobs, the transition to a different type of information and style of presentation should be logical and easy.

From a musical standpoint, the chorus should sound big and memorable. Ideally, the chorus should be easy for listeners to sing along with. This makes your song interactive by letting the listener participate and also makes it easier for a listener to remember the song; it's much easier for a person to remember something they did than something they only heard.

Lift, Channel, or Ramp

"Lift," "channel," and "ramp" are terms used to describe a pre-chorus section that acts as a transition between verse and chorus. Just as an intro says, "Here comes the song," a lift says, "Here comes the chorus."

Musically, a lift can act as a dynamic buffer zone between a laidback verse and an explosive chorus or help prepare a listener's ears for a key change. Lyrically, a lift can be good for enhancing continuity in songs in which the chorus information contrasts sharply with the verse information.

Musically and lyrically, a lift often functions by splitting the difference between two contrasting sections. Lifts should be kept short, one to four lines. When writing a lift, remember that you're taking things from one level to another. Lyrical information in a lift should help connect the verse to the chorus and musical information should do the same. Some lifts are at a plateau, halfway between the feel and melodic ranges of the verse and the chorus. Others start where the verse leaves off and shift gears as they head toward the chorus. A great example of this kind of lift can be found in the Lonestar song "Amazed."

Adding the Bridge

The bridge is a transitional element most often found near the end of a song. Musically, the bridge is used as a break from the repeated sections to keep the listener's attention. Both musically and lyrically, the bridge should be different than the song's other sections. A bridge should be a little something extra. It's a place where you can go outside what the rest of the song is doing and push the envelope a little. To build a bridge, you may choose a different melody, chord structure, meter, information flow, or rhyme scheme.

Often, the end of the bridge is the lyrical and musical climax of the song. In most songs, the bridge precedes the final chorus. If so, it's important for the lyrical and musical information of the bridge, especially the last line, to lead to the chorus.

A bridge isn't always necessary. Sometimes a simple verse/chorus format is enough, or a short instrumental leading into a lift/chorus does the job. Use your intuition to tell you if a song needs a little something extra in the form of a bridge.

A bridge can be a great problem solver in a three-verse song that's starting to feel a little ho-hum. Just take the lyric information of the third verse and write a bridge with it. *Voilà!* You don't lose any information and you still get a nice break to keep the song from getting boring.

Instrumental Passages

In a live band setting, solos and instrumental passages can stretch a two-minute song to twenty minutes or more. As long as the crowd is into it, rock on! But on a demo, you want keep instrumental passages a short as possible. Why? Publishers don't usually care how good the musicians are. They want to hear the song, not the performance. A two-minute guitar solo, no matter how wonderful it is, won't do a lot to advance your song's message and storyline. Publishers need three minutes of radio-playable ear candy that focuses around a hook. Want a cut? Show off your song, not your playing ability.

For a songwriter, instrumental passages exist mostly to provide a break or a transition between parts and to round out a song. If the solo section can be used to reinforce melodic themes from the main body of the song, that's great! If not, keep it short, simple, and "hooky." Make sure the players are focused on the emotional message of the song and not just on showing off their chops. This includes you if you're playing on your own demos. A good solo can add something to a song, but it's better not to have a solo than to have one that gets in the way of your story.

FACT

Approaching a solo from a songwriter's perspective can be a great exercise in melodic composition. Try writing some melodic passages as solos to some of your songs. Aim for something simple and memorable and, if you decide to record it, don't be afraid to let the studio musicians experiment with it.

Getting to the Finish Line

As a songwriter, the ending is the least of your worries. Odds are that the ending you choose for your song will be changed or replaced by the artist or producer if the song gets cut. That said, you still have to figure out how to end your song on a demo and during live performance. Otherwise, you'll be stuck for all eternity playing a song that never ends.

There are countless ways to end a song. Ultimately, you have to decide which one works best for each of your songs. Try several endings and see if one fits the song better than the others. Here are some examples of the different kinds of endings used in contemporary songs. Feel free to experiment with these, change them, combine them, and come up with your own unique ways of wrapping things up.

- **Custom tag:** Musical section or signature lick written to be an ending.
- **Intro tag:** A reprise of the intro used for ending the song.
- **Riff tag:** An ending that incorporates a signature lick or riff from the song.
- **Motive reprise:** A final, instrumental repetition of the main musical theme.
- **Chorus/verse reprise:** Like a motive reprise, but with verse or chorus melody.
- **Hook fade:** Several repetitions of the hook over a fade out.

- **Double chorus fade:** A double chorus that fades out in the second half.
- **Hook dead stop:** A final repetition of the hook, ending in a sudden stop.

Any of the endings that draw from another part of the song may require a bit of tailoring. Tweak and adjust them as necessary. A few tricks to try include slowing down at the very end, modulating the key of a final chorus, or adding a brief rest or bit of silence before a final chord.

Though recorded versions of a song often fade out, you'll need a definite ending for live performance. A tentative ending that trails off uncertainly can undermine your song and make an audience or publisher doubt a song they just heard and liked. A confident ending says that you believe in your song.

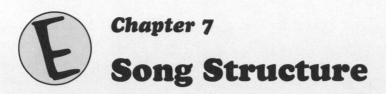

Chapter 7

Song Structure

Once you understand the basic parts of a song and what they can do, you still have to put them in some kind of order. This may sound like a no-brainer, but it can make a big difference in how your song affects the listener. Song structure is a great tool for controlling the flow of your storyline and keeping a song exciting.

Chorus and Refrain

The word *chorus* can mean a lot of different things. Originally, the chorus was an ensemble of actors in Greek theatre who wore spooky masks and chanted or sang in unison (kind of like a choir). Chorus means pretty much the same thing in musical theatre today; you'll still hear actors say, "I tried out for a lead role, but all I got was a part in the chorus." The chorus is there to reinforce the main actors by singing (and sometimes dancing in a "chorus line") along with certain parts of a play to make them sound bigger and stand out—just like the chorus of a modern song.

ALERT!

Some professional songwriters try several different structures for a finished song. Experiment and see which way works best for each of your songs. Try putting the chorus first, switching the order of the verses, or anything else that comes to mind. Take chances; you can always bring it back to the original form.

At times, the term "refrain" has been used interchangeably with "chorus." Technically, the refrain may be considered to be anything that's not the verse. In times past, the verse section was used to set up a story and introduce the song. After the verse alerted people that a song was about to begin, and filled in any "inside" information that the listener might need to understand the song, then the refrain came. The refrain functioned as the main body of the song and could contain several different versions of a chorus along with a bridge and instrumental sections. After the refrain kicked the song into high gear, it never went back to the verse. In the early decades of recorded music, the verse was often left out of a recording due to space considerations in available recording media (many early systems had less than three minutes of recording time) and the refrain was the only part that made it onto the record.

These days, a song part that contains the hook or title and appears more than once in a song is usually called "a chorus." The chorus is still typically the biggest-sounding part of the song and the part most often accompanied by several voices. Fortunately, with the notable exception of a few heavy metal bands, back-up singers are no longer expected to wear spooky masks.

Just because a certain song part, form, structure, or section hasn't been used recently doesn't mean it won't be tomorrow. Tastes change constantly. Nostalgic trends bring back older styles with regularity, and innovations sometimes render an outmoded style of writing suddenly relevant again.

The AAA Song

The AAA, or "triple A," is one of the oldest song structures in existence. The first song was probably a single A, then some early songwriting genius figured out how to copy the melody and meter of "A" and expand his or her song with a similar section. At this point, song structure was born. An AAA doesn't always refer to a song with three sections; it can be a term to describe any song with only one basic lyric section that repeats, so you could call an AAAAA song an AAA for short.

Some of the best-known songs are AAA format and the AAA can cover a variety of genres, everything from "Old MacDonald" and "Amazing Grace" to "The Thrill Is Gone." The advantages of an AAA are that it is almost instantly familiar and easy to learn for a sing-along. AAA songs are great for the campfire, theme songs for organizations, anthems, and children's songs. Since an AAA only has one melodic section, that melody must be incredibly strong.

If you're not an established artist or writer, an AAA song can be an impossible pitch to get past a publisher. An easy fix is to take the hook and fashion a short chorus. Even a two-line chorus, like that of the Stephen Foster song "Oh, Susannah," can increase your song's earning potential significantly.

Figure 7-1

```
I:   1 7 4 1              A:  1 5- 7 4 1 1
     1 4 1 1                  1 5- 7 4 1 1
                              1 5- 7 4 1
A:   1 5- 7 4 1 1             1 5- 7 4 1
     1 5- 7 4 1 1
     1 5- 7 4 1 1        I:  1 7 4 1
     1 5- 7 4 1 1            1 4 1 1

A:   1 5- 7 4 1
     1 5- 7 4 1         A:  1 5- 7 4 1 1
     1 5- 7 4 1             1 5- 7 4 1 1
     1 5- 7 4 1             1 5- 7 4 1
                           1 5- 7 4 1
Tag: 1 7 4 1
                       I:  1 7 4 1
A:   1 5- 7 4 1 1           1 4 1 1
     1 5- 7 4 1 1
     1 5- 7 4 1        I:  1 7 4 1
     1 5- 7 4 1            1 4 1 1

I:   1 7 4 1           A:  1 5- 7 4 1 1
     1 4 1 1               1 5- 7 4 1 1
                           1 5- 7 4 1
A:   1 5- 7 4 1 1          1 5- 7 4 1
     1 5- 7 4 1 1
     1 5- 7 4 1       I:  1 7 4 1
     1 5- 7 4 1           1 4 1 1

I:   1 7 4 1          I:  1 7 4 1
     1 4 1 1              1 4 1 1
```

In modern radio markets, the AAA is almost nonexistent. Occasionally, though, an AAA will come seemingly out of nowhere to scale the charts. Such was the case with Gordon Lightfoot's "The Wreck of the Edmund Fitzgerald," an old-time story song in the style of a sea chanty that caught the public ear in 1976 by adding a modern-day true story and some electric guitar for spice.

"The Wreck of the Edmund Fitzgerald" is actually an AAAAAAA song, where each of the seven sections consists of a double verse. Even though it's basically an AAA song, there are several subtle differences in certain sections, including extra measures. There are also three kinds of instrumental "tags," which are all variations on the intro. One of the tags is different enough that it must be charted as a separate entity. These little touches help the song overcome the prime drawback of the AAA: It tends to get boring to the ears after two or three "A" sections.

In charting this song, you could choose to express the main song section as either an "A" or with a "V" for verse. The chart for this song might look like the one in **FIGURE 7-1**. Don't worry about deciphering the notation system just yet. For now, just look at how the sections are laid out and notice that the patterns of numbers, indicating chords and measures, vary slightly, even between some of the sections marked "A."

The AABA Song

As the music market became more consumer-driven, song styles began to change in response. AAA songs and verse/refrain songs gave way to a form called "the AABA." This form is less repetitive than an AAA, but gets to the meat of the story and melody much more quickly than a verse/refrain song.

In an AABA, the "A" section fulfills most of the common duties of verse and chorus. Like a verse, the "A" section in an AABA usually contains different information each time, though one of the first two A's may be repeated after the "B" section. Like a chorus, the "A" section will usually contain the hook, often at the very end of the section. The "B" section is like a bridge and serves as a break after the first two "A" sections.

Though the former dominance of the AABA has been passed on to newer forms like the ABAB and the ABABCB, you'll still find them making a more than occasional appearance on the charts. Some AABA songs you may have heard are "Don't It Make My Brown Eyes Blue" (Crystal Gayle), "Just the Way You Are" (Billy Joel), and "Yesterday" (The Beatles).

It's important to remember that a song's structure is named by the structure that dominates the song. An AABA song may have an intro or tags, but if AABA is the basic form of the song, you may refer to it as an AABA. Just make sure you put *all* the parts on the song chart.

The ABABCB Song

Modern radio formats generally favor songs that are short and repeat the hook several times in the course of the song. In the last part of the twentieth century and up to now, the ABABCB has become one of the most used forms. This form, along with its siblings, seems to find a perfect balance between variety and familiarity in structure.

In an ABABCB, the structure almost always runs verse-chorus-verse-chorus-bridge-chorus, with the option of an extra chorus at the end that usually fades out over about seven seconds. This form doesn't allow the verse to become tiresome, as it often does in the multiple-verse song forms that don't contain a "C" section. It does, however, give maximum exposure to the chorus (and thus the hook), balancing this by the use of a nonrecurring bridge to freshen the listener's ears before the final blitz.

How many times should the hook appear?
There's no set answer to this. Songs have hit the charts that had no hook at all (though these are very rare) and some repeat the hook dozens of times. If you want to make money, shoot for six or more times. Never settle for less than three.

The ABABCB form is one of the best for commercially oriented songwriting. Examples include "Hurt So Good" (John Cougar Mellencamp), "What's Love Got to Do with It (Tina Turner), and "Sharp Dressed Man" (ZZ Top), which is an unusual variation—it uses the "C" section, musically a bridge, for a guitar solo.

Some variations of this form are ABABCAB ("Back on the Chain Gang" by The Pretenders), ABABCBAB ("Every Rose Has Its Thorn" by Poison), and ABABCABCAB ("It's Still Rock 'N Roll to Me" by Billy Joel). Interestingly, each of these songs has a solo section in a different part: the first, over a recurring intro, the second as a modified third chorus, and the last in the second "C" section.

"ABACAB" and Other Oddities

Of the other popular song formats, the biggest seller is probably the ABAB, which can either be verse/chorus or chorus/verse. Example of this form range from "Back in Black" (AC/DC) and "Margaritaville" (Jimmy Buffet) to "Sugar, Sugar" (The Archies) and "Hotel California" (The Eagles). This form often inserts a long instrumental section in lieu of a bridge, making it a favorite of musicians everywhere. ABABs can get a little stale when they have more than two verses. From a production standpoint, you'll want to do something to differentiate the verses. This is often done by taking the dynamics further down than usual for the last verse.

Myriad variations in form exist. If you look hard enough, you'll find AABACA, ABCBAB, ABCABCB, and almost any other variation you can think of. Rumor has it that the Genesis hit "ABACAB" was named after the order in which the sections appear.

Nonrecurring "A" Sections

One of the oddest song parts, and one that is seldom used these days, is the nonrecurring "A" section. In the early part of the twentieth century, this part was called "a verse," but it bears little resemblance to the verses of today. The nonrecurring "A" section is more of a "pre-song" or verbal intro that sets up the story. This section was usually sung, though sometimes spoken, and bore little musical resemblance to the rest of the song. There were huge lyrical differences, too. Long, dense lines hovered over held chords to create a tension that was broken when the "real song" finally kicked in.

This device is interesting because it freed up the main body of the song to be very simple and singable: All the background information was covered by the "A" section, leaving the rest of the song to say as little or as much as desired. This also allowed for lyrics that were more poetic and vague, because the listener was already let in on any necessary details of the story. For great examples of nonrecurring "A" sections, see if you can find copies of "Stardust" or "I Got Rhythm" with the "A" sections included.

Points of Notation

The way in which song structure is written out varies from songwriter to songwriter. You may see an intro marked as "INTRO," "IN," "I," "A," or "TAG." A verse may be designated "A," "B," or "C," depending on its order of appearance; more common is a "V" (verse). Chorus may not only be marked with the letter appropriate to its order of appearance, but may also be marked "CH" for chorus or, frequently, with a dollar sign ($), a good reminder of the importance of the chorus.

Appearance order or a "B" or "BR" may mark bridge sections. Pre-chorus sections may be marked "PRE," "PC," "LIFT," "L," "RAMP," "R," by appearance order, or even with a drawn ramp or arrow pointing up at an angle. If they occur with every chorus, pre-choruses are often simply written in as part of the chorus. Tags are usually written as "Tag" or "TA," if the tag is a turnaround.

When naming parts for a chart, you may discover that some sections could have multiple names. If your intro is an instrumental chorus and it recurs, it could be an intro, tag, or chorus. Choose the least confusing option. Label it "I" for intro, and it won't be mistaken for a chorus or different tag.

Modified Structures

Every year, thousand upon thousands of great songs go uncut because they aren't different enough to catch a publisher's ear. Songwriters are always looking for new ways of doing things that might make a great song stand out among the millions of other great songs in the world. To accomplish this, they've developed a bag of tricks full of special structural modifications that wouldn't occur to most of us unless we spent a long time thinking about structure and how to change it.

The implied chorus is a neat little timesaver. Used in place of a second or third chorus, the implied chorus goes through any existing pre-chorus sections and starts the chorus normally (usually with the hook), but then doesn't finish, often going to either a bridge, verse, instrumental, or combination of these before going back to a full chorus. Since the listener has already heard the chorus at least once, a little bit of it makes the brain flash back to the previously received information, leaving the brain with the impression that it has heard another chorus.

Merging and Cutting

Merging sections can yield some really cool results. You can try putting one section on top of another, like an extra vocal part singing a verse over the final chorus, or try using the beginning of one section and the end of another. A good way to do this is to write a two-line bridge and then finish it off with the last two to four lines in the form of a verse or chorus.

Sometimes, half a section is all you need to get your point across. This can be especially true of verses. If you've told your story in the first verse and chorus, try writing half a second verse that moves into a bridge or chorus. This move surprises the listener, helps keep his or her attention, and saves time. Remember that it can be a whole lot easier to write a short song than it is to make a long song shorter.

To find more modifications, listen to your favorite songs with a songwriter's ears, check the top-forty countdown, and anything else you can get your hands on. Now that you know what to look for, you'll probably find dozens of tricks and tools you never knew existed. You might also think up a few of your own.

A great exercise for understanding song structure is to analyze several different songs and write out the structure for each, noting any modifications. Start with your favorites and work outward from there. What patterns do your favorite writers use most often? Do you see certain kinds of structures more often in particular genres?

Wraparounds and Turnarounds

Wraparounds and turnarounds are often confused with one another. A turnaround is a song part that is simply a repeat of the end of the preceding section. Turnarounds are often used for intros, short solos, or instrumental sections, and end tags. A common turnaround heard in hundreds of old country songs is a 1 5 1 (or D A D in the key of "D"), but a turnaround can be based around almost any short series of chords, as long as they replicate those ending the preceding pattern. It should be noted that a turnaround may occasionally foreshadow, which is to say it will imitate the end of a part that has not yet occurred. This most often happens when a turnaround is used for an intro.

A wraparound is a literary device used by lyric writers. A wraparound consists of ending the song with the same line that begins it. The wraparound leaves us looking at the scene we came in on from a different viewpoint, having now heard the song. A fine example of a wraparound is the Montgomery Gentry song "Tattoos and Scars," which is an ABABC song that modifies the form by ending the "C" section with the last half of a "B" section before using the first part of the initial "A" section for a wraparound ending. Ⓔ

Chapter 8

Troubleshooting Solutions

Acommon saying in the music business is that great songs aren't written, they're rewritten. Most songs seem great when they're brand new, but problems often become apparent later. Don't despair—this happens to hit songwriters too. The difference is that a hit songwriter usually has an idea of what to do to fix problems in a good song to make it into a really great song.

Interpretation Dependency

So, you played your new song for a few friends and they all got it, but strangers and publishers are getting the wrong idea—they just don't get it. Unfortunately, this means that you just won't get a cut. The problem may be that your song is interpretation dependent; it has to be sung and heard a certain way to make sense because the lyric alone doesn't get the message across.

Irony

For those of you who were baffled by the Alanis Morissette song "Ironic," irony is when the apparent meaning of something contradicts its real meaning. Irony is a subtle device; if you use it in a song without pointing it out, it'll sail right over the heads of most people. Make sure that your intended audience will be able to identify the places in your song that make use of irony. If you have any doubts, it might be best to make the use of irony more clear by either rewriting the line or pointing it out in some other way. If this doesn't work, try saying what you mean.

Sarcasm

Sarcasm is the use of particular kinds of emphasis and delivery that make it clear that a statement is ironical in nature. Like when you go to a party and your ex-girlfriend shows up and says, "It's sure *great* to see *you* here!" Sarcasm can be very funny if used well and interpreted correctly by the recording artist.

FACT

A good way to highlight sarcasm can be to put particular emphasis on one word in a line. Stretching the word and using a slightly higher note can make it stand out. Try this with "Veeeerrry funny" and "Well, excuuuuse me" to get an idea how this can work.

Unfortunately, the use of sarcasm requires some acting ability on the part of the singer. This may severely limit the number of artists who can effectively perform your song. If you hear a particular singer use sarcasm frequently and well, you might consider using it in material written specifically for that artist. For demo purposes, remember that the more exaggerated the delivery, the more apparent the intended interpretation will be.

Clarity Issues

It doesn't matter how timely your message is or how brilliant your metaphor is if nobody understands what the heck you're talking about. If a publisher, or any listener, says they don't get it, explaining and arguing won't help. They have to get it by *hearing the song*, not by hearing you explain what they should have heard. Besides, you can't go around and personally explain to forty million record buyers what your song means. If too many people don't get it, it needs a rewrite.

It's best to develop a circle of people you can get feedback from and play a song for them before you take it to a publisher or pay for a demo. Don't explain anything before you play the song. Ask your critique circle questions about the story line when you've finished. Did most of them get it?

He, She, It

Sometimes solving a clarity issue is as easy as watching your pronouns. Say you've got two guys in your story, we'll call them Bob and Biff. Now, if Bob and Biff are having a legendary fight in the middle of the song and your lyric says, "Then he hit him and he hit him and he hit him again," it's not clear who is hitting whom. It makes more sense to say, "Then Bill hit Biff and Biff hit Bill and Bill hit Biff again." The exception to this would be if you had already made it clear that one person was doing all the hitting, in which case the first version works fine.

To keep a song clear, try to limit pronoun usage to one "he" and one "she" character in a story. Alternately, use a name in the first part of a line that ties to the pronoun in the second half: "The sheriff grabbed the gun and he waved it in the air."

Vagueness

"Stairway to Heaven" is a great song, but what the heck is it *about?* The trick here is that much of the record buying public at the time was into allegory, multiple or hidden meanings, and—let's face it—drugs that made some lyrics appear to make more sense than they actually did.

The song is full of imagery that conjures up a "Lord of the Rings" kind of fantasy world. It's musically beautiful, masterfully performed, passionately sung, and has a kickin' guitar solo at the end. It also came along at the exact right time and was performed by a very popular group.

Here's a simple exercise to do with two or more songwriters. Have each writer bring a song to play. After listening to a song, have all the songwriters (except the one who wrote it) give brief, written descriptions of the characters in the song. Do they match with the author's mental picture of the characters?

A song that's too vague or leaves too much up to the imagination doesn't meet the listener half way. If your song is about a girl, people want to know a little about the girl. Where is she from? Is she shy or brassy? What's so special about her that you had to go and write a song about her? It's great that you still remember your first date with her, but the listener wasn't there, so you need to fill in a few details. Did you go to the drive-in or roller-skating? Did you show up in jeans to find her wearing formal attire? What did you eat?

You don't have to overload the listener with details, but give enough of the picture to make someone want to fill the rest in. Ideally, you want an average person who's just heard your song for the first time to be able to tell you what it's about and remember a few details.

Assumed Information

Let's say your song begins with the following lines: "The alarm clock went off and she said, 'honey, it's time to wake up!' / I had to get goin' or else I'd be late for the bus."

You can see the scene in your head: It's the first day of seventh grade, he got an alarm clock for his birthday, but his Mom still calls up the stairs like she always has. She's called him "honey" since he was a little baby. As a young man, he's starting to feel a little uncomfortable with the nickname, yet it's hard to let go of the stability and comfort of childhood. You can see the house, smell the coffee and eggs, and hear the AM radio playing in the kitchen.

Unfortunately, a listener could hear the same two lines and picture *this* scene: It's Monday morning. He always sleeps through the alarm because he's always tired. His wife, knowing this, gently wakes him. They only have one car and he has to catch the city bus downtown to his job so she can pick up the kids after she's done with hers.

Holy cow! How'd *that* happen? Well, you assumed a lot of information that you didn't tell the listener, so the listener's imagination filled in what you didn't say. Let's try a rewrite and see if it gets a little clearer: "The alarm clock went off, but she still yelled up the stairs 'boy, wake up'/ I had to get goin' or I'd miss that big yellow bus."

By adding the "but she still" in the first line, it becomes apparent that "she" has been yelling up those stairs for a while. So, it's someone he knows. It also firmly establishes that she's not in the bed with him. She calls him "boy," so either he's really a boy or it's someone with whom he's very familiar or both. A big yellow bus must be a school bus. So, he must really be a boy, which means she must be his mom. It all makes sense now.

FACT

Unless you show them otherwise, listeners assume certain kinds of information. Most listeners assume any kids in your song have two parents who are still married. Most also assume the song takes place in modern times. Make a list of other "gimmies," and be sure you spell out anything that disagrees with the status quo.

The TMI Syndrome

Of course, there is such a thing as too much information. A few deft brushstrokes can sometimes paint a picture. A few details can make a scene seem more real. Too many, though, and the picture can become confusing and cluttered. How much is enough? You'll have to decide for yourself. The nice thing is that you almost always have time to take out or put in a few things before you take a song to a publisher. Finding the right balance between too little information and too much is one of the things that can make a good song into a great song.

Let's say you're writing a song about two junior-high sweethearts from the point of view of the girl, who's looking back at the event as a grown woman. You decide to describe the boy with the following lines:

He had fourteen freckles underneath his blue eyes
Six of which were of significant size
Three on his nose, five on each cheek
And one under the lips I longed to hear speak.

What's your point here? Is the song about freckles? If it is, that's okay. If not, let's decide what's important here and do a rewrite. The fact that she remembers exactly how many freckles he had after all this time says that he made a big impression on her—that's good, keep it. However, people get that idea without having to know how big the freckles were or the exact location of each one. Let's see if we can use the space more efficiently and get some other stuff in there with the freckles:

Fourteen freckles underneath his blue eyes
I tried to kiss 'em all on the fourth of July
There was one between his chin and his lower lip
Wouldn't y'know that's the one that I missed.

What kinds of details should I add?
That depends on what you're trying to say. Need to reinforce that someone's a little wild? Don't just have them pull up in a fast car, make it a *red* car, and have it skid to a stop as they smile. Don't *tell* the listener, *show* them.

Cute or Trite? Sweet or Sappy?

If you can get them on the radio, love songs only have to make sense to people who are totally in love and not anyone else, right? Well, you can make a lot more money by writing love songs that make sense to the rest of the world. Think about the songs you listened to with your first love. Looking back, some of them are pretty sappy, right? Some of them would probably have embarrassed you even back then, if someone had caught you singing them to each other out on lover's lane.

The problem is, songs that might sound great to someone in love can put off an average listener and make the average publisher (who has heard a gazillion of these) want to strangle you before you can write again. To get the most out of your love songs—and survive your next publisher meeting—you want something that not only appeals to starry-eyed lovers, but to anyone who's ever been in love and anyone who ever hopes to be.

It's All about Dosage

Writing a love song is like making sweet tea. Not enough sugar and it's not sweet tea; too much, and it'll make you sick. Look for a balance that's somewhere in between. Find a way to say it sweetly, without being sappy or cute or trite. A little tension and/or humor can be a big help in keeping the listener from lapsing into a diabetic coma every time your song comes on.

Meter Adjustments

So, your song's almost done but you're having problems with the meter. The third line of the second verse sounds good, but it just doesn't match the third line of the first verse. It's so different that you can't just leave it, and it's bugging the heck out of you. You've tried rewriting it a zillion times with different words and word orders. You even reworked the rhyme scheme a couple of times to try and get something new happening. You actually tried changing the story to get a line that would fit. And yet, not one of these options has you any closer to a workable line.

You're out of gas. You've consulted books, played it for all your co-writers, prayed and fasted, and thrown darts at a thesaurus. There's just nothing left to do, is there? Actually, there's always something you can do. There are bound to be word combinations you haven't tried yet. Make a list of the ones you've tried—all of them, every single one. Make a list of possibilities for lines that say the same thing from a different angle. Make a list of other things this verse might say. Cover all the ground you've already covered, take a break, and cover it again. Even Sherlock Holmes didn't always catch things the first time. Make sure you haven't missed something. Oh, and here's a solution you might have missed: If the line sounds good the way it is, why not change the third line of the *first* verse to match it. Sometimes, it's just that simple.

Melodic Difficulties

Or you may run into the following problem. The words are perfect. The meter is perfect. The song is three minutes and twelve seconds of perfection. It just sounds a little weird in places and doesn't blow you away in others. You thought it would work itself out if you just sang it for a week or two. That didn't happen. It's time to sit down and fix the problem.

Differentiating Parts of a Song

If the melody is good but it just doesn't go "bang" when it hits the chorus, there are a number of ways to fix this problem. First, look at the overall melodic range of the song. Is it too narrow? If so, try moving the chorus melody up a third or the verse melody to a fifth harmony in the octave below the melody. You might have to make some adjustments, but it's a starting point.

In a song with very small melodic range, modulating the key can be a way to differentiate sections. This is especially true in songs with sections that repeat back-to-back. For a great example of multiple modulations, listen to the Tommy Roe song "Dizzy."

Now, let's take a look at the *tessitura*—a factor describing where, within the melodic range of a song, a certain section spends most of its time. If you have a good melodic range in the song, but the parts still sound a lot alike, look at the tessitura to identify problems. It could be that the verse has a couple of low notes in the first line, then jumps up into chorus territory for the remaining three lines. To solve this, try reserving the top few notes of the melodic range for chorus use only. The opposite can be done as well, with a few notes on the bottom being used only in the verse. Overall, you generally want a lower tessitura for the verse and a higher one for the chorus. This doesn't mean things can't overlap, just that they should have significant differences.

Pay Attention to Continuity

What if the melodies of two adjoining sections are so different that they don't seem to connect? Sometimes this can be a tessitura problem. Look at where the notes are in the end of the first section. Are they more than half an octave away from the notes that begin the next section? If so, you can try changing the melody of the last line of the first section to "walk up" into the next section. Alternately, you might try starting the first line of the second section lower and "walking up" from there. Sometimes a combination of these two approaches can work.

If that doesn't do it, you might consider writing a two-line lift that provides a buffer zone. A lift usually has elements of the melody and meter of both sections. Sometimes, though, it will be totally different from one or both sections. The important thing is for the lift to create a workable musical connection to the sections on either side of it to help make the transition work. Of course, it'll probably need lyrics and it might make your song too long, so make sure you have extra time and something to say.

Too Much Range

The vocal range of many performers spans about an octave and a half, and getting outside this territory can limit the number of artists who can sing your song. Of course, if you know for certain that your song will be performed by Celine Dion or Mariah Carey, go right ahead and reach for the sky. Otherwise, you'll want to try and make your song exciting without resorting to multi-octave jumps. Besides, you want the listener to be able to sing along, right? When you realize that one of your songs might be "a little rangy," you need to find a way to decrease the melodic range.

Avoid Too Much Modulating

Modulating (changing to a different key) can freshen things up but it can also lead to range problems. Modulation works well in a song with a relatively small melodic range. The bigger the melodic range of a song, the less room you have to modulate without significant changes to the melody. If a modulation is causing your problem, try modulating to a key closer to the original key. If that doesn't work, leave the modulation out. Most modulations are either a half step or whole step up.

Switching the key of a section can be a way out of trouble. It can, however, open a whole new can of worms. Unless the song has a relatively small melodic range, you'll have to have to figure out how to get back to the original key for the next section. Always look ahead.

Trouble-Spot Transposition

If the whole chorus is too high, try moving the whole thing down to a harmony below its present position. If it's just that some spots in the melody go too far outside the normal range of the song, there are a couple of different ways of transposing them while leaving the structure intact. First, try using a harmony of the melody in that spot. Take the trouble spot and figure out a harmony (third or fifth usually work the best) and play the harmony lower or higher than the melody, depending on what you need. Sometimes a spot transposition will make it necessary to change a few surrounding notes to make things blend.

Necessary Sacrifices

Troubleshooting isn't always fun. Sometimes you'll have to get rid of a perfectly good line or word simply because that's what the song needs. There will come a time when you have to cut out the best line in the song because it doesn't fit, doesn't rhyme, or doesn't belong.

Remember that it's the song that's important. Don't let stubbornness stop you from getting a cut. Always be willing to examine your options. Would you really want to lose out on a payday just because you couldn't find a rhyme for "purple" and refused to put your main character in a blue dress?

Get used to making the necessary sacrifices and looking at the big picture; when you do start getting cuts, publishers, producers, and recording artists are going to commit far more horrible atrocities to your songs than you ever envisioned.

Imagine someone taking out a line in your song that mentions a particular brand of vehicle that's in competition with the kind of vehicle the artist is paid to endorse. Now imagine someone replacing your line with an awful line that doesn't make sense and doing so without even *asking* you to rewrite the line in a way that works. Imagine that the song becomes a big hit and gets played a lot on the radio. Every time you hear it, you think "Oh, my God. That line is *horrible* and the whole world thinks I wrote it." Now imagine the size of the checks you receive for the song. Imagine a lot of zeroes on them. It can't repair the sense of hurt and violation, but it sure helps. Ⓔ

Chapter 9

Playing an Instrument

Most successful songwriters—especially those who write melodies—play an instrument. To the beginner who is not a singer or musician, the musical part of songwriting can be a bit daunting. Make the effort; music business professionals tend to take a songwriter much more seriously if he or she can write a melody (even a bad one) and play an instrument (even a little bit).

The Benefits

Perhaps the most important thing that playing an instrument can bestow upon a songwriter is respect. Publishers, producers, A&R reps, recording artists, and other songwriters will be more likely to respect you and your songs if they know you can play. Of course, there's someone even more important than those people: You, the songwriter, will have more confidence and self-respect if you know that you can write and play a song all by your self without any help from anyone.

FACT

If you're already a professional musician, you may be able to use your skills to help advance your songwriting career. Many professional songwriters have made business connections by playing live and/or recording for other people. There is nothing more valuable to you, business-wise, than a direct connection to an artist or producer.

And that's not all. If you play an instrument, you won't have to rely on others to figure out the chord progressions to your songs. You won't have to hire a musician to play for you at an open mike or writer's night, and you'll be able to communicate musical ideas more clearly and more quickly to other musicians in both live and studio settings. This gives you power and independence.

It also means that you won't have to get that embarrassed, apologetic look on your face when someone asks you to play something you wrote. When it comes to proving that you're a songwriter, playing one of your songs is much more convincing than pointing to a notebook or waving a CD.

Brainstorming with an Instrument

When it comes to the actual writing of a song, playing an instrument can open up a whole range of options. Doodling around on an instrument is one of the most popular methods used by successful songwriters for coming up with new ideas.

Sometimes just learning a new chord or experimenting with a different groove or time signature can be all it takes to start you writing a hit song. Playing an instrument can also make for better communication and a more balanced workload when you co-write with another player.

What If I Have No Talent?

You don't have to be a handwriting or calligraphy expert to write great lyrics. You also don't have to be Eddie Van Halen or Mozart to write a great song with the help of an instrument. It's just another tool in your toolbox and it's used in a much different way by a songwriter than by a musician. This is true even if you are Eddie Van Halen.

Instruments are a songwriter's tools for setting moods, building grooves, figuring out chords and signature licks, arranging, trying different keys, working on harmonies, and composing motives or even whole melodies.

Luckily for you, songwriting is different from painting or sculpture in that you can redo a part as many times as it takes to get what you want. This means you can make a million, or a billion, mistakes on your instrument and it won't matter one bit. All that matters is the *one* time when you come up with the part you need for the song. Let's use baseball as an analogy. How well could you play baseball if you could take as many swings as you needed to hit the ball? That's what playing an instrument is like for a songwriter. Come to think of it, that's what songwriting is like: You just keep swingin' until you hit it, then run with it and let the publisher (umpire) decide if you're safe or out.

Learning to play an instrument, even badly, can enhance your songwriting immeasurably. Some of the worst musicians in the history of the world have been some of the greatest songwriters. Unfortunately, some of the best songwriters have been overlooked because they didn't try to learn at least a little about the music side of the music business. To return to the baseball analogy, the best left-fielder in the world can't hit a home run unless he or she steps up to the plate and swings.

> **Am I too old to start?**
> You're never too old to start playing an instrument. You may never become a virtuoso, but, then again, you just might. Jazz great Wes Montgomery was in his mid-thirties when he first took up guitar and was so awful at first that even his wife wouldn't listen to him.

Choosing Your Instrument

After deciding to take the plunge and learn an instrument, you are immediately faced with a sea of options and a medium-sized lake of decisions. As a songwriter, you'll want to pick an instrument that leaves your mouth free to sing, so put away that bassoon fantasy for a minute and think about a more realistic choice.

The Most Obvious Options

Acoustic guitars and electronic keyboards are by far the most popular instruments for songwriters. Why? Because they're versatile, relatively affordable, and used in most kinds of music today. Keyboards offer maximum versatility. A good electronic keyboard can have thousands of different sounds, from pianos to cellos to elephant noises, and can act as a workstation for arranging and sequencing.

An acoustic guitar is tops for portability. It's easy to throw in the car for a co-writing venture, party, campfire, or solo writing session by the lake, and you don't need electricity to use one. Guitar is the instrument most likely to be easily borrowed at an open mike, writer's night, or party. Most publishers have an acoustic guitar right there in the office.

Of course, there's nothing stopping you from deciding to take up the mandolin, banjo, cello, accordion, or any other instrument to augment your songwriting. Still, guitar and keyboards are the easiest to get lessons for and work well in more genres than most other instruments. Eventually, you may decide to expand and add more instruments, get an electric guitar, or buy a piano to augment your songwriting and instrumental studies. This is a fine idea. For now, though, it'll be cheaper, easier, and more productive to start with the basic keyboard or acoustic guitar.

Just because you write on piano doesn't mean that you are restricted to writing piano songs. The same holds true for guitar and other instruments. Learn to use your imagination to come up with parts or ideas that can incorporate different instruments.

Using the Computer

These days it's entirely possible to compose and play a whole song on the computer. With the exception of live playability, a computer can do anything a keyboard or synthesizer can—and more. Computers can make all the sounds, stack them on top of each other, control dynamic parameters, and even tell keyboards what to play and when. Some programs will even allow you to orchestrate your song in standard notation and have the computer play it back for you.

The computer can be a great instrument for those with motor nerve disabilities or other physical challenges that make playing an instrument difficult. With a computer, your musical ability is determined solely by your knowledge of the program, your artistic vision, and the hardware or software you choose for the job.

Sequencing and Loops

Like many modern keyboards, computers with the right software can be used as sequencers. What is a sequencer? Basically, it's a program that controls what kind of sound gets made and when. With a sequencer, you don't have to be able to play perfectly to make it sound as if you did. You just have to be willing to take the time to key in the exact information for the notes you wish to be played.

Another popular application for computers in songwriting is the use of loops. Loops are pieces of songs, ranging from less than a second to a whole section, that you can arrange and rearrange inside the computer to make a "music bed" for your song. A loop can be as simple as a drum beat and as complex as a whole band. Some people make their own loops, others use "factory" loops from various looping programs. In the past, many songwriters have used loops made from digitally sampling other people's records.

ALERT!

Be very careful if you use samples of other people's work. Chances are that a borrowed drum sound or horn hit will go unnoticed, but if you use a recognizable part of someone else's song, you could be breaking the law and you might end up owing money—and lots of it—to the writers, recording artists, and record company.

Buying an Instrument

Once you've decided what instrument you'd like to play, the next step is to acquire it. While it's true that some people have started out on a borrowed or rented instrument, you may find that having your own will help you stay committed.

You (Sometimes) Get What You Pay For

You can find a playable guitar or keyboard for a beginner for under two hundred dollars, but how do you know what playable is when you don't play? If you plan to buy a better instrument, sometimes a little thing like the year, color, make, or model can mean a difference of thousands of dollars on otherwise identical instruments. What may appear to be a brand-new, top-of-the-line instrument might fall apart in a year, while that beat-up old thing in the corner might still sound great when your great-grandkids play it. The absolute best way to get what you need and avoid getting ripped off is to take along a friend who is an experienced player and knows about the brands, styles, and prices of the type of instrument you're looking for.

New versus Used

A new instrument is like a new car: It looks new, it smells new, it shines and sparkles. It also costs a lot more. But electronic keyboards become obsolete after a few years. Parts become harder to find and the new models always have more options. Pianos last longer, but they only have one sound. Besides, do you really want to carry a piano around? Your best bet is probably either a new keyboard or a gently used one that is less than five years old. Have a keyboard-playing friend explain features like onboard sequencing, sampling, FM synthesis, and the various forms of MIDI (Musical Instrument Digital Interface) compatibility. These are all things you'll want to know before you buy.

ALERT!

If you get one of the cheap stick-on pickups or the kind that fits in the sound hole, you will not make a lot of friends out of writer's night hosts. Most of these are very low output and hard to dial in. Instead, opt for an under-the-saddle system with an active pickup. You'll spend a little more, but it's well worth it.

Unlike most computers these days, a good guitar when properly maintained can last well over a hundred years. An acoustic guitar made with good wood and a lacquer finish starts to sound better as it ages, usually hitting peak tone at somewhere between fifteen and fifty years of age. On the other hand, substandard wood, cheap machine heads, poorly aligned bracing, bad glue joints, and a host of other things can render a seemingly perfect, brand new guitar unplayable within a year or two. For these reasons, a used guitar is often the best way to go. Features to look for include an adjustable truss rod in the neck and a solid (not laminated) top. Features that are nice to have but not crucial (because they can all be replaced) are a porcelain or bone saddle and nut, strap buttons at the tail and heel, and tuning gears with a ratio of at least 16:1. If you have the money to invest and want to start with a really good guitar, some of the brands most often used by professional songwriters and musicians are Martin, Takamine, Taylor, and Gibson.

You will probably want an electronic pickup in your acoustic guitar that allows you to plug in for live performances. If the instrument you want doesn't have a pickup, you can buy a good one for about $150 (including installation) in most places. Some pickups are simple affairs that you just plug into and let the soundman worry about the rest. Others have built-in volume and tone controls, equalizers, and other fun toys. The 2001 models of some companies began including built-in tuners.

Where to Look

New instruments can be found in music stores and mail order catalogues like *Musician's Friend,* and are increasingly available online. Used instruments may be a bit harder to track down. Some music stores carry used instruments and equipment. A few even specialize in used and vintage gear. (If you find one of these, it's usually a great place to hang out, talk shop, and hear stories.) Pawn shops, yard sales, garage sales, auctions, classified ads, and "trading post" style newspapers are all places where you might find a deal on a used instrument.

If you don't know a lot about the kind of instrument you intend to buy, be very careful about buying used instruments or any instruments sold by mail-order or through online stores and Internet auctions. With some of these buying methods, you may be agreeing to take merchandise without warranties or return options.

Room to Grow

Instead of getting the cheapest possible instrument, one that may sound horrible and be difficult to play, your best bet may be to get a good one that will leave you some room to grow. It's awfully hard to get motivated to practice on something that even a pro couldn't get a good sound out of.

This doesn't mean that you need an expensive, professional-quality instrument to get started, but you'll probably want something that you can still use a year from now without being distracted by the playability problems of a shoddy instrument. When you do your shopping, have that same friend play the instruments you're serious about buying. Listen to how they sound. Ask your friend which ones play well and which are good deals for the price. Buy your friend lunch and make an afternoon of it, trying out several instruments in different locations before making your final decision. A little extra time spent on finding the right instrument can save you a lot of time and money in the long run and make the experience of learning to play a lot more fun.

Learning How to Play

The hardest part about learning to play an instrument is learning to be patient with yourself and not giving up. You have to give yourself permission to be bad for a while, maybe as long as a couple of years. This can be tough, especially if you're surrounded by other songwriters and musicians who are accomplished players. If you want to feel better, ask one of your favorite musicians how bad he or she was during the first few months of playing. The answer may surprise you. Rather than be intimidated, look to these friends as a source of encouragement and inspiration. Someone probably helped each of them get started and most of them will be glad to pass it on.

Ways to Learn

The options for learning an instrument are almost unlimited. You may want to employ several at once or switch off from time to time. The best way to start is probably with lessons. Group lessons are offered at some colleges and community centers and are usually affordable. Private lessons are more expensive, but the one-on-one attention is worth it if you're serious about learning.

Either way, make sure you find a teacher you can communicate with and with whom you feel comfortable enough to state your goals, ask questions, and take a direct hand in your lesson plan. Most music stores offer private lessons with accomplished, reputable teachers. You can also find private music teachers in the classified ads of your local newspaper, on music store bulletin boards, through local music schools, or by asking friends who play.

Always record your lessons, so you can check how things are supposed to sound and hear the exact words of your teacher instead of trusting to memory. In this way, you can take in more material and absorb it later on your own time. Ask for detailed explanations of anything that seems difficult or unclear.

Instruction books can be another great way to learn your instrument. Literally hundreds of books are available for guitar or piano instruction. The advantages of learning from a book are that it's usually very affordable and you can pick a book that concentrates on the things you want to learn. If you're starting from square one, figuring out a book and an instrument at the same time may be too much to juggle, so you might want to consider taking lessons for a while, then adding in some independent study from a book.

Videos and software, while sometimes a bit more expensive than books, can provide a more accessible learning experience, with information presented in sound and video formats as well as text. When you can watch and hear someone play the lesson being learned, it can make understanding it much easier. Once you've learned how to play a little, you may also find learning opportunities in instrument-specific magazines. For those on a limited budget, the Internet may offer some solutions; in the past few years, a number of Web sites, some of them free, have begun offering lessons and learning materials online.

How Good Is Good Enough?

When have you learned enough to start using your instrument as a writing tool? Songs have been written that use only one chord and thousands of songs have been written around a pattern of three or four chords. You might be able to start using your instrument immediately. Don't get frustrated if you don't instantly get the results you want and don't feel as if you have to use your instrument for all of your writing sessions. Be patient, but persistent, and work your instrument into your writing regimen at a pace that you feel good about. Eventually, you'll probably find that not only will playing inspire you as a writer, but writing will also inspire you as a player. As you become familiar with your instrument, you will begin to relish the challenge of picking out the music in your head and using the instrument to make it a reality.

Improvisation has been an important part of songwriting from the early days of music. Many songwriters describe coming up with melodies and signature riffs as a process of making lucky mistakes while improvising on an instrument. Improvisation is an essential element of Renaissance, Baroque, blues, jazz, rock, and many other styles of music.

As you practice your lessons, listen for sounds that inspire you. See if you can learn the chords to some of your own songs. If you don't have these charted, your teacher or co-writers can probably help. Once you've got a handle on some basic chords, start experimenting with different chord patterns, grooves, and rhythms.

As you learn and your musical skills grow, your instrument will become more productive as a writing tool. How far to take it is up to you. You may decide, as many great writers have, that the basic chords and rhythms are enough for you and leave the fancy stuff to the producers and studio musicians. On the other hand, you may find, as Sir Paul McCartney, Prince, and Camille Wallin have, that fluency with half a dozen instruments helps you express yourself more clearly and gives you more writing options than a basic working knowledge of just one instrument. For now, concentrate on getting started. You can decide the rest later.

Chapter 10

A Crash Course in Music Theory

Music theory is extremely useful, non-toxic to artists, and doesn't have to be intimidating. You're probably thinking, "That's what they said about algebra!" Fair enough, but you've got a choice. Would you rather try to decipher a book's worth of abstract theory crammed into one chapter or learn *how* songwriters use theory and where to learn more? This chapter will give you an introduction to the aspects of music theory that you really do need to know about if you want to be a songwriter.

What Do You Really Need to Know?

How much music theory does a songwriter need to know? You might as well ask how many brushes a painter needs or how many instruments should be in a band. How much theory you'll need is up to you. If you're a classical composer, you'll probably want a college-level education in theory and composition. If you're a film, TV, or jingle writer, it *really* helps to know how to orchestrate and write out parts. If you're a songwriter who hopes to hear his or her songs on the radio someday, the amount of theory you need to know can be determined by how many options you'd like to have, how many styles you'd like to explore, and how much money you'd like to make.

FACT

Starting out as a rock musician with no knowledge of formal music theory, Frank Zappa became increasingly interested in theory and compositional techniques. He went on to become a respected innovator in rock and jazz and one of the premier classical composers of the twentieth century. He even invented a new form of musical notation.

Did the part about the money get your attention? Like any other advantage you could name, an education in theory doesn't guarantee success, but it *can* give you a distinct advantage in certain situations—it can help you to write better songs, more songs, and more kinds of songs. That can mean a lot more money in the long run. Do you need to know music theory to be a successful songwriter? The answer is no. You don't need it in precisely the same way you don't need a vehicle to get from New York to Los Angeles. You *can* get there by walking, but a car, train, or plane is a faster, easier, and more certain way of getting there.

Where Can I Learn Theory?

Now that you know some of the things theory can help with, you still need to know where to find all this precious information. Will you have to take ten years off and study in a monastery in northern Bavaria or, even worse, take out a student loan and go to school full time? Luckily, you can start learning on a purely part-time basis and there are several affordable options for doing so.

Buy a Book

Hundreds of books are available on the subject of music theory. Check your local library first and get an idea what's out there. Make sure you find a book that starts from square one and covers things in an easy-to-read style. A book on advanced modal harmony isn't a good starting point.

Once you know what you need, you can find it online and/or order from your favorite bookstore. Use a highlighter to emphasize key points. Give yourself tests and put what you learn into practice.

Take a Class

Most colleges and universities have classes in music theory. Call the ones in your area and ask about an introductory music theory class. Have them send you a brochure with a course description. Ask if you can talk to the teacher to see if the course covers the material you need at a level you can understand. If you want a private music tutor, most piano teachers and many guitar teachers are well versed in music theory and will teach the basics for the price of instrument lessons. Another option is to take some theory-intensive piano or guitar lessons. This way you learn theory, performance, and how the two work together, at the same time.

Software for Standard Notation

Perhaps the easiest way to learn to read and write music is with a computer program. There are a number of interactive programs available with tutorials explaining the basics. Some let you click and drag notes, print sheet music, hear what your creation sounds like, and move things around until they sound right. These programs can be are also great for writing melodies and arranging.

Hundreds of software programs are now available for various musical applications. Because of this, many large music stores now have a software section where you can buy music software, ask questions, and compare programs to see which one best suits your needs.

Music Charts

A chart is a representation of a song's basic chord structure and arrangement. Charts are a necessity in the studio and can also come in handy in live settings. Some nightclubs in major music hubs have chart jams, during which a singer/songwriter can get up and sing with the band and have them play along with the charts. This is scary, but fun.

California charts are used by some studio musicians, by many beginners, and by some touring bands who already know the key in which a song will be performed. A California chart is usually written with the chord name, followed by slashes to denote the number of beats a chord is played. There are many variations of this system, but a California chart for "You Are My Sunshine" might look like this:

C////   C////   F////   C////
F////   C////   C//   G//   C////

However, the most popular charting system is the Nashville Number system, which allows you to use the same chart for a song in *any* key. This system can also be used to explain much of the theory you need to get off to a good start.

The Nashville Number System

The first thing you need to know is called "the universal scale." Remember roman numerals from grade school math? That's all the universal scale is. In case you don't remember, here are the numerals you'll need, in order, from one to seven: I, II, III, IV, V, VI, VII. Now, remember that "Do Re Mi" stuff from music class back in school? Match it up with the Roman numerals (see **TABLE 10-1**).

Table 10-1							
I	II	III	IV	V	VI	VII	(I)
Do	Re	Mi	Fa	So	La	Ti	(Do)

Okay, let's explain a little and then build a little more. There are seven notes in a major scale, the eighth being the same note as the first, but one octave higher. If you're in the key of A, then "I" or "Do" is an A note. If you're in the key of C, "I" is a C note, and the major scale goes C, D, E, F, G, A, B, and it would line up as in **TABLE 10-2.**

Table 10-2							
I	II	III	IV	V	VI	VII	(I)
Do	Re	Mi	Fa	So	La	Ti	(Do)
C	D	E	F	G	A	B	(C)

All the Notes There Is

What about all that sharp and flat stuff? The C major scale doesn't have any of that. That's why it's the easiest. If you always wrote in C major, that'd be about all you need to know. Since you might get bored with writing in C major for the rest of your life, let's work the rest of the notes in, so that we have more options (see **TABLE 10-3**). In the music biz, this is called "all the notes there is," which drives English teachers nuts. What you're about to hear makes classical composers faint, but it *works,* so who cares if it's wrong? Notice the little "b" by some of the notes? That means flat (lower than). The symbol for sharp (higher than) is "#." So, a D# is the same as an Eb. That's why you don't see any sharps in the scales in **TABLE 10-3**—they're redundant and have been left out for your convenience.

Table 10-3											
I	bII	II	bIII	III	IV	bV	V	bVI	VI	bVII	VII
C	Db	D	Eb	E	F	Gb	G	Ab	A	Bb	B

You'll also notice that the flats are written before the Roman numeral instead of after. This is to separate it from any flats occurring elsewhere in the chord, like a bIII chord with a bVIII note in it. That will actually make sense very soon but, for now, focus on the universal scale (**TABLE 10-4**). Highlight it, memorize it, let it be your friend.

Table 10-4											
I	bII	II	bIII	III	IV	bV	V	bVI	VI	bVII	VII

Scales and Modes

As you saw before, the seven notes of the C major scale correspond with the numbers in the universal scale, but what about other keys? Just write the notes under the universal scale in order, starting with the note that's the name of a new key. So for the key of D, the scale would look like the one in **TABLE 10-5**.

Table 10-5											
I	bII	II	bIII	III	IV	bV	V	bVI	VI	bVII	VII
D	Eb	E	F	Gb	G	Ab	A	Bb	B	C	Db

To find the notes of a D major scale, see which ones line up under the numbers without flat symbols: D, E, Gb, G, A, B, and Db. This works for finding any major scale and, if you know the code, for finding other scales and modes (see **TABLE 10-6**).

Table 10-6						
Scale			**Notes**			
Major pentatonic	I	II	III	V	VI	
Lydian	I	II	III	bV	V	VI	VII
Mixolydian	I	II	III	IV	V	VI	bVII
Natural minor (Aeolian)	I	II	bIII	IV	V	bVI	bVII
Melodic minor	I	II	bIII	IV	V	VI	VII
Harmonic minor	I	II	bIII	IV	V	bVI	VII
Minor pentatonic	I	bIII	IV	V	bVII	
Phrygian	I	bII	bIII	IV	V	bVI	bVII
Dorian	I	II	bIII	IV	V	VI	bVII
Locrian	I	bII	bIII	IV	bV	bVI	bVII
Blues	I	bIII	IV	bV	V	bVII	
Hungarian	I	II	bIII	bV	V	bVI	VII
Neapolitan	I	bII	bIII	IV	V	VI	VII

By the way, the technical name for the major scale is Ionian. All these scales and modes have different sounds and feels. The Dorian mode will give you that "Santana" sound, the Phrygian mode can give the feel of Spanish flamenco music, and the two pentatonic modes are good for rock, pop, and country.

How do I find notes on an instrument?
On guitar, the notes made by the open strings are (fattest to skinniest) E, A, D, G, B, and E. Move up one fret, and you move up one note. So, on the A string, you'd go A, Bb, B, C. Pianos go in order, so ask a friend where the C note is, and you can easily find the rest.

So, if you wanted to find the Mixolydian mode for the key of E, what would you do? First, write down a universal scale, then write "all the notes there is" under it, starting with the key you're in (E). (See **TABLE 10-7**.)

Table 10-7											
I	bII	II	bIII	III	IV	bV	V	bVI	VI	bVII	VII
E	F	Gb	G	Ab	A	Bb	B	C	Db	D	Eb

Now, use the code for Mixolydian and line up each Roman numeral with the corresponding note in the key of E. What you should get is an E Mixolydian mode in **TABLE 10-8**.

Table 10-8						
I	II	III	IV	V	VI	bVII
E	Gb	Ab	A	B	Db	D

Chords

But wait, that's not all! You can also use the Nashville Number system to find chords. In a given key, put together the notes that correspond to the following numbers to make the chord shown in **TABLE 10-9**.

Table 10-9				
Chord	**Notes**			
Major chord	I	III	V	
Minor chord	I	bIII	V	
Major sixth chord	I	III	V	VI
Seventh chord	I	III	V	bVII
Major seventh chord	I	III	V	VII
Minor seventh chord	I	bIII	V	bVII
Suspended second chord	I	II	V	
Suspended fourth chord	I	IV	V	
Half diminished chord	I	bIII	bV	bVII
Diminished chord	I	bIII	bV	VI

So, an E major chord is made up of E, Ab, and B. An E minor chord would be E, G, and B, just a one-note difference. This table will come in handy not only for finding chords, but for naming the chords in your songs. Say you've got a song in the key of C and the second chord in the song has the notes A, E, G, and C. Putting the notes in numerical order, you'd have I bIII V bVII. Looking through the codes, you'll see that those notes make a minor seventh chord. There's a lot more useful stuff you can learn about chord construction, but this'll get you started.

When converting chords to numbers, all aspects of the chord (minors, sevenths, etc.) stay the same. If it's a B diminished chord in the key of A, it'll be a II diminished in numbers and a C# diminished in B. This holds true for transposing as well: Chords change names but not essential properties.

Transposing

Yes, folks, the Nashville Number system slices, it dices, and it even transposes your song to a new key. How? Say you've got a song in the key of D, with the chords D Em A and G, but that's too high for the singer. You need to put the song in the key of B. First, put the chords into numbers with the universal scale (**TABLE 10-10**).

Table 10-10											
D	Eb	**E**	F	Gb	**G**	Ab	**A**	Bb	B	C	Db
I	bII	II	bIII	III	IV	bV	V	bVI	VI	bVII	VII

So the chords are I, II minor, IV, and V and the chord pattern is I, II minor, V, IV. Starting with the new key, write all the notes under the universal scale so they line up with the chords from the original key and the universal scale (**TABLE 10-11**).

Table 10-11											
I	bII	**II**	bIII	III	**IV**	bV	**V**	bVI	VI	bVII	VII
B	C	**Db**	D	Eb	**E**	F	**Gb**	G	Ab	A	Bb

The chords in the new key would be B, Dbm, E, and Gb and the chord pattern would be B, Dbm, E, Gb. Once you get familiar with the number system, you won't even have to transpose, you'll be able to play a numbers chart in any key. That's one reason that writers and studio players use this system.

There are many variations on the number system. Each bandleader will have his or her own ways of doing certain things. A look at the charts and a quick conversation before going into the studio to figure these things out can save you from a communication breakdown in the middle of a costly session.

Charting with the Nashville Number System

Now, for the really fun part. The universal scale is also the building block for the Nashville Number system of charting songs. This is why the flats are written before the numbers—to prevent confusion with the chord information that's written on the chart *after* the number. So, in the key of C, C would be an "I" or "one" chord, F would be the IV, and G would be the V. What about minors, sevenths, and all those other things?

Information used to modify a chord is written in the exponent position, so in the key of C, a D7 would be written II^7. Minors are written by using a minus sign after the number representing the chord, so a D minor in the key of C would be written II^-. Suspended chords are written with "sus" followed by the number representing the degree of the suspension, all in the exponent, II^{sus2}. The symbol for major is a small triangle in the exponent, $II^{\blacktriangle}$. This is only used when a major needs to be specified, as in a D major seventh chord. For augmented chords, the exponent is a plus sign, II^+ and for diminished chords an exponent of "0" is used, II^0. For this reason, you may hear a studio musician refer to a C diminished chord as "C with a cookie." A chord, unless otherwise noted, lasts for a whole measure and lines usually run four measures long. To put more than one chord in a measure, underline all the chords in that measure and, if desired, write in the number of beats each chord receives over the chord.

FACT

A commonly used way to structure a chart is to denote sections by putting the section symbol (CH or $ for chorus, V for verse, and so forth) on the far left with a box around it and then leaving space between sections. This makes it easier to keep track of where you are when playing the song.

Here's a chart for "House of the Rising Sun" in A⁻. Songs in minor keys are usually written in the key of the relative major because, most of the time, it ends up being easier to write and read that way. The relative major can be found by finding the bIII of the minor key, and the relative minor of a major is the VI of the major key. The relative major of A⁻ is C, so **TABLE 10-12** is in C.

Knowledge of the Nashville Number system is usually passed down from one musician or songwriter to another. Perhaps the only available book that explains this system in detail is Chas Williams's *The Nashville Number System* (2001). It would be well worth your time to locate a copy of this book for further study.

Table 10-12			
Chart for "House of the Rising Sun"			
VI⁻	I	II	IV
VI⁻	I	III	III⁷
VI⁻	I	II	IV
VI⁻	III	VI⁻	III

The Rest of the Theory

The Nashville Number system doesn't explain all the music theory you need to know and there are some little things like rhythm and harmony that you might want to take a look at if you want to make millions of dollars.

Harmony

From Ancient hymns, Renaissance choirs, and barbershop quartets to the Statler Brothers, the Temptations, and N'Sync, vocal harmony is one song element that almost never goes out of style.

Studying the harmony styles of current bands can help you write songs with those groups in mind. Certain kinds of melodies and chord structures lend themselves to certain kinds of harmony arrangements and vice versa. Knowing these things will help you to write a song with the kind of harmonies you want or find the right harmonies for a song you've already written.

In a broader sense, harmonic theory will help you understand how instruments and voices work together, and how bass lines, chord structures, and other instrumental parts work within a song to build harmonic structure that surrounds your melody and reinforces it. This gives you more power to influence things like prosody, dynamics, and "feel" in your songwriting.

Knowledge of harmony can be a troubleshooting tool. When the chords of a song and the vocal harmonies sound right separately but clash when put together, check to see if they have conflicting harmonies. If so, they may form chords that sound unpleasant to the ears. Change one or the other to fix this problem.

Rhythm

Knowledge of rhythm helps you make sure that everything synchs up. It can aid in finding better flow and symmetry in your lyric meter and communicating with bandleaders, studio musicians, and co-writers.

Familiarity with different kinds of beats expands your groove options for songwriting. Knowing the difference between a straight beat and a shuffle or between a Bossa Nova and a Samba saves you from having to communicate by making mouth sounds or pounding on the nearest flat surface.

Analyzing the Greats

Most songwriters can proudly list several other songwriters who influenced them and readily admit to studying hit songs and what makes them work. Without some grounding in theory, this means a lot of guessing and trying to blindly capture the feel of something.

Music theory can help you to understand exactly how a song is put together and why it works. This gives you more options and information to work with and leaves you more time for writing your own songs.

FACT

These days, rhythmic differences are the main factors defining various genres. Learning the rhythms of a particular style of music can be the first—and most important—step to being able to write songs in that genre. Knowing a little about rhythm can put you on the path to becoming a very versatile songwriter.

Theory as a Troubleshooting Tool

In addition to being a valuable compositional tool, an aid to communication, and a potential money saver, music theory can also help in solving problems and fixing trouble spots in your song.

Being able to instantly analyze the meter in the first stanza will help you make the next one symmetrical without all the head scratching and vague notions that something doesn't feel right. When chords that should work clash and harmonies don't fit the style of your song, knowing the theory behind these elements will give you solutions to the problems. When the chart is wrong or a part needs to be changed, theory can save you time and money in the studio. Wouldn't you like to be able to explain to a sax player or drummer exactly what you want? Do yourself a huge favor; devote some time to learning how music works. It'll pay off in the long run.

Chapter 11

Entering the Big Leagues

At some point, you'll have to decide whether songwriting is a hobby or a career. Songwriting as a hobby can enrich your life in countless ways as you continue down the path to family, security, and a better chance of happiness—or you can risk everything and go for the big leagues. But be forewarned: The odds of making even a meager living as a songwriter are astronomically small.

Making a Commitment

If you're actually thinking of trying to make a career of songwriting, there is really only one way to do it—to do it ALL THE WAY. You have to make and keep a commitment to songwriting, be prepared to make sacrifices, and do so with the understanding that you have better odds of winning a casino jackpot.

Great songwriters leave Nashville, New York, and Los Angeles every day, heads hung low, never to return. However, some songwriters who are pretty good end up getting the jobs that the great ones missed because they made the commitment, did everything they had to do, and followed through without stopping for anything. Imagine going through basic training with no drill instructor to make you do all the things that you must do and learn all the things that you must learn. Can you be that tough on yourself?

Still willing to go for the high stakes?
Sit down and have a talk with yourself. Ask yourself what you're willing to give up to be a songwriter. Talk it over with family and friends; make sure you have the support you'll need to do this.
If you still want to try, good luck and read on.

Getting Organized

The biggest weak spot in a songwriter's game plan is usually organization. You have to treat songwriting like a small business, with you as the owner/operator. If one in ten songwriters is capable of writing great songs, only one in a hundred works hard enough to achieve that goal. Maybe one in a thousand songwriters stays focused and organized and does all the things that it takes to get those great songs cut. Of all the talented, hardworking songwriters in the world, it's usually the most organized who make a living at it.

Just writing is not enough, you need to come up with a game plan and stick to it. What kinds of songs should you be writing? How will you get them recorded? Who will you get to listen? If you don't have a business plan to get from where you are to where you want to be, guess where you'll end up? Out of business. Sit down and make a plan of attack, even if it's just to figure out what you need to know to make a plan. Repeat as necessary.

ALERT!

Don't let the business and planning aspects of your songwriting career intrude on your writing. When you're working on a song, devote your full attention to it. Songs are the product your company deals in. Lousy product means no sales.

Scheduling Time

In order to write at the professional level you will need to devote massive amounts of time to the art, the craft, and, eventually, the business of songwriting. Unless you are independently wealthy and willing to live like a monk, this means scheduling your time wisely to get it all in.

Time to Write

For most songwriters, this is the easiest part of the job and the most pleasant. Still, have you ever spent forty hours in a week writing songs? How about twenty or even ten? If you get a publishing deal, you may be expected to sit down in an office with a co-writer for three or four hours, twice a day, five days a week, and come up with something good regularly. This means being able to work through writer's block and writing well even when you are not particularly inspired.

Why write when you're not inspired? Ask an Olympic medalist if he or she competes and trains only when inspired. It's usually an inspired performance that earned the medal, but that performance wouldn't have been possible without years of training every day and competing in hundreds of events.

So, schedule writing sessions and stick to them. It's easy to let yourself slide because a favorite show is on or your friends are going out somewhere. Remember, if you don't work, nothing will get done. Make a minimum hourly commitment to songwriting each week. If ten hours a week is all you can do, then start there and build on it. You'll be amazed at how much better you'll write after a year of writing more often.

Try sitting down and writing for four hours. It's a lot harder than you think. You may have to work up to it, but it's worth the effort: Writing *more* will help you write *better*. It sharpens your skills so that you're able to write a great song when inspiration strikes.

Time to Learn

In addition to writing songs, spend time learning more about songwriting. Even hit writers spend time studying the craft. There are books and magazines galore about the different aspects of songwriting and publishing, and there are songwriting forums on the Internet where songwriters from all over the world "talk shop," discuss craft and technique, and critique each other's work.

Analyzing the craft aspects of current hits is another great source of information. Set aside some time each week to learn more about songwriting, then make a point of applying what you have learned when you sit down (or pace the floor) to write.

Time for Ideas

Set aside time to generate ideas and to compare the kinds of ideas you've been using with the ones on the radio. What types of hooks and styles of storytelling are being used? Even better, what kinds haven't been used? Some ideas require weeks of incubation before you know how to incorporate them into songs. Sometimes an idea will stick in your head and demand to be written. This is a good sign.

Time to Edit

For many songwriters, the hardest part of the writing process is editing and rewriting. It can be difficult to go through a beautiful song that came in a rush of inspiration and sort out what to cut, what to keep, and how to fix the broken or missing parts. For this reason, most songwriters have huge piles of works-in-progress and a small stack of finished songs.

ALERT!

Paying attention to how co-writers approach things can be a great source of information because you get to see things from inside the process. Don't let it distract you from your own work, but be aware of what's going on across the table.

If you believe in a song, don't let it sit there, gathering dust and slowly going out of style. Schedule time each week to rewrite, fix, polish, and finish songs. Remember, it doesn't matter who's ahead halfway through a race, or even an inch from the finish line. What matters is who finishes and when. To win, you must finish, so focus on the finish line.

Support and Feedback

It's hard to be objective about your own songs. Sometimes you'll think you have a surefire hit and publishers will give you a look that says, "Did someone leave a dead possum in here?" Other times, you may have a future hit right in front of you and not know it. You must believe to succeed. Support and feedback can play crucial roles in learning to believe in your songs.

Moral Support

It's easier to have faith in something if you're not alone in your belief. Build a support group of people who like your songs. Start with friends and family, and then develop a circle of other writers and musicians who believe in you. Finally, look for publishers who see your potential as a writer (and can see it without asking you for money). As the number of people who believe in you grows, it will be easier for you to believe in your abilities and in your songs.

Financial Support

Sooner or later, somebody has to spend money on your songwriting career. Probably, it will be you. Ask yourself what you can do to put some cash into your business. Is there something less important than songwriting that's eating up your demo money? Can you do without four hundred TV channels? Could you live with cutting your bowling back to once a week? How much studio time would that Hawaiian vacation have bought?

Start an account for your songwriting business and put money in it every week. Make a minimum weekly cash commitment to your career. If you have a good week and can put back a little extra, that's great, just make sure you put in at least the minimum amount every week and don't spend it on anything but songwriting. You'll be surprised how fast your stash will grow. Keep track of how you spend your songwriting money. Save all your receipts: Hopefully, you'll need them someday for tax writeoffs.

FACT

Many songwriters sell CDs of their collected demos and put the profits into more demos. Some of the many songwriters who are also performers put back all their tip money or gig money to help cover songwriting expenses. Think of some more ways you can generate operating capital for your songwriting business.

Support from your spouse or family can make all the difference. Many successful songwriters received financial help from their families or spouses before making it big. Many also lost their spouses and/or estranged their families over money issues before they made it, so it's important to discuss boundaries beforehand and know what kind of support you can expect and for how long.

Finding an Investor

If there's a way to get "outside" money for your career, it can help take you over the final hurdle. The most important thing to ask yourself before looking for an investor is, "Am I really ready to do this?" If you're still three years away from being a hit writer, you'll just be blowing money that you could use later and losing a valuable contact in the process. When you're ready, make a list of the wealthiest people you know. Make sure they all get the opportunity to hear your songs, either live or recorded. The next time one of them says, "Gee, your songs are so good, I don't understand why you're not on the radio," talk to them about the business side of music. Explain about the costs of making good demos, postage, gas money, hotel bills, and any other expense you regularly incur as a songwriter.

Of course, these people will probably want something for their investments. Selling part of the publishing on your songs in return for professional quality demos is one option. Just remember, a publisher usually wants a *minimum* of half of the publishing rights on a song, so try to keep as much as you can to bargain with later. Sometimes investors will put money into a recording project more easily than a demo project. If you're a great performer, talk with investors about making a record. This gives them a product they can hear, see, and touch. Offer the investor the title of Executive Producer and a percentage of sales. That way, you keep your publishing open to use elsewhere. And *always* have a lawyer examine and explain any contracts you are asked to sign.

Constructive Criticism

The flipside of support is criticism. It's just as important in helping you to believe in yourself and reach your goals. Starting with your support group, build a circle of people whom you trust to give you honest opinions about your songs. Have other songwriters and musicians who are as good or better than you point out trouble spots and suggest changes. Ask publishers what they like and don't like about your songs. Songwriting forums on the Internet usually have critique boards where you can give and receive feedback. Some songwriter's organizations, like NSAI, offer a professional critique service for members. Some songwriters even pay a critique service to go over their songs with a fine-toothed comb.

Don't worry about whom you agree with. The important thing is to get as much feedback from as many sources as possible and then analyze it to see what it means. This is a great way for you to get a more objective picture of your songs and of yourself as a writer.

Look for patterns in feedback to help spot your strengths and weaknesses. Do most people love your melodies and say very little about your lyrics? Do people say that your uptempos all sound like something from twenty years ago? Do your other writer pals all drool over your hooks? Listen to the positive and the negative. Ignoring the good things you hear about your writing can keep you from being able to build on your successes. Discounting all the bad things means you'll make the same mistakes again and again.

ALERT!

Learn when to bend and when to stand your ground. Just because a publisher wants to change your song doesn't mean you should; just because you were inspired when you wrote it doesn't mean it's perfect the way it is. Try to look at your song from more than one perspective before deciding.

Of course, you can't take everyone's advice. Your grandma may love your old-time pop ballads, but she's not a publisher and she's not buying a million records this year. The kid next door might hate hearing you put a hip-hop beat in a modern country song, but that doesn't mean it won't work. Learn to sort the information you receive and look for the patterns. Do certain subgroups react in a particular way to something about your song? If you find that a number of people react strongly to something in your song, either positively or negatively, then examine it and see what makes it work, or not work, as the case may be. Listen to everybody, then figure out what it all means and what you want to do about it.

Going Public

As you progress and develop a repertoire of songs, you will want these songs performed in a live setting. Along with recording, live performance is one of the truest tests of a song. Seeing how strangers react to your song in a live-music setting will be very beneficial for you in terms of seeing the result of your work.

Playing Out

If you can sing, even if it's just enough to get the song across, then you need to get out there and sing your songs. When you play a song for a live audience, you have to get inside the song from the viewpoint of a performer instead of as a writer, to get the story and the emotion of the song across to the listeners. If you can do it, then it's possible for other artists to do it. If you can't, it may help point out the weak spots in your song.

If you're scared about "playing out," many songwriting associations and clubs offer the opportunity for live showcases in a supportive atmosphere. Being surrounded and encouraged by other songwriters can help take some of the stress out of playing your songs in a live setting.

Start with a low-pressure situation, like an open mike night, and work your way up to a showcase or "in the round" setting. Performing frequently will help take the fright out of stage fright. You need to become comfortable on stage so that when you play in front of publishers at a big-time writer's venue you won't feel so intimidated. Decide on a place and set a date. Practice until you're sick of your own songs and then practice some more.

When you take the stage, concentrate on connecting. Remember that the performer is the link between the song and the listener. Be confident and be a transmitter for the song. If you don't feel it, nobody else will. If they can't hear you, they can't hear the song. Giving a halfhearted performance of a great song is like showing the Mona Lisa in a dark, windowless room with one candle; it doesn't matter how great a masterpiece you know it is if no one else can see it.

Finding Someone to Sing Your Songs

It's also good to get others to perform your songs. The more people sing your songs, the higher the chances that they will be heard by the right person. Look for bands and singers in your area who are looking for songs to perform or record. Before you pitch to an act, make sure to get a good idea of what they sound like and only give them songs that fit what they are doing. Otherwise, you're wasting everybody's time. Pay special attention to acts that already have label interest; even if your song doesn't make it onto their major label CD, it could still get heard by the record company.

The Internet is another place to find people who might be interested in singing your songs. Many forums and bulletin boards have areas for singers and bands currently looking for songs. This can be especially true of recording artists from Europe, Asia, and the former Soviet Union. Because of the popularity of music from the United States and the United Kingdom, these acts are often looking for songs with English lyrics and an authentic feel that might help them break through on the charts.

ALERT!

While foreign markets can be great places to get cuts, make sure you have your songs registered with your PRO (Performing Rights Organization) and keep track of how they are doing. Some songwriters have had huge hits and didn't make a penny because they didn't have a PRO and a publisher to collect foreign royalties.

The Importance of Having a Life

When you start seeing results from devoting time and money to songwriting, you'll probably want to devote even more to your career. You'll notice that the more you invest in songwriting, the better your songs are getting and the more frequently you're coming up with good stuff. Demos are costly, but it's so much fun to hear your song come alive. You'll wish you could spend all your time and money on songwriting and recording.

This is good, to a point. Just remember that you have to live enough to have something to write about. Don't completely lose touch with your life. That date you canceled last Friday to stay home and write? What if it might have inspired your best love song ever? Could that camping trip you passed up (to save for a demo session) have put you more in touch with yourself and given you some crucial insight? Ⓔ

Chapter 12

Writing for the Commercial Market

You've learned all the fundamentals of songwriting, established a writing regimen, and started organizing for the "big push." Now it's time to look at the big picture, catch up with the market, and start writing songs that can get cut. Catching up to the market, and staying there, is an ongoing process in the life of a professional songwriter.

Viable Formats

At any given time, there are several genres that are "hot." In 1982, new wave, reggae, traditional country, and heavy metal all had a good year. In 1992, rap, alt, hip-hop, and line-dance country scored big. In 2002, the nu-soul, bluegrass, alt country, jam, and singer-songwriter genres did well. Knowing what's hot or, even better, what's going to be hot, can boost your earning potential.

Current Market Styles

When a new genre becomes successful, opportunities exist for those who can write radio-friendly songs or co-write with artists in that genre. A perfect example of this is the collaboration of producer-songwriter Glen Ballard with alternative singer-songwriter Alanis Morissette on her "Jagged Little Pill" CD.

Instead of waiting for a new sub-genre to become huge, then scrambling to catch up, keep an eye on emerging styles; study what makes them different, and write a few songs in those styles. You'll have a head start if it becomes the next big thing.

ALERT!

While it helps to be able to write in any musical style, don't write a song that goes against your moral style. In other words, don't write a "cheating" or "gangsta" song unless you wish to make a public endorsement of those things. Remember, if it's a hit, you have to live with it for a very long time.

Other Options

Tracking the work of influential artists is one way of keeping up. Some recording artists either stay ahead of the market or help determine what the next big thing will be. Garth Brooks, Elvis Presley, The Beatles, Prince, Nirvana, and Madonna have all enjoyed periods when it seemed that they could do no wrong. During those times, when one of these acts put out an album, others raced to put out similar material. These following acts need the right kind of songs in a hurry, and that's where you come in. Keep track of what innovative mega-stars are doing to see what kinds of songs are likely to be in demand.

An option taken by some songwriters is to write songs that will sell in nearly any market. The "timeless" style is difficult to learn, or even define but, for some, it has proven to be worth the effort. To get an idea of this kind of writing, study the songs of Marvin Hamlisch, Marilyn and Alan Bergman, and Burt Bacharach and Hal David. Many Beatles songs, like "Yesterday" and "The Long and Winding Road," fit the timeless category as well. Timeless songs are harder to pitch than songs that capitalize on current trends, but they keep longer without spoiling.

Keeping Up with the Competition

To get a staff job at a publishing house, you have to be better than someone else who is about to be let go. To get a cut on an album, your song has to be better than songs written by the artist, the producer, all their friends, cousins, friends of cousins, and all the writers at the publishing companies who handle the artist's and producer's songs. You have to have an edge. To compete, you must not only be a great songwriter, but also a well-informed one.

Once you start writing "ahead of the market," you may have to wait for some of the more conservative people to catch up. If you have a cutting-edge song that a publisher doesn't get, run it by him again in a few months if the style is still hot.

Listening to What's Out There

As a professional songwriter, part of your job is to keep up on current hits and top artists. You need to know what kinds of songs are being cut and which artists are selling the most records. This helps you decide what kinds of songs to write and where to pitch them. Of course, you shouldn't write anything you don't like. A better way is to find what you do like about current hits and styles and then use that to write a song that you, and everyone else, will love.

Billboard and R&R

Reading the charts and trade magazines helps you keep up with current formats. When people talk about the charts, they're usually referring to the charts in *Billboard* magazine. *Billboard* lists the top songs and albums in pop and several other genres. In addition, *Billboard* has articles on musical trends, hot artists, statistics for top grossing concert tours, and other music news. *Billboard* is a great resource for finding out what's selling and getting airplay.

Radio and Records, R&R for short, has charts and articles on the music biz, but the emphasis is more on demographics, market trends, and the business side of things. R&R uses a slightly different formula for its charts than *Billboard* does, so reading both and comparing can give you a more balanced view of the market.

Knowing what's playing on the radio helps you to write songs that get played on the radio. Having an idea what will be the next trend can help you decide what musical directions and lyric styles to experiment with to stay competitive in the marketplace. Writing in a current style can be the difference between being a "good" songwriter and a professional songwriter.

FACT

One way to keep up with all the trade magazines without starving to death is to have each person in your peer group subscribe to one publication, then share the information. Your local library may carry *Billboard* or R&R. Some songwriting organizations, like NSAI, provide a free library for member use.

Good Songs, Great Songs, Hit Songs

With hard work, most songwriters can learn to write a good song. With hard work, talent, and more hard work, some writers learn to write great songs. With hard work, talent, more hard work, careful study, even more hard work, and some luck, a few fortunate souls write hit songs.

Many gifted songwriters spend their entire lives turning out one masterpiece after another and never have a hit because they refuse to bow to some of the conventions of the radio format. That's their choice. Other equally talented songwriters spend their lives turning out one masterpiece after another, get filthy rich in the process, and retire young.

The Road Less Traveled

To catch the public's ear, a song must be either better or different (or, ideally, both). Better songs come through hard work and talent; "different" is partly a matter of choice. We all work with the same twelve notes, yet some people find totally new combinations. Listen to John Mayer's blend of folk, alt, rock, and jazz. He's not doing anything radically new; he hasn't invented any new notes or chords; but he combines familiar elements and influences in a way that sounds fresh to our ears. The Beatles, Hank Williams, and other musical pioneers have done the same thing; they took what was and found a way to do it differently.

Finding a new way of doing things is probably the hardest task for a songwriter to accomplish, but it can have the richest rewards. Those who come up with the next trend can gain not only financial success, but also a place in history. Innovations are often nothing more than the result of a willingness to experiment, combined with the songwriter's influences and process. Being conscious of this can help you to refine and better understand the differences that work. Being different can help you stand out in a sea of songwriters. Don't force it, but be open to it.

A Matter of Length

If you want to hear your songs on the radio, keep them short. Two-and-a-half to three-and-a-half minutes is considered the ideal length for a single. Longer songs get recorded, but it's usually the shorter ones that get on the air. Try timing your songs as soon as you have a verse and chorus; this can help you set up a structure that has space for the necessary information while keeping a reasonable length. Remember, if everything is in place and a song is too short, you can add a solo. A good exercise is to try writing a one-minute song that tells an entire story.

ALERT!

In general, short songs stand a better chance of getting radio play. However, cutting out important information or speeding a song up to an uncomfortable tempo can ruin your song. A great song with a comfortable tempo that's a little too long has a much better chance than a song that seems incomplete or rushed.

Hook Reinforcement

The best product in the world would be hard to sell if nobody knew what to call it. The hook is your song's brand name; it lets people know what the song is called and tells them something about it. On a simpler level, it's what people will ask a DJ for when they call in. A hit song usually has a hook that's well placed and appears frequently. Having a great hook, placing it where it stands out, and building the rest of the song to reinforce it greatly improves your chances of a hit.

Depth Cuts

Not every song you write has to be a three-minute single in the newest style. Sometimes a song demands to be written a certain way. Some stories take longer to tell and some ideas need to be written in a specific genre. Sometimes you have to break some rules. Rather than force a song into an ill-fitting mold, let it be what it is and follow where inspiration leads you. When this yields an exceptional song, go ahead and run it by your feedback group. If they go nuts over it, play it for a publisher or two. Don't hold your breath, but see what happens.

Occasionally a song that breaks a lot of rules is so absolutely brilliant that a publisher will "go to bat" for it. "Strawberry Wine" is a great example of this: It's a five-minute, ballad-tempo waltz about a taboo subject (losing virginity) that was a huge hit. It's the perfect tempo and beat for the feel of the song, the melody is fantastic and has a bittersweet prosody, the story is beautifully told, and the subject is handled in a very tactful manner that made a normally off-limits topic accessible and market friendly.

While "Strawberry Wine" is a rare exception, most records have at least a few songs on them that aren't even intended to be singles and, because of that, can break a few more rules than usual. These are "depth cuts"—songs meant to round out the recording with some missing elements and help to push the artistic tone of a recording project in a desired direction. You won't get rich on depth cuts, but they can help you to establish a reputation and hold on to your publishing deal.

FACT

In the early days of his career, Nashville singer-songwriter Jim Lauderdale built such a reputation for depth cuts that record companies and recording artists would specifically request a Jim Lauderdale song to enhance an album.

Writing for Yourself or Your Band

If you're a singer-songwriter or a songwriting member of a band and have hopes of getting a record deal, there are a few things you might want to know. Writing for a specific, unsigned act that you're a member of has challenges and rewards not found elsewhere within the realm of professional songwriting.

Forging a Sound

For a recording artist, great songs—even hit songs—aren't always enough. You need songs that show off the singer or the band and have a distinctive sound that people will be able to recognize. When you hear an Aerosmith song, you *know* it's an Aerosmith song. Would Travis Tritt sound right singing an N'Sync song? Probably not!

There are a number of factors that work together to create a musical identity for a successful group or artist. The most important aspect of forging a sound usually centers around the voice of the lead vocalist or vocalists. You need melodies and musical styles that showcase the lead vocals and allow the singer to shine. The wrong kind of song, even if it's a great song, can make a fantastic singer sound like an amateur.

Vocal harmony choices can influence the musical identity of a group. Alice in Chains, the Beach Boys, and the Judds all have identifiable harmonies that make it easy to recognize their songs. Write songs that lend themselves to the vocal and musical abilities of the act.

It's wise to define the specific genre of the act. Not that you can't go outside the lines of that genre, but it's good to be able to say, "We're a modern country band" or "It's kind of like Dave Matthews with some elements of Widespread Panic and Barenaked Ladies." Record companies have to be able to label a band before they can sell its work.

Bringing in an Outside Writer

Here's a little secret: Big names from Bon Jovi to the Dixie Chicks, bands that write many of their own songs, sometimes choose to work with professional songwriters. Why would a big star who's written a ton of hits want to do such a thing? A co-writer will bring different strengths and ideas to the table. Working with an established songwriter can help in identifying what's universally appealing about an act and refining those qualities to get a crossover hit.

Bringing in an outside writer can also shake things up and help keep an act from getting into a rut. Once an artist or band has established a musical identity, it can become increasingly difficult to come up with new ideas and still remain within the parameters of that identity. It can be also be hard to work new musical elements into an established sound without alienating the fan base. An outside writer may bring a more objective viewpoint to the table that helps an act to stretch a little without losing what's good about what they already have.

What to Do with the Leftovers

Sometimes you'll write a great song that just doesn't fit your style or the style of the band you're in. Try to think of whom the song might be good for and pitch the song to any singer or band that you think might be a good match. Bryan Adams, Skip Ewing, and Patty Griffin are all well-respected recording artists who have found that songwriting can be a door opener, an extra source of income, and a creative outlet outside of a recording career.

Sometimes you may pitch a song you've already recorded. Van Morrison's recording of "Have I Told You Lately That I Love You" is beautiful, but Rod Stewart's version made him a lot of money. Billy Joel has had his share of hits, but one great song he wrote and recorded didn't climb the charts—until Garth Brooks made "Shameless" a #1 hit.

FACT

Aside from being a moneymaker, songwriting can also help your career as a recording artist by proving you can generate hits and by putting you in touch with the right people. Songwriting success helped launch the careers of Don Williams, Carole King, Willie Nelson, Lucinda Williams, Neil Sedaka, and Phil Vassar.

Writing Songs for Others

Say you're an eighty-year-old songwriter who weighs twelve hundred pounds. You have an inoperable mole the shape—and approximate size—of Paraguay on your forehead, a half octave range, and a voice that sounds rather like a duck with bronchitis. It's likely that you may encounter some difficulty getting a record deal and might consider focusing your efforts on writing songs for other people to record.

Thinking Past Your Personal Limitations

It's important to know that you can write songs that exceed your own performance limitations. Even if you can't sing anything with complex trills or a big range, you must be able to write for people who can. You might not be able to play some chords or grooves without making mistakes, but you can write them and let the studio musicians do the playing. Learn to think beyond what you can do; with songwriting, the only limitation is your ability to imagine.

Learn to write songs that sound good for other voices than your own. This goes for lyrics, too. With a little study and effort, an eighty-year-old grandmother could write a song from the viewpoint of a young soldier. By the same token, a big, burly biker could write a convincing song on the joys of motherhood.

Writing with the Artist

One of the best ways to get a cut is by writing with a recording artist. Think about it: If you were doing an album, would you rather record someone else's song or one that you helped write and will get writer's royalties on?

While it's probable that you can't just call up Alan Jackson or Missy Elliot and ask to write with them, you can start by writing with the up-and-coming singers in your town, especially if you live in a music hub. Learn their styles and get to know them. Learning to work well with artists can really pay off when you get a staff job at a publishing house and have access to major label recording artists.

A great approach for writing artist-specific material or writing with a recording artist is to imagine them singing the lines as you write them. This will help in your choice of vowels, trills, and language and help to make your song a better fit for the artist.

Chapter 13

Recording Your Songs

Writing great songs doesn't do you much good if the world never hears them. Since it would be impractical to go door to door, playing your songs six billion times, and most publishers need something that they can listen to at their convenience and copy for pitching, you might consider recording your songs.

Demo Options

Once you decide to record your song, you must decide what kind of recording to make. The options range from a live recording with the onboard mike on your jambox to a full-production master recording, which may cost you tens of thousands of dollars.

Worktapes

A worktape is a rough recording that helps you remember a song and lets you hear what it sounds like so you can make decisions for the next step. Some staff writers also use worktapes to run new or unfinished material by their publishers for feedback and constructive criticism. Worktapes can be recorded on just about anything—a jambox, micro-recorder, or a full-blown digital studio.

The most important consideration in making a demo is that the vocals can clearly be heard above the music. The melody and the lyrics are what make up a song; anything else is just window dressing. If you're afraid of forgetting a really cool instrumental part, record it separately.

GVs and PVs

Guitar/vocal (GV) and piano/vocal (PV) demos are sometimes good enough for pitching, especially on ballads. Most publishers will tell you that they can always spot a great song by listening to a GV or PV, but many of them are either wrong or lying. It's up to you to figure out if a GV or PV is enough for a given song. If you believe that a particular song can be pitched with a demo in this format, make sure to put as much care into the recording it as you would for a full demo; it needs to be clean, clear, and balanced, with a performance that gets the song across well.

Home Recording

There's a middle ground between making a worktape and paying for time in a professional studio. If you have a little time, some money, and a do-it-yourself attitude, buying some home recording gear can, in the long run, save you time and money and help you learn about the recording process. These days, the options for home recording are virtually limitless and can be tailored to fit most budgets.

The Four-Tracks

The best-known piece of home recording gear is the four-track recorder, which is relatively inexpensive (often under a hundred bucks, used) and easy to use. A four-track has four independent tracks, which means that you can record guitar, vocal, bass, and drums, or any other combination of four inputs, with each on its own track. Moreover, four-tracks are available in various analog and digital formats and most have built-in mixers. The best use for a four-track is for working out ideas before going into the studio.

FACT

Most professional songwriters will tape a song as soon as it's done, then do a GV and/or home-recorded multi-track version before beginning a full production demo. Using these different stages can help you iron out the bugs in your song and make production decisions before going into the studio.

More Tracks

Cassette-based systems are also available in six- and eight-track configurations and reel-to-reel machines have up to twenty-four tracks. As you subdivide an analog tape into more tracks, it leaves less room for each track. This can result in lower fidelity and more "bleed through" between channels. Because of this, you may want to consider using a one- or two-inch reel-to-reel system for analog systems over four tracks. (Digital systems don't have this problem.)

Reel-to-reel recorders don't usually have built-in mixers. If you choose a reel-to-reel system, you'll need a mixing board with at least as many channels as your recorder has tracks. Some digital recorders have in excess of fifty tracks and most have built-in mixers.

For making full production demos, the minimum number of tracks you'll need in a system is sixteen. Twenty-four gives you more to play with and thirty-two can handle most sessions. It's easy to use up tracks on a big production: Say you've got a song with a lead vocal, an acoustic guitar, and a click track to keep time so that other players may add their parts later. To these three tracks, you add a drumkit, kick, snare, hi-hat, two rack toms, and a floor tom (each with its own mike and track), and two overheads for cymbals. That takes us up to twelve tracks. Now, let's add bass, electric rhythm guitar, lead guitar (in stereo, no less), piano, organ, mandolin, steel guitar, and fiddle. We're up to twenty-one and counting.

Should I buy studio time or build a studio?
That depends on how much time you want to devote to learning recording techniques. Many songwriters do both. If you want to learn, start with a used four-track and work your way up. Meanwhile, you can still use a professional studio.

Let's add three-part harmony backup vocals, which are often stacked (recorded twice) for a fuller sound. The producer decides to stack the lead vocal in a few key spots, and then the lead guitarist comes up with a great harmony part for his solo (in stereo, of course). The acoustic guitar is buried in the mix: Stacking will help the problem. We're now up to thirty-one tracks, barely enough room left for that all-important kazoo part. See how fast things add up?

Removable Drive Systems

Some digital recording systems have drives by which recordings can be stored on jazz, scuzzy, or other removable media and reinserted later for further work. This is good, in that it leaves the information in a soft or rewritable form while freeing up onboard memory for other projects. The limitation of this type of storage system is that these media don't always have sufficient capacity to store an entire project. Most removable drive systems have onboard mixers; some have automated mixing capabilities, onboard effects, and nonlinear editing options.

Internal Hard Disk Systems

Many stand-alone digital recorders have an internal hard disk, like that of a PC, for onboard storage and virtual workspace. Without a removable media drive, these systems can be limiting; once the memory's full, you must mix the project and delete the tracks before moving on to the next project, so you can't remix, redo, or add tracks at a later date. A hard disk system with a removable drive is a great option for home recording. Most units have onboard mixing and digital effects processing. Some have limited mastering capability.

Computer-Based Recording

The future of recording probably lies with computer-based systems. Professional studios now offer computer-based recording in addition to, or instead of, traditional two-inch analog tape machines. Many of the top songs on the charts today were recorded on computer-based systems.

FACT

Digital recording is a fast-changing industry these days. Whenever a new system takes over as the next big thing, many studios rush out and buy one. This is your chance to buy last year's model from them at a great price.

Costs for computer recording systems vary widely; some companies offer free software programs for turning your home computer into a simple studio, while high-end systems can run upwards of $50,000. A smart shopper can find a professional system for under $20,000. That may sound like a lot, but remember that an analog system of similar capabilities would have cost several hundred thousand dollars a few years back. Computer-based systems often have features not found in analog systems. These include:

- Built-in digital effects like reverb, delay, and chorus.
- Nonlinear editing capability that lets you jump instantly to any point in the song, cut and paste whole sections, and remove or add single words or notes.
- Nondestructive editing capability that allows you to "undo" changes.
- Sample/loop ability that you can use to sample sounds and build loops.
- Onboard sequencing for making samples, loops, and MIDI information into a complete music track for your song.
- Automatic vocal tuning for pitch trouble and perfect, automatic harmonies.
- Amplifier/speaker simulators that can simulate hundreds of vintage combinations at a fraction of the cost (and volume).
- Pre-amps for "warming up" mike signals or boosting signal on low-level tracks.
- Compressor/limiters to even levels, stop peaking, and add warmth or sustain.
- EQs and mastering programs for shaping the sound of your recording project.
- Automated mixing that lets you compare mixes and automatically control effect and fader levels so you can focus on listening instead of twisting knobs.

ALERT!

Don't get in over your head with recording gear. You can easily spend $100,000 on stuff you don't need and can't operate. Start small, take your time learning the process, and keep doing demos at a professional studio until you're ready and able to do your own.

Another nice thing about computer-based recorders is that the signal path is much shorter and cleaner than systems using outboard gear. This means a cleaner, stronger signal; a better, clearer recording; and fewer patch cords to buy.

Finding Good Mikes

Microphones are often overlooked in terms of importance. The microphone is the first thing that a voice or miked instrument encounters, and it greatly influences the sound of a recording. That fancy recorder won't do you much good if you have a fifteen-dollar mike.

Different mikes are made to handle different sound pressure levels and work at different distances and in different directional patterns. A '57-style mike is great for snare drums, speaker cabinets, and other "hot" signals. Condenser mikes are perfect for ambient applications like overheads for cymbals, acoustic instruments, choirs, and symphonies. Shock-mounted capsule mikes are great for close-up recording of vocals and acoustic instruments.

The most important part of any piece of recording gear is the manual. Before you buy a used piece of recording equipment, make sure that the manual is included or, at least, available from the manufacturer. Many companies now offer manuals online. Also, check the Internet for a BBS or user group for your gear.

Outboard Gear

Even if you have tons of cool built-ins, you may want a particular effect that the onboard stuff doesn't provide. In that case, you can buy a stand-alone unit to do the job. These separate processing units are collectively called "outboard gear."

Some of the various effects and processes that can be obtained from outboard gear include reverb, delay, chorus, flange, envelope follow, graphic EQ, parametric EQ, compression, limiting, and pre-amping. Digital multi-effect units are available that combine several of these functions. Analog versions are usually limited to one or two functions but may sometimes have better sound or finer control parameters, depending on the effect and model.

A good starter set for your studio might include an analog mike pre-amp, a digital multi-effect processor (reverb, delay, and so on), a thirty-one band graphic EQ, a four-band parametric EQ, and an analog compressor/limiter. When you shop for new toys, ask the seller to explain what they do and how to achieve the desired results.

The Players

You have a great song (or several) and now you're ready to record, either on your own or at a studio. It's time to decide who will play which parts. Budget, location, and project goals may all influence these decisions. You have several options for filling personnel needs and you can mix and match different options.

Have a Band

If you can find good players, being a member of a band can be a very cost-effective way to do a recording project. A dedicated band can put in the kind of rehearsal time that would cost a fortune with studio musicians. If the band writes together or wants to release a CD, get everybody to chip in.

Of course, this means that more people will be part of the decision-making process. The drummer will probably want the drums way too loud, the guitar player will want a solo, and eventually you're dealing with tension among band members; as a result, you've got nothing but bad tracks and an ugly project.

Recording projects have been the end of many good bands, so it's a good idea to clearly delineate who will make which decisions before you go into the studio. If you can't afford a producer, bribe the engineer with beer or donuts for some opinions (he's been put in this position before and still has drumstick fragments in his skull from the experience).

Remember this: No matter how many rehearsals you've had or how many gigs you've played, recording is a different process. People will get nervous and their brains will lock up, parts that worked great at the gig will suddenly have glaring flaws, and all singers will hate the sound of their own voices on a recording. Some of the best live players are awful in the studio and vice versa. The recording studio is a different environment and requires a different approach. The main rules for recording your band are these: Before recording, practice until you're sick of the songs, then practice for three more weeks, and, when in doubt, simplify.

Be a Band

Maybe you're one of those guys who can play everything well. Prince is famous for being able to play virtually any instrument found on any of his records. If you fit this description, great!

But even if you can't play everything, you can still do most of the tracks yourself: These days, a good sequencer and synthesizer combination can cover drums, keyboard parts, and bass. All you have to do is program the tracks instead of playing them. Some instruments are notoriously hard to replicate with a synthesizer, but you can sequence whatever works and hire out what's left.

Hire a Band

Most studios have connections with studio musicians, and some studios even have a "house band" on call. In any case, the studio can probably recommend players. Get players who read charts and a bandleader who can write them. That way, you can communicate ideas precisely and quickly.

FACT

Studio musicians are usually hired by the session rather than by the song. Make sure that you have several songs charted, but don't be disappointed if you only get a few songs recorded. Most union musicians also have a cartage service deliver and set up their equipment. You are expected to pay for this service.

In music hubs, most of these players are members of the Musicians Union, which means they may cost a little more than the guys down at the Antler Club back home, but union session players can be pretty amazing. With a good bandleader and charts, a lot of these cats nail it on the first take, which can save you money on studio time and rehearsals.

Also, professional session players know how to set their equipment for the right sound in the studio. This saves time and money as well.

Choosing a Singer

Okay, the studio and players have been chosen. Now somebody has to sing your song and put some heart into the performance, or your great song may never go anywhere but a Music Row dumpster. Engineers and publishers can usually recommend vocalists. If you don't live in a music hub, your options may be limited to jingle singers and local bar band vocalists. If you live in a small town, move—or at least look in the nearest big town.

When to Sing Your Own Demo

Most songwriters insist on singing their own demos. Do the guys who build racecars insist on driving them in the Indy 500? Maybe you should rethink things a little bit. Even if you're a fantastic singer, your voice might not be right for a particular song. Remember, when it comes to pitching songs, it's the *song* that matters, not your artistic vanity or hopes of a record deal.

If you can't find someone who can sing your song better than you, then sing your own demo. Otherwise, look for a voice that's similar to artists to whom you might pitch the song or close to the one you heard in your head when writing it.

Boy or Girl?

When it comes to many songs, it doesn't matter whether the performer is male or female. As a matter of fact, you may want to put some effort into writing songs that are either nongender specific or have two different versions of the lyric—this doubles your chances of getting a cut. If you can afford two demos, one with male vocals and one with female vocals, then go for it. All things being equal, go with a male singer; the theory is that many male singers will shy away from a song with a female vocal on the demo but most female singers aren't scared by a male vocal demo.

While it's good to have a song that can be sung by a male or female performer, don't sacrifice quality to force a song into a mold that won't fit. If a song is obviously much stronger one way than the other, go with what works.

Mixing a Song Demo

Mixing is a stressful task. Get a good night's sleep before a mixing session. When in doubt, listen again. Don't be afraid to tell the engineer what you want but listen to any advice he or she may offer. Odds are that an experienced engineer has heard more sessions than you and your three closest friends put together.

Four Mixes

When you mix your demo, you need at least four mixes:

1. **Minus one mix:** This mix has the music, but no lead vocal; it is useful for trying different singers, singing over for your own CD project, and for karaoke night at the Antler Lodge.
2. **Radio mix:** This version should be as close as possible to perfect; it's great for playing for the folks back home and for your personal listening pleasure.
3. **Vocal up mix:** A mix with the vocals louder than normal, so publishers can hear the words.
4. **Vocal *way* up mix:** An extra mix many songwriters are advised to make, in case the "vocal up" mix isn't as dramatic as you thought.

As you check your mixes, you may notice that your songs sound different on other systems than they did during mixing. All speaker systems sound a little different—in some cases, the differences are pretty dramatic. It's best to check your mixes on several different systems before sending them off for duplicating or mastering. Many studios have several sets of speakers for testing mixes. Also check mixes in your car, home, and anywhere else you can think of.

Don't start mixing after a day, or even a few hours, of tracking. After a few hours of listening, your ears get "tired" and things sound different. Always start a mixing session with fresh ears and never go longer than five or six hours at a time.

The Last Step

Mastering is the final phase of a professional project. In the mastering process, the radio mix is split into many different tracks by frequency, which are compressed and tweaked separately, then mixed back together. This makes the recording sound more even and helps each part stand out without covering up the others. Also, mastering can boost the overall level and make the recording sound better on a variety of playback systems.

Simply put, mastering is the difference between a great demo and a "radio ready" recording. Does your project need to be mastered? Unless you plan on getting airplay, probably not. If you have plenty of cash and want to take a great recording up another notch, mastering can do that. Many computer-based recording systems have mastering capability. You might experiment with this, but remember that mastering is an art all its own. Most mastering engineers are specialists who do nothing else. An amateur mastering job can ruin your project. Ⓔ

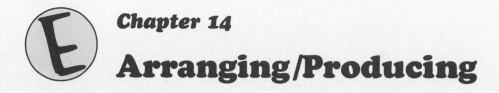

Chapter 14

Arranging/Producing

The charts, players, singers, and engineer are ready. The recording should work out like magic, right? It might—as long as you have a magician or two handy. When it comes to producing great songs, keep in mind that without designating someone to oversee critical recording decisions, your project will more than likely sound like a train wreck.

The Producer's Role

Just as a songwriter needs to learn to think like a songwriter, there are thought processes and perspectives that are unique to a producer's job. A producer should be able to envision several kinds of production for a given song, hear various instrument parts and harmony arrangements in her head, and have a good idea how everything will work together in the studio. As a producer, it's your job to know how different tempos, time signatures, grooves, effects, recording techniques, and many other elements will affect the impact of a song on listeners. A producer has to be equal parts arranger, musician, recording engineer, songwriter, and A&R rep.

FACT

A large percentage of successful producers are also hit songwriters and respected musicians. Many songwriters become producers so that they can more fully realize their artistic visions without having to rely on a producer to get it right. Glen Ballard, Mutt Lange, Jimmy Jam, and Terry Lewis are all multi-talented writer/producer/musicians.

That may sound like a lot to learn and, in truth, it is. Remember, though, that a producer doesn't have to actually do all these things. A producer just has to be able to imagine the way a song should sound and communicate those ideas to the performers. A guitarist thinks about the guitar part. A singer thinks about the melody and the lyric. A drummer thinks about—well, nobody is really sure what drummers think about—but producers have to think about all these things and how they work together to help a song reach its artistic and/or commercial potential. The producer has to see the big picture and steer a recording project toward the intended goals of the recording artist and the record company, hopefully with a result that radio station program directors and listeners will all enjoy.

Train your brain to hear production possibilities. You can start by listening to your favorite songs from a production standpoint. Pay attention to how everything fits together, from the drums, bass, and other rhythm instruments to the backup vocals, lead instruments, and lead vocals. Listen to the effects and the way parts get louder and softer. Pick a specific part and follow it through the song. Where does it come in and out? How is it mixed? What does it add to the song? Was anything special used to reinforce the chorus, hook, or bridge?

Shortly, you'll begin hearing songs in a different way. You'll hear how production and arrangements work to strengthen a song. When you have this down, move on to songs in different genres to see what's unique about production for those styles. Now, move on to current hits and the production styles that are hot right now.

Finally, start imagining these elements in your own songs. Learn to hear a full production in your head by building it a track at a time. Keep at it until you can imagine different grooves, styles, and combinations of instruments on any song you hear. That's what a producer's brain is supposed to do. Adding production ideas to the writing process can give another dimension to your writing and help you take things up a level.

When is a producer needed?
Any time you record, one or more people are making production decisions. There is always a producer. If nobody else is doing it, then you are the producer. If you are unaware of this, your production will suffer and it's the producer's fault.

How a Song "Feels"

When it comes to production, it's important to establish a song's groove. From a writer's perspective, groove refers to the style, genre, or type of beat used for a song. From a production standpoint, groove also means the "pocket" or feel laid down by the rhythm section and/or the playing styles employed by various schools of musicians. Knowing the ins and outs of various grooves is one of the things that can help a producer "make" a song.

Genre Grooves

A genre groove has the feeling of a specific type of music. The Garth Brooks country hits "Ain't Goin' Down 'Til the Sun Comes Up" and "Papa Loved Mama" are both fast rock shuffle grooves. Brooks's cover of the Little Feat song "Dixie Chicken" is a Cajun shuffle groove used predominantly in zydeco music; his mega-hit "The Dance" uses a groove common to modern folk music. Because of the production and the musical identity of the recording artist, these songs are all considered to be country. Properly used, genre grooves can add the moods, flavors, and prosodic elements of other styles to a production.

FACT

A drum machine can be an invaluable tool for trying multiple styles and grooves on the same song. You can program examples of a few dozen different grooves and beats into your drum machine, then try them all with each new song, adjusting the tempo to a comfortable spot.

Geographic Grooves

Some grooves are geographic in nature; you may hear someone refer to a Detroit, LA, Bakersfield, Nashville, or London groove. This means that the feel is similar to one used by the studio players from that area. Detroit players may push the beat a little for a high-energy feel. London players usually play right on top for a very steady feel. Chicago musicians will often pull the beat for a smoky, lazy feeling, and New Orleans players may push or pull, depending on the moment and the song.

Sometimes the feel of these grooves is caused by tension between various instruments within the group rather than between the ensemble and the "true" beat. This is especially true of the relationship between the bass and drums and between those two instruments and the others. Spend some time talking with studio bassists and drummers. They can be great sources for groove history and information.

Group Grooves

Certain artists or groups have become so associated with a particular kind of groove that the mention of their names communicates the desired feel for a song. This kind of groove information is very specific and, if all parties involved are familiar with the reference, can really help to zero in on the right feel. You might spend half an hour writing out or discussing the theory behind one of the different grooves in the Dixie Chicks song "Goodbye Earl," when just saying, "It's a Buddy Holly thing" might be all you need to do.

Certain songs can also make for easy references to particular grooves. If you say "Blueberry Hill," you don't have to explain what a triplet feel is or how New Orleans musicians apply a "swing" to that feel. Mention "Moondance" and you might save a whole afternoon of re-explaining the groove in a different way for each musician. Referring to a particular artist or song helps the mind to hear a part instead of imagining it as an abstract concept.

A good exercise, and a good way to prepare for communicating different groove ideas during a session, is to find two or three well-known song examples for every groove in your catalog. While you're at it, learn what each of these grooves is called by its genre and/or beat.

Genre and Style

What genre or style will your song be performed in for the demo? This can be a toughie. Your song might sound perfect as a straight-ahead blues tune. It sounds cool that way, but cool doesn't buy groceries. Selling fifty thousand units is considered a big sale for a blues record. Wouldn't you rather pick a genre that routinely sells in the millions?

Style is different than groove. Style is more a function of where the song will be marketed. A song written in one style or genre can often be successfully marketed in a different, more profitable style by carefully mixing the right elements of the two styles together. Groove can influence this, as can instrumentation, the way a song is mixed, and who sings the song. A change in one or more of these factors can sometimes take a song into markets never even dreamed of by the songwriter.

A great example of this is the Collective Soul song "Shine." In the original version, it's a psychedelic alt-rock song. The same song, as performed by Dolly Parton and Nickel Creek, becomes a reverent Americana/gospel song with a touch of bluegrass. The lyric and melody are the same, the tempos are close, the groove isn't all that different, but the production and vocal delivery made a big, crunchy rock song that would terrify most country fans into something that was radio-friendly to the country market. People who would have switched channels on the original version were suddenly rushing out to buy this great new country version.

Learn to separate style, genre, and groove from the song in your head. Think of your song as a car. Melody and lyrics are what make a song; they are the motor that makes it go and the frame that holds it together. Production elements are the added features like body style, leather seats, and choice of colors that help the car appeal to different groups of buyers. If you have any doubt about this, listen to the band Hayseed Dixie: They have recorded an entire album of bluegrass using songs originally written and recorded by the heavy metal group AC/DC.

When attempting to write or produce a crossover project, don't automatically assume that halfway between two genres is the right place to aim. Each song is different and will require specific attention to what factors from each genre will influence production values, groove, instrumentation, vocal delivery, mix, and lyrical and melodic elements.

Splitting the Difference

Often, a song, artist, or production that hits a middle ground between two genres has a wider market appeal. The Eagles, Lynard Skynard, and

Bruce Springsteen are all rockers whose influences from country music gave them a market edge. Conversely, Travis Tritt, Montgomery Gentry, and Charlie Daniels are country artists whose rock-n-roll leanings draw fans from both genres. The trick with crossover songs and production is to draw fans from other markets without alienating fans of the primary style. If you can do this, you can really cash in.

This is especially true if you can take a song from a given genre and pull it toward a pop sound. Shania Twain is a country singer, Eric Clapton is a blues artist, and No Doubt is a ska band. However, all three have managed to score on the pop charts and outsell the competition in their respective genres. Both as a writer and a producer, you need to understand what's important about a genre to the majority of its fans and which of those elements can be used to appeal to a wider audience.

A, B, C, or All of the Above

For some songs, several production styles might work. It's up to the producer to determine which style will best carry the song, both artistically and commercially. Your decision may be affected by current market trends; if a movie soundtrack suddenly makes bluegrass the hot new thing, you might want to demo your song as bluegrass instead of traditional country. Your decision may also be influenced by your connections. If your song would work as a country ballad or a modern R&B "boy band" song, but all your connections are in the R&B scene, the choice is simple, at least for now.

Choosing a Tempo

Give ample consideration to choosing the perfect tempo for a song. You can change a guitar part after the tracks are done, you can punch in or computer-tune a pitchy vocal line, you can add a choir and a symphony after the fact, but unless you want to start over, you're pretty much stuck with the tempo you choose.

You can slightly alter the tempo on most recording systems with a function called "pitch control." Why is it called "pitch control"? Because when you slow down or speed up a recording, it alters the pitches of the notes you hear in playback. If you move the pitch control too far up, the voice track will sound like a chipmunk on helium; too far down and it'll sound like Godzilla on Valium. The industry terms for these unwanted effects are "munchkinizing" and "demonizing."

The point here is that you need to carefully consider what tempo is right for a song before you start laying down tracks. Tempo affects the groove and feel. A couple BPM (beats per minute) too fast and the whole thing sounds stiff and rushed. A little too slow and the song can drag and sound sloppy. Experiment with different tempos before making a worktape and use the tempo you think works best. Use a click track from a drum machine to count things off; that way you can use the BPM indicator to see exactly what tempo you intend to use. When demo time arrives, solicit the opinions of the engineer, players, and demo singer.

Pitch control has actually been used as a recording technique by some producers. Working with The Beatles, Sir George Martin found that electric slide guitar parts have a unique tone when recorded with the tape slowed down and played back at normal speed. Other producers have done the same with background harmonies to improve pitch.

Instrumentation

Choosing the right instruments for a particular song is one of the most difficult, yet fun, parts of the producer's job. Try to imagine "Margaritaville" without the steel drums or "Turn the Page" without the sax part. Even better, try to imagine "Margaritaville" with sax and "Turn the Page" with steel drums. Yikes! Just as much as the groove or style, instrument choice can influence the overall feel of a production and help position a song for success in a given market.

Certain instruments lend themselves to particular genres of music. When you hear a banjo, what do you think of? How about pedal steel, turntable scratches, violin, conga drums, or distorted electric guitar? Each of these instruments instantly conjures up a specific kind of music. Knowing this can help you mix and match instruments for a particular flavor or feel.

Some instruments work well for several styles of music. A Hammond B-3 organ can be used for a Bach Toccata or a classic rock song like "Freebird." An accordion might bring to mind polka night at the bowling alley, but it's also important in zydeco, Mexican country music, and some of John Mellencamp's roots rock. There are no rules concerning what instruments can't be used for a given style. You might use mandolin on a rock song (like Rod Stuart's "Maggie May") or synthesizer on a country song (like Shania Twain's "Man, I Feel Like a Woman"). Classical-style string arrangements have been used in many different genres to "sweeten things up" and help a song's pop crossover appeal. This is where a producer has to go with instinct and hope he or she will make the right decision.

Familiarizing yourself with the differences of the major instrument brands can be a big help. Want a twangy country guitar? You probably need a Tele through a Twin. Classic rock? Try a Les Paul through a Marshall. Gritty blues? It might be a Strat or an ES-335. Ask musicians about different instruments.

If you have enough tracks and enough money, you can experiment with the instrumentation, but don't get too carried away: Your ultimate job as a producer is to choose the combination of instruments that will best accentuate the song.

Sonic Impact

The most ephemeral and intangible, yet most important, part of a producer's job is to make sure that when the last knob has been turned and the final mix burned, the song has that something special that makes people remember it. This is called "sonic impact." It's that thing you can't quite put your finger on that makes some songs stand out. There are probably a few songs that you can remember hearing for the first time because they made a huge impact on your perception of music. They were different or better than anything else you were listening to at the time. These songs, for reasons that are difficult to pin down, stick in your head year after year. That's what sonic impact is.

There is no guaranteed way to achieve sonic impact, no magic formula that works every time. Skill, luck, intuition, and timing all play a part in a song's sonic impact. The important thing is to be aware as recording progresses, listen for elements that bring out the magic in a song, and capitalize on them when you find them.

Often, when a new production style accompanies the birth of a new style or genre, the first few years see a lot of songs with major sonic impact. Why? Partly because they are the first songs to ever sound that way. Hundreds of songs have a similar production, groove and performance style to Chuck Berry's "Johnny B. Goode," but his song was among the first to explore that particular musical branch and thus garnered a permanent spot in the public music consciousness. Honing your production skills and keeping up on current production trends can give you a better chance of being in the first wave of a new trend.

Key Changes

Key changes are sometimes written in by the songwriter as a natural occurrence (like in Cheryl Crow's "Every Day Is a Winding Road"). Just as often, though, a key change is a production decision made when a song seems to be bogging down at a certain point. This kind of key change is usually used between back-to-back verses (like in George Jones's "He Stopped Loving Her Today") or to give a final chorus a little extra "oomph" (as with Bon Jovi's "Livin' on a Prayer"). Key changes sometimes add just enough difference to a song to keep the short attention span crowd from tuning out.

Although a key change is a convenient way to solve a problem without changing the lyric, melody, or structure of the song, it's easy to overuse this quick fix. Before you change keys, ask yourself if the song needs anything extra. If a song is rolling along just fine, a key change can muddle up a good thing and make charting, playing, and singing the song more difficult.

ALERT!

If something definitely needs to be done, make sure a key change is the right thing to do. Might the song be better helped by a rewrite, edit, or structural change? If a key change is what's needed, you'll usually want to keep it to a half step or whole step, so as not to move the melody out of the singer's range.

Solos and Instrumental Passages

The producer often has the last say over where solos and instrumental passages will be placed in a song, how long they will last, and what form they will take. Your goal as a producer is to use solos and instrumental passages to frame the song in a way that enhances the overall impact of the lyrics and melody. This means adding signature licks, instrumental chorus, or smokin' solos and also knowing when a song doesn't need any of these things.

Once you have the arrangement worked out, time it. It's easy to let a song go over four minutes, which hurts the chances of getting airplay. Sometimes a compromise must be made between art and commerce. Be brutally honest in these decisions. Is that solo really necessary, or just really cool? Don't hurt the song's impact just to make it shorter, but get as close to three minutes as you can without losing anything vital.

The most common compromise, and one which seems to satisfy the most people, is to make a "single edit" for radio play and an album version to go on the CD. Some computer-based recording systems can cut pieces out of a song and edit the remaining parts together. This saves time and money over recording two versions. Ⓔ

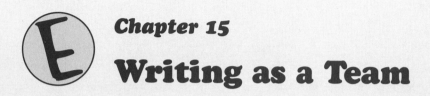

Chapter 15

Writing as a Team

If you started out working alone, the concept of writing a song with another person can seem alien. However, once you get your feet wet, you may find that, like thumb wrestling, chess, and dating, songwriting is much more fun when two people are involved. Many songwriters have discovered the benefits of collaboration, but there are a few things you need to be aware of before you start.

Great Teams

Lennon and McCartney, Bacharach and David, Ashford and Simpson, Goffin and King, Boyce and Hart, Rogers and Hart, Rogers and Hammerstein—many of the world's most enduring songs have come from co-writing teams. With some teams, one person writes lyrics and the other melody (like Gilbert and Sullivan). Other teams collaborate on all aspects of a song or mix and match responsibilities, depending on circumstances (like Lennon and McCartney). Every team has a different dynamic and a different process. Just as you developed a process for writing by yourself, you will have a different team process for each co-writer you work with.

Two heads are better than one; when it comes to songwriting, two heads working together can be better than three or more working separately. The right chemistry in a writing team can yield a song better than either of the writers would have come up with alone or with other co-writers. No one understands why, but few in the music business doubt that it's true. Some teams just have something special. Ideally, this is what you're looking for, a co-writer that you click with.

To start a co-writing session, many professional songwriters talk about life for a while, discussing current events, personal lives, childhood memories, or any number of other things, looking for an idea that moves both writers. This also helps you build a rapport and develop a sense of each other's viewpoints.

The Joys of Co-Writing

No matter what your strengths, weaknesses, or skill level, there's someone out there just waiting to write a song with you. Even if you don't find that special someone right away, co-writing offers advantages that make it a worthwhile endeavor. At the very least, you'll have more ideas and options to work with—your co-writer may have the perfect idea for tweaking one of your songs to make it great.

For many writers, the co-writing process is more productive and enjoyable because it offers the chance to toss ideas back and forth in a dialogue rather than having to sit alone in a room and puzzle things out. The addition of another perspective can make problem solving easier. Co-writing helps with questions of subjectivity; you can simply ask your co-writer, "Will people get it if we say . . . ?"

Co-writing can be a great learning opportunity. In a co-write, you'll see firsthand how someone generates and develops ideas, turns a phrase, and edits a song. And there are business advantages as well. If you both hold staff positions with different publishers, you'll have two companies pitching your song. You'll double your contacts for getting a song to the right people and the chance someone will recognize one of the names on the lyric sheet. Co-writing is a great way to get to know other writers better and to become known to their publishers, other co-writers, and contacts. In a business that revolves around networking, this is priceless.

When should I start co-writing?
If you are a complete (lyrics and melody) songwriter, you can start co-writing as soon as you have the basics down and can write a whole song. If you write only lyrics or only melodies, you may begin co-writing as soon as you can write a complete melody or lyric.

Finding Co-Writers

Your local songwriting association or branch of Nashville Songwriter's Association International (NSAI) is an excellent spot to meet potential co-writers. You can also meet songwriters from all over the world at Internet songwriting forums and chatrooms. Of course, if you live in a music hub, there'll be a lot more writers around, possibly even a music scene of clubs and coffeehouses where songwriters hang out and perform. Open mike and writer's nights have a distinct advantage over some of the other places you might look for co-writers: You get the opportunity to hear people perform their songs before you actually begin working with them.

A Word of Warning

In music hub cities, there's a delicate set of manners involved in asking someone to co-write. You shouldn't ask anyone to co-write until they've heard some of your songs. Be prepared to give potential co-writers a CD to check out. If you are an unknown writer (i.e., you don't have a paid staff-writing position or any major label cuts), don't ever ask an established writer for a co-write. This is considered extremely bad form. If you know an established writer, you may ask his or her opinion of your material. If you are friendly acquaintances, you might ask for an opinion on a few demos. You might even suggest to an established writer who has befriended you that you look forward to the day when you are well enough established to co-write with someone as talented as he or she. All this is fine, but you must never ask point blank for a co-write with an established writer.

Be careful when getting to know a potential co-writer. Don't give out your home address to someone you haven't met. Instead, arrange to meet first in a public place. Remember, just because someone writes songs, even great ones, doesn't mean he or she isn't a serial killer, con artist, or long-distance service telemarketer.

Why is this such a big deal? First, most publishers have the right to approve co-writers for their staff writers, and it can be a hassle to get approval for an unknown when your other co-writers have hits, cuts, or are professional staff writers. Second, if it weren't considered impolite to ask, established songwriters would be inundated with thousands of co-write offers from every idiot who ever wielded a pen or strummed a guitar. This rule keeps established writers from having to say, "No" a hundred times a day and from having to deal with irate or hurt songwriters demanding to know why not. Hopefully, you'll someday have the opportunity to be grateful for the protection offered by this rule. In the meantime, find co-writers on or slightly above your own level who are working hard to get to the next one.

Compatibility

Sometimes you can put two hit songwriters in a room together and nothing happens. Sometimes you can put two pretty good songwriters in a room together and magic happens. Occasionally, for reasons unknown, you can put a songwriter in a room with a potted plant or a Border Collie and that writer will come up with a better song than he or she would have alone.

If It Ain't Broke . . .

When the right time, place, and people all come together, the result may be a great song. If your collaboration with a newbie is yielding great results every time, stop worrying about what should be happening and keep writing great songs. If your co-writer only contributes a few lines to each song, but they are the perfect lines needed to complete the song, stop whining and keep writing great songs. Remember, 50 percent of a million dollars is more than 100 percent of nothing. Your goals are to write great songs and make a living. If it works, go with it.

Even with your favorite co-writers, you may hit a dry spell or slump now and again. Instead of giving up, try adding something different to your process or taking a little break. Don't worry; odds are that things will return to normal or even get better.

We Need to Talk

Sometimes co-writers just don't click, and it may be for reasons totally unrelated to how well you like each other or how good a writer you both are. Don't be alarmed when this happens. It often takes several sessions to begin building a rapport with a new co-writer. If, after several nonproductive sessions with someone, you feel like there's a problem, schedule a "no-write" session to talk about process and get to know each other better. If you get to the point that you feel like both parties are just wasting time, suggest some time off and try again later.

Where Is This Relationship Going?

Make sure that you and your potential co-writer have compatible goals. The last thing you want is to find out that your co-writer is only interested in composing Portuguese disco music, when you've committed your life to the pursuit of the perfect heavy metal polka. Likewise, if your ultimate goal is to be a hit writer, but your co-writer sees songwriting as a hobby and wants to write ten-minute campfire songs, there may be problems.

That being said, as long as you have some writing goals in common, you might learn more from someone with a different set of musical experiences than from someone who writes the exact same kinds of songs as you. Before you write with someone, discuss your writing goals and influences and trade songs so that you can each get an idea of how the other writes. Remember that fluency in different styles helps to ensure a long career as a songwriter. If a co-writer is a potential source of information in this regard, count that as a plus and learn all you can.

FACT

Gilbert and Sullivan, arguably the most successful writing team of the nineteenth century, had very different personalities, lifestyles, goals, and approaches to writing. Still, because of mutual respect, commitment to quality, and a great—if inexplicable—writing chemistry, they overcame these differences and enjoyed a long reign at the top.

Irreconcilable Differences

In addition to differences of personalities, goals, and musical styles, you may find that you have a different writing process than someone else. Some songwriters pace, some sit quietly, and some prefer to lie on the floor, gazing at the ceiling. Compulsive snackers, pencil tappers, hummers, strummers, whistlers, and weepers are all to be found amongst your would-be co-writers. What if you chain smoke during writing sessions, but your potential pen pal has psychic asthma and starts making little wheezing and coughing noises before you even get one lit? Is your co-writer a day person? A vegan? A compulsive nose picker? It all makes a difference. Things that wouldn't bother you at most times might drive you right up the wall when you're trying to create. Most songwriters are as defensive of the idiosyncrasies in their processes as they are offended by those of others. Know in advance what you and your co-writer can deal with and what you can't.

Ultimately, what matters are the songs you come up with. It might be worth getting up a little early or going outside to smoke if the resulting songs are good enough. If you can't find an environment that suits you both, try passing songs back and forth and working separately. With a little communication and compromise on both sides, these things can usually be ironed out.

I Want a Divorce!

Sometimes it just doesn't work. A co-writer rubs you the wrong way or you don't write well together. You can't devote an infinite amount of sessions to working things out. In most cases, people you don't like aren't that fond of you either and will be more than happy to call it quits with no hard feelings. If you just plain don't like someone, odds are that you won't write great songs with that person. Even if you do get some results, you'll dread each session as it approaches and probably leave feeling depressed and drained.

ALERT!

If you question a co-writer's ethics or have trust issues, terminate the relationship. Be polite and discreet and try not to burn bridges or alienate anyone, just get out and stay out. Your songs and your reputation could be at stake.

If you like someone, but you just don't write well together, save the friendship and move on. Songwriting is supposed to feel good. If it doesn't, you're doing it wrong. Most songwriters prefer to work with people they know, like, and trust. That way, the worst thing that happens in a session is that you spend some time with a friend, doing something that you both enjoy.

Setting Ground Rules

Despite its many advantages, co-writing carries some baggage that solo writing doesn't. You and your co-writer will need to come to an agreement on certain points or at least agree to disagree. Here's a partial list of issues you may need to discuss.

1. Will the co-written work be a fifty-fifty split in terms of copyright and royalties, no matter who writes what? Or will the split be based on total contribution?
2. Who decides when the song is ready to be recorded or performed?
3. Must both writers agree on arrangements and matters of performance?
4. How will demo costs be split, where will the demo be made, and what is the budget for recording?
5. Who will produce the demo or have a say in the production?
6. What happens if one of you isn't happy with the song?
7. What if one of you brings a partially completed song to the table and ends up wanting it back?
8. What if one of you wants to bring in a third co-writer?
9. How will disagreements over lyrical or melodic content be resolved?
10. Who will bring the potato salad?

The answers to these questions might seem obvious, but it's unwise to assume anything that's not spelled out in advance. You might get together with your potential co-writer a few days before your session to discuss some of these points.

It might be a good idea to discuss the planned length of your session beforehand. Most co-write sessions last three to four hours, but you may wish to go longer if you feel you're on to something. You might also want to leave a little extra time between sessions in case this happens.

Written Agreements

Some songwriters, especially in New York and LA, prefer to clear up any questions or doubts in advance by using a written co-writing agreement. If you decide to use a co-writing agreement, make sure that you have one that has been drawn up by an entertainment attorney. Otherwise, it may prove to be worthless.

Some songwriters, especially in Nashville, may be insulted if you ask them to sign a co-writing agreement. These people believe, perhaps not wrongly, that you shouldn't write with someone you don't trust. Many of them also believe in an unwritten code of co-writing etiquette that sometimes contradicts what the law has to say about co-writing. Whether you prefer an ironclad contract or a handshake, make sure you get at least one of the two.

The Unwritten Rules

Though some songwriters, and most lawyers, may believe differently, there are rules of etiquette ascribed to by most professionals. If you bring an idea or partial song to the table, it's still yours unless you use something your co-writer came up with. Unless otherwise stated, all co-writes are shared fifty-fifty. The song is done when you both agree it's done and not a minute sooner. Unless otherwise agreed upon, demo costs are to be shared equally, and so are decisions regarding recording.

No other writers will be brought in on the song unless both writers agree. As long as no substantial changes to the lyric or melody have been made, each writer is free to perform and record the song as he or she sees fit. Small disagreements over content should be handled either by compromise or by agreeing to disagree. Larger disagreements should be handled before pitching the song. If the two writers cannot come to an agreement or agree to pitch two different versions, the song goes on the shelf and stays there. If only one co-writer has a deal and his publisher is fronting the demo money, that writer or his publisher will make all decisions regarding the demo.

There's more, but you'll learn it as you go. If you want to know about a particular subject, ask your co-writer how he or she feels about it. Mostly, the unwritten rules are about mutual respect and treating your co-writers the way you'd like to be treated.

Don't assume that all songwriters are aware of the laws or the unwritten rules and etiquette procedures that govern co-writing. Always make sure you and your co-writer understand and agree to all the terms, written or unwritten, to which your songs will be subject. If you have the smallest doubt, ask.

Different Types of Writers

One of the most important things to know about yourself is what kind of writer you are. You need to be aware of what you bring to the table as a co-writer. You also need to know your weaknesses, so that you know what to work on and what kinds of co-writers to seek out. For the same reasons, it's important to learn what kind of writer your co-writer is. There are many types of songwriters and most writers combine two or more of these types.

Lyricists

Lyricists are people who write words for songs. Famous lyricists include Hal David, Charles John Quarto, and Bernie Taupin. Lyric writing is, in part, a highly stylized form of poetry, with many sub-genres and schools of thought in practice. A lyricist should not only know how to write a lyric that lends itself to being put to music, but also how to write a lyric to an existing melody.

Most beginning songwriters, lacking musical prowess and having had at least some experience with language, mistakenly regard themselves as lyricists by default. These writers forget that most of the other songwriters in the world grew up reading, writing, and talking as well. If you really want to call yourself a lyricist, expect to spend years studying and perfecting your craft, just as you would to be a composer of music. To be a true lyricist requires poetic and storytelling skills surpassing those of most English professors. Plus, there are several times as many would-be lyricists as there are melodicists and songwriters who can do both put together. If you want to be a professional songwriter, it's worth your while to learn something about music.

Melodicists

Melodicists write the melodies for the song lyrics. As with a lyricist, a good melodicist can either write his or her part first or add it to an existing work. Some music theory and experience with an instrument are recommended for those who wish to specialize in melody writing. Arranging and producing skills also come in handy for a melodicist, as lyricists aren't usually much help in these areas.

Additionally, you should spend at least some time learning how to write lyrics. Remember that you're in competition with a lot of songwriters who can write melodies and lyrics. Even if you never become proficient at writing lyrics, a bit of study can help you to understand your co-writers.

FACT

From a legal standpoint, unless otherwise agreed in writing, lyric and melody are each worth 50 percent of the song and you own 50 percent of each melody or lyric you help write. If you only work on the melody or lyric and co-write that part, you will only own 25 percent of the song.

Other Forms of Contribution

In addition to lyrics and melodies, there are many other contributions a writer can make to a session. Some people are good at starting songs and coming up with ideas; others are great at finishing them.

"Song doctors" or "fixers" are natural-born troubleshooters. "Groove" writers specialize in grooves. Vibe writers, much like a potted plant or

Border Collie, have the unique ability to make a song better just by being present for its creation. They just put off a vibe that makes other writers work better.

Carrying Your Weight

To build a reputation as a good co-writer, make sure that you do your share of the work. Even if someone else is a better or more experienced writer, being prepared, working hard, and being ready to contribute your best work to a song will help to make sure that you attract and retain skilled co-writing partners.

Many songwriters prefer to make the first co-writing session with another writer a "getting to know you" session where each writer shares some of his background, views, and goals and the two writers trade songs and discuss ideas and processes without worrying about coming up with a song.

Do Your Homework

Learn a little about your co-writer before the session. Get a CD of his or her songs and listen a few times to get a feel for your co-writer's style, strengths, and weaknesses. If a number of the songs on the CD are co-writes, ask your co-writer about the nature and extent of his or her contributions. If you know that your co-writer is especially strong with melodies, bring some lyrics for which a melody has been eluding you. If he or she is an uptempo specialist and great with grooves, and you're not, let your co-writer take the lead on these things.

Learn something about your co-writer as a person, too. Does he or she have a spouse or children? What interests or beliefs do the two of you have in common? What unique experiences can your co-writer draw upon? Knowing the person you're working with helps you to communicate and makes your co-writes better.

Bring Your Best

If someone is worth co-writing with, he or she is worth trusting with some of your good ideas. Not that you should give away your best hook during the first session, but if you both come in with your B material, the session will probably not yield much. Always bring a few good hooks or ideas and maybe a few songs for which you think your co-writer may be the right finisher or fixer. Bring an open mind and keep it that way.

Your co-writer may have some radically different ideas that might help make the song a potential hit. Always hear out your co-writer and carefully examine any ideas he or she feels strongly about, even if they directly contradict what you had in mind. Bring your instrument, your toolbox, and a recorder, so you don't lose any good ideas. If you're writing at someone else's office or home, bring a beverage and any munchies you might need for the session. You might even ask if you could bring your host a beverage as well.

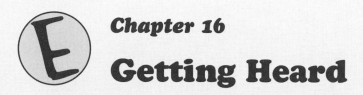

Chapter 16

Getting Heard

A fantastic demo of a killer song doesn't do much good unless somebody hears it. "Somebody" doesn't mean your mom, friends, or even your local DJ. You need *Somebody* with a capital "S." This where most songwriters are stumped. Who is this somebody, and what is it that this person can do for you? And how do you get this somebody to hear your work?

Find a Music Hub

For an aspiring songwriter, there are only a few cities in the United States that really have any importance; 99.9 percent of all publishers with enough juice to do something for you are located in these hub cities. Regional scenes pop up from time to time; some flourish and become permanent hubs; some fade after a few years. New York has been a hub since the late 1800s, Seattle for only a decade. Right now, Nashville, New York, and Los Angeles are the major players.

Nashville and LA have only been hubs since the 1950s. Keep abreast of up-and-coming music hubs: The best time to establish yourself is when a new scene springs up. A little attention to trade magazines will keep you clued in.

Many of the smaller hubs specialize in one or two kinds of music: Detroit is known for hip-hop and rap, Miami for salsa and dance music, Austin for the singer/songwriter and alt-country genres, Seattle for alt, grunge, and metal, Atlanta for hip-hop, nu-soul, and modern R&B, and Minneapolis for the "Paisley Park" pop/R&B/rock/funk crowd. These hubs are fairly exclusive in terms of genre, so if you want to be a country-western songwriter, Detroit might not be your best bet.

The Decision-Makers

There are a lot more people who can decide that a song won't go on a recording project than there are people who can decide it will. At a publishing office, the receptionist, copy boy, or janitor may also serve as a song screener; after all, chances are they are also songwriters, musicians, or singers. Even if they're not, they probably know more about the music business than you do.

Screeners may include the catalog manager (copy boy), executive assistant (secretary or gopher), and the intern—an unpaid student job for those who hope to land a job in the music industry after college.

Screeners weed out the songs that have long intros, sound "muddy," or are just plain horrible. Most songs never make it past this first level: You'd be surprised at what sounds horrible after listening to a hundred songs a day for a few months. Screeners mostly handle mail-ins and drop-offs. This means that getting an actual appointment may sometimes bump you up a level.

FACT

Treat everybody in the music business with respect. Fortunes can change fast and that secretary could be a VP within a couple of years or the mailroom guy might get an artist deal. Don't be fake or overdo it, just treat everyone as you'd like to be treated.

After the screeners, there are professional managers and pluggers. Professional managers handle the day-to-day supervision of the staff writers and help guide their careers. Pluggers take songs from the publisher's catalog to pitch to A&R reps, producers, and artists. If you make an appointment at a publishing company, you may meet with a professional manager or a plugger. The top decision-maker at a publishing house is usually the creative director.

The Real Decision-Makers

People who can actually decide to put a song on a record are the artist, the label's A&R rep for that artist, and the producer of the artist's recording project. It's usually tough getting a song to even one of them. If it weren't, we wouldn't need publishers. Sometimes the members of the artist's touring band can get a song heard, depending on how close the artist is with the band. Merchandise managers (the T-shirt people), bus drivers, live sound engineers, or the artist's personal assistant or instrument technician might get your song heard on a good day. Roadies probably don't have a great chance. Gardeners, dentists, and others probably aren't a good bet, as their professional relationship to these people is not a musical one. It's considered bad manners to try to pitch to the spouses or family members of the artist, producer, or A&R rep unless invited to. It's okay, however, to give anyone a free CD for his or her own enjoyment.

ALERT!

Don't expect someone connected to pitch for you just because you gave him or her a CD to play for a VIP. If someone's nice enough to take a CD, leave it at that. If he or she is impressed enough to play it for the person you're trying to impress, you'll hear about it.

Big Fish, Little Fish

You might run into problems trying to get the creative director of a big New York publishing company to listen to your songs. It's probably going to be easier to get someone at Bob's Bait Shop and Publishing in East Nostril, Arkansas to check out your stuff and give you some feedback. Heck, you might even get 'ole Bob himself to listen if the fish aren't biting. The problem is that Bob probably can't do much for you, unless you'd be willing to accept night crawlers as pay.

You're really wasting time trying to get to either of these guys. One is unreachable (for now) and the other can't help your career. You need an attainable goal that moves you forward. Shoot for small- to medium-sized publishers in music hubs. These people won't be as easy to get to as 'ole Bob, but with a little persistence, you can get them to listen to your songs and they can do something for you.

Pitching Your Songs

Whether it's to a recording artist, a publisher, or a bus driver, at some point you'll have to pitch your songs to someone. Most songwriters focus on pitching to publishers in hopes of getting a staff deal that they think will be the end of their pitching days. A staff deal can be a wonderful thing, but many hit songwriters still participate in pitching their own songs. Who wouldn't buy a car from Henry Ford?

How to Get a Publisher to Listen

Have you ever called, e-mailed, or written to a publisher and asked for an appointment or permission to send a CD? Most publishers, caught on the right day and not pressured too much, will make an appointment to listen to a couple of your songs. Get a copy of *Songwriter's Market* (it's a big book that lists a lot of publishers and their submission policies) and start making connections. Most of the listings show some credits for publishers who actually have cuts.

FACT

When you start pitching, you'll need a separate toolbox. Set aside a place for cataloging and storing demos and make folders for contacts, appointments, and lyrics, and for tracking activity with each publisher (when you met, what you played, and the response). Keep a few demo packs in your briefcase and car for chance meetings.

Have you ever gone to Nashville, New York, or LA and looked in the phone book under music publishers? Try it sometime. Start making calls. Tell the person who answers the phone that you're a songwriter and you'd like to either send some material or come in and play a few songs for someone. You might only get one positive response for every ten calls, but it only takes one "Yes." If you want a publisher to listen to your CD, you have to be patient. Don't come across as desperate; be self-assured without being cocky.

Persistence is the key. If someone says, "No," call back in six months. If someone says, "Yes," follow up ASAP. After someone listens, ask if you can submit more material in the future. If you are fortunate enough to get a "Yes," then send more songs and/or schedule another meeting every one to three months, depending on the publisher's schedule. At this point, you arc finally in the game. You may allow yourself a little victory dance, replete with hoots and hollers, as soon as you are in a private place.

What to Present

When someone says he or she will listen, don't inundate your new contact with every song in your catalog. Present your best three or four songs, on CD, with lyric sheets. Most publishers prefer lyric sheets in all capital letters, in Times New Roman font and twelve-point type or larger, with black lettering on white paper. Try to keep each song to one sheet and don't put two songs on the same sheet.

Never explain your songs unless asked; if you have to explain a song, it's not written clearly enough. Be polite, be on time, and don't be alarmed if the person you meet isn't—publishers are busy people. This person is doing you a huge favor by listening. Last-minute things pop up all the time in the music business. Don't be surprised if your meeting gets pre-empted in favor of a last-minute pitch to an artist or producer. Reschedule and move on to the next goal.

Even if you play live, have a CD ready. Remember, your hope is that this publisher will want to keep some of your songs to play for someone else. This may require repeated listening, and he or she may also wish to play your songs for other people in the company before making any decisions. Don't ask for a deal or a contract. If a publisher wants to offer you one, he or she will not hesitate to say so. Ask for feedback.

Make sure to double-check the spelling on all your lyric sheets. While poetic license may allow a songwriter to use incorrect grammar to make a point or illustrate a scene, poor spelling tells a publisher that you're either lazy, not terribly bright, or both. If you have any doubts on a word, look it up.

Pitching by Mail

If there's just no way that you can get to a music hub to pitch in person, you can try mailing your songs to publishers. This works better if you've already had at least one previous meeting in person. Call or write first and get permission to send your work, or your songs will be thrown away unheard. Ask for the name and/or title of the person to whose attention you should send your package.

Don't put clever slogans like "Open Carefully, contents HOT!" The publishing staff has seen them all a million times. It won't score you any points. Likewise, fancy labeling and embossed lyric pages just tell a publisher that you like to waste money and remind him or her that you're "not from around here." Don't expect to hear anything back on mail-ins. Even if a publisher likes your songs, you won't usually get a response unless there's something that he or she wishes to place under contract. Wait at least a month before a follow-up call after a mailing. When you call, ask for feedback and see if you can send three or four more songs. Repeat as necessary.

Hire a Plugger

If you can't make it to a music hub often enough, or there are people that you just can't get in to see, you may want to acquire the services of an independent plugger. This includes dropping off CDs and, if possible, making in-person pitches to A&R reps, artists, and publishers. A plugger with a good track record can be worth some money. An unproven plugger is in the same boat as you and should work for less than an established plugger.

How do publishers and pluggers know who's looking for songs?
Aside from personal contacts, publishers and pluggers use specialized newsletters called "pitch sheets," which list who's looking, what they're looking for, when they need it, and who's accepting submissions. Subscriptions to some of these publications may cost over a thousand dollars a year.

Before hiring a plugger, ask for references and find out if he or she has pitched anything that actually got cut. Some pluggers, if they really believe in your songs, may offer to work for a percentage of your publishing rather than a flat fee. This is fine, as long as the agreement states that he or she only gets that percentage on songs that he or she gets recorded, commercially released, and distributed by a major label. Again, have the contract reviewed by an entertainment lawyer, or you may be sorry.

Forwarding Services

Recently, a number of companies have sprung up that offer forwarding services to songwriters. Taxi and Tonos are the two big players in this industry and, though the jury is still out on how well forwarding services work, they seem promising.

The way most of these services function is by charging you for each song they evaluate, then passing along the best ones to publishers and producers. You may submit a thousand songs and never get one forwarded or you may get half of your submissions sent on. If these companies grow and build reputations in the music business, they may become a legitimate alternative to publishers.

The upside to using a forwarding service is that they don't usually want your publishing rights. In addition, some of these companies offer feedback and/or critique services that may be of help to up-and-coming songwriters. The downside is that you will be charged for every song that you send, regardless of whether or not it gets forwarded. Also, forwarding services don't pay a draw, give you an office, fix you up with co-writers, or help with demo costs as a publisher would.

Is a forwarding service right for you? Maybe, but think it over carefully; most of these services charge an annual membership fee in addition to per-song charges.

Web Presence

These days, one of the best tools a songwriter can have at his or her disposal is a professionally built Web site. It can be the virtual equivalent of an office, retail store, message center, fanzine, demo catalog, and resume all in one.

Setting up a Web Site

A number of companies offer free Web space where you can build your own site with the easy set-up instructions provided. This is a great way to start. When you get tired of having a Web address that's longer than some of your lyrics, graphics that look like they belong on someone's refrigerator door, and barely enough space for a picture, much less a song file, you might consider spending some money on space and hiring a Web site developer.

Among the things you can put up on your Web site are:

- Downloads and/or audio streams so that people can listen to your songs.
- Lyrics from your songs.
- Accomplishments, reviews, and bio information.
- A credit card server or a link to an online store for selling CDs, t-shirts, and other merchandise.
- A calendar of gigs where you'll be playing your songs.
- A guestbook where people can leave messages or get on your mailing list.
- A picture, so people have a better idea of who they're dealing with.
- Pictures of your dog, dressed like Kiss's Gene Simmons last Halloween.

It's important to get a domain name with your name in it. It helps make you easier to find in a Web search and reinforces your name to anyone who sees it. If you can't get yourname.com, you might try .net, .biz, or yournamemusic with one of those three suffixes. Be creative—it's your job!

MP3 and Realaudio

CDs use a file type called a "wave" file. In a computer, you may recognize these files by the suffix *wav* after the dot (mysong.wav, freebird.wav). Wave files are high-quality audio but, at the present, are too big to be of much use on the Internet.

Currently, the two major formats used for song files on the Internet are MP3 and RealAudio. Most CD-burning programs have an option for turning a CD track into an MP3 file. Read instructions carefully; there are different kinds of MP3 files and you want to make sure you get the right one for the application you have in mind. Realaudio tracks can be "ripped" from CDs with the Realproducer program.

Some people have begun using Internet song files to pitch songs. Several online publishing houses have sprung up in the last few years. Most of them were immediately bought up by large publishers and closed. The future may see a lot of pitching done via Internet. A DSL, cable, or Broadband connection allows good-quality audio to be downloaded quickly or streamed. As soon as most publishers have these faster connections, look for Internet pitching activity to skyrocket.

Single Songs and Spec Pitches

Many smaller publishers will either offer you a single-song contract or, if they know and trust you, a spec pitch. On a single-song contract, you temporarily assign a publisher the publishing and administration rights to your song. In exchange, the publisher will attempt to get your song recorded by a major label.

If the publisher accomplishes this within the period specified in the contract, that publisher gains control of copyright and publisher's royalties for your song for at least thirty-five years. The publisher may pay for a demo, give you money, advance you a small amount to be recouped later, or none of the above.

On a spec pitch, someone pitches your song with the understanding that, if he or she gets it cut, you'll sign over all or part of the publishing as soon as you receive confirmation of the song's status from the record company. Spec pitches are fairly common in Nashville, but less so in other places. Don't expect an advance, help with a demo, or anything other than a pitch from a spec deal. With a spec pitch, be even more scrupulous than if you were under contract: If you ever burn someone on a spec deal, you may never work again.

Beware of the Sharks!

For the most part, the music business is a pretty nice place. Publishers take half your royalties and give you demos, a draw, and a plugger. Record companies take your songs and give you a few pennies per unit sold. Everybody takes and gives, and everybody is happy. However, some people want to take all your money and give you nothing of any value in return. These people are called "sharks."

Sharks aren't always easy to recognize. They may have impressive credits, own big studios, and drive expensive cars. What you don't know is that these people may have either exaggerated their accomplishments or fallen out of the loop, and that they use their credentials and studios to separate gullible songwriters from their life savings, which is how they can afford those fancy cars.

When Should I Pay Someone?

When should you pay a publisher for a demo? How about never? It's part of the publisher's job to provide front money for demos. For a staff writer, half of this amount is usually recoupable from mechanicals collected by the publisher from the label, but it's never paid directly by the songwriter to the publisher. It's a conflict of interest for a publisher to sell demos or studio time to a songwriter with whom they are doing business as a publisher. Anyone who tries to do this is a shark and not worth your time.

ALERT!

There is one circumstance under which you might receive a legitimate bill from a publisher for a demo. If you, as an unsigned songwriter, co-write a song with a staff writer and that writer's publisher pays a studio for a demo on your song, you owe that publisher your half of demo expenses for that song.

Other Shark Species

There are many types of sharks. Most companies that advertise in magazines looking for lyrics or poetry are sharks who will get around to asking for money soon enough. Companies that offer to set your lyrics or poetry to music, for a price, are mostly sharks. Think of it this way; someone who wants to set your lyrics to music will, if he or she truly believes in your talent, want a co-write and 50 percent ownership of the song instead of money. Many of these places use the same music beds and melodies on hundreds of lyrics. Publishers usually spot these unoriginal productions in the first few seconds. Your song will then enjoy a brief career as a would-be Frisbee on its way to the trashcan.

Any company that offers to put you on a compilation disc to go to publishers or record companies, for a price, is probably a shark. Are you starting to see a pattern? The only people who should ever ask for money to do something with your song are the studio people and musicians (for making demos) and independent pluggers (for making copies and pitching on your behalf).

A Word about Contests

Songwriting contests are a fun way to get your feet wet and maybe even get some recognition. Some contests have celebrity judges and offer big prizes and studio time to the winners. What a contest probably won't give you is what you really want; a song on the radio, a big cut, a staff deal, or a contact in the biz.

Most of the time, the odds of winning a big contest are worse than the odds of getting a staff deal. While some legitimate contests really do have big prizes and celebrity judges, most are moneymaking ventures first and foremost. If a contest is free to enter, or has a small entry fee and prizes you could actually benefit from, go ahead and have fun. Otherwise, spend your money on demos.

Some contests, especially progressive contests, can be huge rip-offs that end up costing the winners thousands of dollars. In a progressive contest scam, local competitors pay a small entry fee. The winners (there are usually several) usually receive a prize certificate, some local press, and/or a radio appearance. These winners then pay larger fees to compete in state and regional competitions before moving on to the finals, for which the entry fee may be over a thousand dollars. The finals are usually held in a music hub. Winners are responsible for their own transportation, lodging, and meals. Over a hundred winners may compete for a grand prize (usually a value-inflated demo package disguised as a recording deal). Nonwinners are usually invited back for the next round of finals. The contest organizers have generated several hundred thousand dollars in revenue with very little financial outlay, and it's all perfectly legal.

FACT

Legitimate contests can be a good move for the aspiring recording artist, especially if they involve televised finals that could give you exposure. The band Sawyer Brown and singer Troy Gentry of Montgomery Gentry both followed big contest wins with bigger successes.

There is such a thing as a legitimate progressive contest. In one of these, there is either no entry fee or a small, one-time charge. A legitimate progressive contest will usually have a well-known sponsor and will pay your travel expenses on anything past the regional level. Some bands and artists have been discovered in these contests. Caution: Read all the fine print before entering any contest. You may be giving away your publishing rights when you sign the entry form.

Chapter 17

Legal Basics

This chapter could easily be called "whatever you do, ask a lawyer first or you'll be sorry," but that's kind of a long title. While this chapter has some examples of how things might work, much of the information has been simplified to make it understandable. It is not meant to show you how to conduct your legal affairs—you will need your own lawyer for that kind of information.

Copyright Laws

Other than the ability to write a great song, a copyright is a songwriter's most valuable asset. A copyright is a set of exclusive rights granted to the creator of a work for a certain amount of time. Copyrights are a way to encourage people to create literary and artistic works; by giving creators exclusive rights to copy, distribute, and sell their works, it makes creating profitable. If not for copyrights, any bum with a computer could copy your song, put it on the Internet, and even sell copies without giving you a penny. A copyright gives you ownership of the song and legal protection from copyright infringements.

> **What kind of lawyer do I need?**
> Any lawyer is probably better than no lawyer, but what you really need is an entertainment attorney—a specialized kind of lawyer who knows the terms and loopholes used in music business contracts. It's a good bet that the publisher has an entertainment attorney who knows every trick in the book. Fight fire with fire.

Only You!

"Exclusive" means that only you, the songwriter, or someone to whom you assign your copyrights, has control over your work. Basically, the exclusive rights you have under copyright law cover the following:

- The right to make copies—either printed, audio, or visual—of the copyrighted work
- The right to distribute these copies
- The right to perform the work
- The right to display the work
- The right to make new works based on the original work

Furthermore, these broad rights translate into hundreds of more specific rights. Technically, all you have to do to get these rights is put your song in fixed form, like on paper or a recording. From that moment on, you have a copyright on your song. Registering that copyright with the Library of Congress is something you must do in order to protect your rights and cash in an infringement. All you have to do to register your copyright is fill out a form and send it in, along with a copy of your song and a fee to cover paperwork and storage in the archives.

What Copyright Doesn't Cover

You can't copyright the ideas or topics you write about, even if you're the first person to think of them. If you figure out a totally new way to look at love, nothing prevents every other songwriter in the world from writing a song using the exact same viewpoint. The same is mostly true for hooks and titles—they're up for grabs.

ALERT!

Order and duration of notes are part of a copyright, but particular notes are not, so much as the mathematical relationships between them (thirds, fifths, etc.) is. This means that changing the key, and thus all the notes in a melody, does not make it a different song.

However, if you in any way give the impression that your song is related or the same as someone else's, you could be in legal trouble. Common phrases and clichés can't be copyrighted, neither can chords or chord patterns. Also, the notes and words you use aren't new, so you can't copyright them.

Giving up Copyright

The only problem with all these exclusive rights is that it's hard to make money without getting rid of most of them first. What? That doesn't make sense? Okay, let's put it this way: Most of these rights are assigned to a publisher when you sign a contract. The publisher will then, hopefully, get your song recorded, collect money for use of the copyright, and give you a share of the profits. The rights you keep after assigning the copyright to a publisher are whatever rights are spelled out in your contract and the right to money from performance royalties.

FACT

European copyright law includes the concept of moral rights, which are retained even when you transfer copyright ownership. These rights protect your song from being purposefully butchered in the studio or used in a porn film without your consent. In the United States you don't have these rights, unless they're specified in your contract.

Copyright Term

Copyright term is the period for which you have exclusive rights. The term of protection offered to copyright holders has come a long way. The 1710 Edict of Anne provided a twenty-one-year term of exclusive rights. The first U.S. Copyright act, passed in 1790, provided only fourteen years of protection, but was renewable for another fourteen.

The term offered to member nations of the Berne Convention went up to the life of the author plus fifty years in 1908. The United States increased it to a total of fifty-six years in 1909 and signed the Berne Convention in 1988. The "Sonny Bono" Bill added another twenty years to the Berne convention's "life plus fifty" provision. If you assign your copyright to a publisher and don't get a reversion in the contract, you may apply for one after thirty-five years and possibly get it back.

Copyright and Co-Writing

With respect to co-writes, in a song with a lyric and a melody each is considered to be worth 50 percent of the copyright. Furthermore, even if one writer composes the entire lyric, and the other the entire melody, each owns 50 percent of the melody and 50 percent of the lyric. So if you write a melody and your co-writer writes a lyric and you put the two together and call it a song, your co-writer now owns half of your melody and you own half the lyric. Neither of you can reuse that melody or lyric without your co-writer's permission.

Unless otherwise agreed, all co-writers on a song are assumed to have an equal share. The key words here are "unless otherwise agreed." Some writers actually go through a song lyric with a pen, marking which lines came from whom, and then figure up a percentage ownership based on the number of lines each writer contributes. In the music business, the term for this kind of person is "obsessive freak."

Exceptions to the Rule

There are exceptions to the exclusivity of a copyright. The laws allow for use of your work in research, criticism (like reviews), commentary, and news reports, as well as by some nonprofit, charitable, educational, religious, and governmental institutions—as long as it doesn't interfere with your exclusive distribution rights, sales, or the value of the copyright.

For instance, a reviewer can quote a couple of lines from your song without violating your rights, but if that reviewer prints a whole verse and chorus, he might be stepping over the line. If he prints your whole song, it would probably be interfering with your ability to control the distribution of copies. A teacher could play your song as a teaching aid or make a copy of the lyrics to your song for use in her class without paying a royalty. If, however, the teacher made copies for everybody in the class to keep, that might be an infringement.

Voluntary and Compulsory License

When it comes to recording, the copyright holder can only control who makes the first commercial recording of a song. The first time your song is cut, the record company must obtain a voluntary license from your publisher. The publisher doesn't have to grant this license, which can be a good bargaining chip. Once a song is licensed the first time, anyone can make an original recording and make copies for sale by applying for a compulsory license and paying the statutory mechanical royalty rate. This only applies to making records for sale to the public for their personal use: No one can use your song in a commercial or for TV, movies, or background music without permission of the copyright holder. Anyone who legally buys a copy of your song has the right to make a copy for personal use, but not to publicly display (like on a Web site), distribute, or sell copies.

Although songs have been protected by copyright for a long time, until 1972 there was no U.S. law preventing the unauthorized copying and sale of records. Bootleggers could apply for a compulsory license, pay statutory rate to the publishers, and make and sell copies without paying the artist or record company a dime in royalties.

Copyright Infringement

Infringement is what occurs when one party (meaning a person, group, or company) violates another party's copyright. Examples of infringement could be illegally copying or distributing someone else's copyrighted work or claiming ownership of a work that's substantially similar to someone else's copyrighted work. Depending on the type and severity of the infringement, the skills of the lawyers involved, and the disposition of the judge on a given day, a "guilty" verdict in an infringement case could have results ranging from a "cease and desist" order prohibiting further infringement to fines and damages totaling millions of dollars.

Concern over copyright infringement is also a factor on the inside of the music business: Some of the newest genres like electronica and rap rely largely on taking samples and creating loops directly from the work of other songwriters and musicians. This raises the questions of who should receive credit and royalties for a given work and how they should be divided.

Fighting Back

What can you protect against infringement? The lyric and the melody are the parts protected by your copyright. What does that mean? The closest thing to a tangible explanation is that the lyric is a work resulting from the order in which you place the words and the melody is a work resulting from the order and duration of notes. Thus, if a work duplicates a substantial portion of the patterns of order and/or duration of notes or words in your work, it might be infringing on your copyright.

Might? Well, you may also have to prove that the authors of the other work had access to yours. If you write something, show it to no one, and put it in your attic and someone a thousand miles away who's never even met you writes a similar work, you might have a hard time getting any money out of a lawsuit. If it was not the person's intent to violate your rights, it's considered a "no harm, no foul" situation. If you have a good lawyer and a copyright registration predating the other person's work, you might get a portion of his or her copyright and/or a "cease and desist" order.

This reinforces once again the importance of copyright registration and of publicly performing your work. If you register your copyright, you establish with certainty a date after which any similar works may be suspect. If you perform publicly, especially on radio or television or in a touring act, you increase the odds of proving that access to your work was readily available and that infringement was intentional, which is a criminal offense, carries tougher fines and punishments, and the possibility of a higher damage award to the copyright holder.

What is a copyright notice?
A copyright notice consists of the copyright symbol, ©, the name of the owner, and date of the copyright. This gives fair warning to potential violators that a work is copyrighted. Using the words "all rights reserved" is good, too. Unless you use a notice, your rights aren't completely protected.

Prepare to Be Boarded

Perhaps the biggest concern of songwriters these days is the issue of Internet song piracy. By some estimates, ten of billions of copyright violations are occurring every year. Music pirates are illegally downloading songs from the Internet and making copies of downloads without paying the songwriters, publishers, recording artists, or record companies.

This has caused a slump in the music business. However, if piracy problems can be addressed, songwriting revenues could hit an all-time high. Downloadable music reduces material, packaging, transportation, and warehousing costs to zero, so records can be sold for far less—people can buy more records and we can all make more money.

International Copyright Law

Everything you've learned so far applies to U.S. copyright law. Things may be different in other places. Most of the European nations and many other countries around the world have agreed to follow the basic copyright laws of the Berne Convention. There are also other treaties and conventions covering copyright and intellectual property rights that some countries follow, but a number of things in each are left to the discretion of member countries.

Many countries that are not part of the Berne Convention have radically different copyright laws. Some have no laws protecting you and your songs. Every country is different. You could probably study for the rest of your life and not know half of the copyright laws in the different countries of the world.

It's very important to know that you'll need a different publisher, called "a sub-publisher" or "sub-pub," in each country where your copyright is recognized and your song is making money. Sub-pubs represent your copyright interests in their respective countries and collect your nonperformance-based royalties for a percentage of the song's earnings in that country. The idea here is that the sub-pubs know the laws in their country and, since sub-pubs work on a percentage, will do their absolute best to collect all monies due and help your song achieve its maximum earnings potential.

Single-Song Contracts

Before you get a staff deal, you'll probably get a few offers for single-song contracts. This is like a one-night-stand when you're looking for a relationship but, when you're lonely, the attention is nice. Just be careful and use a lawyer. If you play your cards right, you might even meet a nice publisher and settle down.

FACT

Almost all publishing contracts contain the words "standard contract." It's something publishers or their lawyers put on the contract to make it appear standard, like it's the one everybody signs. There's no such thing as a standard contract. Question anyone who suggests otherwise.

When it comes to single-song contracts, you need to pay attention to the agreement on reversion—when you get the rights to your song back. Reversion is always a good thing. When you sign your contract, there should always be a reversion clause saying that if the publisher doesn't get your song "on hold" or cut within a certain amount of time (usually six months to a year), you get it back. According to some agreements, you may have to pay back any advances and half of any demo expenses to get reversion.

The Fine Print

Fine print on a single-song agreement might stipulate a small time window during which the songwriter must request reversion in writing in order to receive it. Pay close attention to this if you want your song back. Also look for the provision that the publisher is to be reimbursed for "reasonable expenses" pursuant to pitching or marketing the song, either if the song gets cut or before reversion occurs. Compensation to the publisher for these costs should come from the publisher's share of the royalties. If there are no royalties, the publisher hasn't done his or her job and isn't entitled to a dime in expenses. Other dirty tricks include the following:

- Paying mechanicals on the wholesale price, but collecting a percentage of retail.
- Paying you in cents per unit, so you don't see what percentage the publisher is making.
- Paying 50 percent of the *net* instead of the *gross*, which lets the

publisher deduct the rent, utilities, staff pay, his or her salary, and lunch before paying you.

- Paying 50 percent of the gross, but only on a limited list of income sources. (Getting paid on the gross is good, but make sure the percentage is based on "all receipts.")
- Taking larger chunks of smaller sources of income like foreign royalties or film and video rights.
- Reserving the right to issue licenses at a reduced rate. (This would allow your publisher to offer its affiliated record company your songs for next to nothing.)
- Making deals with owned or affiliated sub-publishers in which income is not computed "at source."

ALERT!

All's fair in love and publishing. You may sometimes be faced with a choice between a deal that doesn't seem equitable and no deal at all. This is a toughie. In the music business, the only way to ensure fair treatment is by having enough success to demand it and an attorney to enforce it.

These are some of the most common tricks. There are hundreds more. Many of these are found in staff deals as well. Before you sign a contract, it's not a bad idea to have it looked over by a lawyer.

Staff-Writer Contracts

Staff-writer contracts, also known as "staff deals" or "term songwriter agreements," are what most songwriters dream of—until they get one. When you finally get offered a staff deal, you will probably have been living on mac and cheese for a couple of years. You will be tempted to sign the first contract that offers you the possibility of groceries in return for control of your life's work and half your future income. If you don't have a lawyer, you will get ripped off.

There are a million things you can ask for. Some of them, you might get. Of course, there are a thousand songwriters standing in line behind you, most of whom will gladly sign a contract without even reading it. Almost any deal is better than no deal. Negotiate the best deal you can and get on with writing great songs.

Most staff deals involve an advance of some kind. Instead of blowing it all on pizza and beer, see if you can get an entertainment attorney to help negotiate your contract in return for payment from your advance. Think of it as an investment in your future. The money you save might be your own.

Draw, Advances, and Recoupment

Most publishers offer their staff writers a draw, which is a small advance on future royalties. This is not a salary. It's more like a loan that you pay back with your royalties. If you sign an exclusive agreement granting a publisher the rights to all your work created within a given period, you should receive a draw to live on while you write full time. (Make sure it's in the contract, or you might not get it.) How much draw you get is something you have to work out between you and the publisher. Remember, a draw isn't free money; it's an advance against future royalties. Most staff deals also provide advances for making demos, but you should only be liable for half the demo budget, not all of it.

Your contract will probably have a clause giving the publisher control of everything you've already written, with the exception of stuff you've already signed away. This is pretty standard, but the publisher might fail to mention that it's also standard to pay for these songs. How much will vary, depending on how many songs you have and how much the publisher wants them.

All these advances get paid back. This is called "recoupment," and it comes from your share of the royalties that your publisher collects (mechanicals, synch rights, etc.) and nowhere else. If you're a gazillion dollars unrecouped, the publisher can't take your car or garnish the wages from your paper route. All he or she can do is get you a cut and collect the money that way. Still, being recouped is good. It means your publisher is happy, because your songs are making money and you don't owe anything. It also means that you get paid royalties from your publisher instead of paying back advances, so everybody's happy.

More Fine Print

You'll have a minimum number of approved songs, usually between ten and fifteen, which you must write in each year of the contract. "Approved" means that your publisher thinks they're great. This doesn't mean that you can bring in fifteen co-writes. Your minimum is in *whole* songs—that's thirty two-way co-writes or forty-five three-way co-writes. For this reason, many writers are reluctant to co-write a song with more than one person.

Your initial term will probably be for one to three years, with several renewable one-year options at the publisher's discretion. This means that if you start getting hits, they can automatically renew your contract on the same terms. Ouch! On the other hand, if a publisher has been good to you, worked hard to get you cuts, and helped you to grow as a writer, a few years paying that back isn't so bad.

Smaller and newer publishers will often do a little "catalog building." They may keep a promising writer under contract for a while without making demos or pitching anything, then terminate the writer's contract and wait for another publisher to make the investment in demos and pluggers. When the writer starts getting cuts, the previous publisher can then sell the copyrights on all that writer's songs in his or her catalog for a huge profit. If your contract doesn't guarantee demos and pitching, the publisher doesn't have to provide them for you, so you may be in danger of working with a catalog-building publisher.

Cross-Collateralization

This one is so nasty, it gets its own section. Cross-collateralization is a state where recoupment owed for one thing (like draw) can be taken from another (like your artist's royalty on your own project). Some people even try to cross-collateralize between different members of a writing team. This is bad and wrong. Make sure that your draw isn't recoupable from anything but the money your publisher collects for you as a songwriter. If the publisher wants to be able to recoup from any other source, like performance royalties or songs you may write after the term of your contract, refuse and tell everybody you know what happened.

Co-Pub

Co-publishing, or co-pub, is a wonderful thing that happens after you get some hits. It means that you not only get whatever money you have coming as a writer, but also a portion of the publishing income. This portion is usually tallied after administration and overhead costs have been taken out. It's crucial to have your attorney oversee the wording of your co-pub deal. Otherwise, you'll end up with your publisher's yacht listed as an overhead cost and you'll get next to nothing.

Before You Sign Anything

One last word of advice: Before you sign any contract, get to know something about the people you're doing business with. Find out what the contract says, and what it means. A little detective work might save you a lot of money and years of misery, not to mention the anguish of watching your songs die on the vine.

Checking References

Most reputable companies will be happy to tell you about what they've accomplished and whom they do business with. Follow up on these references and see if they pan out. If someone tells you he or she wrote or published a big hit, find out the title and artist, go to a record store, and see if it's true. Call the local Better Business Bureau and see if any complaints have been filed against the company and/or if they are considered in good standing.

Always take some time to think things over before signing a contract; you can't change your mind once you sign. Take it home. Have your lawyer look it over, along with any staff writers you know. If anyone ever pressures you to sign on the spot, something is probably wrong and you should consider walking out.

If you're living in a music hub, it's usually pretty easy to ask around and find out what kind of person you're dealing with. Talk to some other publishers and see what they have to say. Track down writers who've dealt with the company and find out if they were happy with the way things turned out. The music communities in most hub cities are fairly tight-knit. If a publisher has a reputation, good or bad, chances are that you know somebody who can attest to it. Do Web searches on the names of the publisher, employees, and the company.

Finding an Entertainment Attorney

You can find entertainment attorneys in most music hubs. Look in the Yellow Pages. Ask friends in the music business for a recommendation. Finding an attorney who lives in the hub where you do business is a good idea; he or she will be likely to know the people you do business with and maybe even make some connections for you.

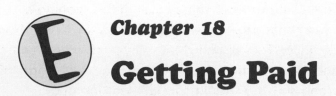

Chapter 18

Getting Paid

This is the fun part, right? Yes, if there's anything left when the math is done. A hit song generates several different income streams, and while it's nice that there are so many ways to get paid, there's a different payment formula for each one and usually several ways to get ripped off. To protect yourself, you may even consider finding a good accountant.

Performing Rights Organizations

The law says that no one can perform a copyrighted work in public unless they get permission from the copyright owner. Getting permission generally involves money. This law is the best thing to happen to songwriters since the introduction of copyright laws. Getting written permission for each individual song could be tough for a radio station that plays hundreds of songs a year and time-consuming for writers and publishers, so some very special companies came into being to handle this part of the business.

Performing rights organizations, or PROs, grant "blanket" licenses to radio and TV stations, networks, venues, and other music users that allow them to use all the music owned by the songwriters and publishers represented by that PRO. In return a music user pays the PRO, and most of that money gets distributed to the songwriters and publishers. PROs represent hundreds of thousands of writers and publishers in the United States alone and frequently use this clout to lobby for songwriter's rights.

FACT

Before PROs, most songwriters made little money. A songwriter's income came primarily from the sale of sheet music. Performance rights, though legally protected, were mostly paid on the honor system. This meant that, aside from the major vaudeville venues and large concerts, songwriters and publishers rarely saw a penny in performance royalties on their works.

ASCAP

Founded in 1914, ASCAP (American Society of Composers, Authors and Publishers) was the first performing rights organization in the United States and is the only one owned and run by the songwriters and publishers who are its members. ASCAP is a nonprofit association; its board of directors is elected by the membership.

ASCAP is very active in representing songwriters before the U.S. Congress and has, for nearly a century, initiated reforms in copyright law that benefit and protect songwriters. ASCAP pays performance royalties on songs solely based on the type and estimated number of performances they receive. It also sponsors seminars, showcases, grants, and award programs for promising writers. To join ASCAP, you must be a songwriter, publisher, or a songwriter's heir.

BMI

BMI stands for Broadcast Music Incorporated. Like ASCAP, BMI is a nonprofit company. Unlike ASCAP, you don't have a vote or a say in running it. BMI was started by radio broadcasters who were unsatisfied with ASCAP. Competition between the two organizations keeps both PROs working fairly hard to keep members happy and loyal. Long ago, ASCAP was pretty snooty about allowing country and R&B writers into the organization. BMI was willing to profit from anyone, regardless of genre, and decreed an open door policy. It didn't take ASCAP long to see the costly error of its ways, but many older writers feel an allegiance to BMI because it welcomed them when no one else did. BMI pays based on estimated performances but gives bonuses to songs that get a lot of play, meaning that there's even more money for the big hits and less for the small fry.

In order to collect money for performance royalties, you and your publisher must both be affiliated with the same PRO. For mid-sized to large publishers, this often means incorporating two or three different companies, one for each PRO, so that they can work with any songwriter regardless of his or her PRO affiliation.

SESAC

SESAC (Society of European Stage Authors and Composers) is a for-profit company. This gives them the ability to woo you if they really want you by doing things that wouldn't be kosher for a nonprofit. SESAC generally pays faster than U.S. PROs, but may pay less overall. SESAC is small, but it looks like they'll be around for a while.

Around the World

Almost every country in the world has at least one performing rights organization. If you live outside the United States, you'll need to join a

PRO in your own country. Many PROs, like Performing Right Society (PRS) in England and the Society of Composers, Authors, and Music Publishers of Canada (SOCAN), are affiliated with ASCAP or other U.S. PROs to make international royalty collections easier.

Choosing a PRO

There is no "best" when it comes to PROs. They all have their own advantages and ways of doing things, and they all pay about the same. Find out which one is right for you. Ask for information packets from all three. Visit a nearby branch office and try to get a vibe. Call ahead for an appointment with a writer rep who will explain things. Writer reps are wonderful people who spend their time helping songwriters.

You won't get to negotiate anything about your PRO contract. You will once again be presented with a standard agreement. Read it over and sign it. Most PRO contracts are indefinite or automatically renew every so often, so make sure you know how to get out of your contract. With some PROs, this isn't easy.

Registering Your Work

You also need to register each song with your PRO. If you check the database at your PRO's Web site, you'll find that for most titles, anywhere from one to several hundred songs exist. Your PRO is too busy collecting money for you to keep track of what you've written lately. To get paid for a song that is getting played, you must let them know that it exists.

You may hear people talk about "a poor man's copyright," a letter that you mail to yourself with a copy of your song inside that then gets postmarked and left unopened. This has never been tested in court and probably doesn't offer you very much protection. Getting a real copyright registration is your best bet.

Notifying your PRO of a new song is easy—all you need to do is register the song by using a simple form. Some PROs now have online registration; check your PRO's Web site to see if this service is available. Registering songs with a PRO doesn't usually cost anything.

Performance Royalties

Performance royalties make up a major chunk of a songwriter's income. This money is generated by broadcasts and public performances of your song. It doesn't matter who's singing your song, what label it's on, or if it's live or recorded—you should still get paid for it. Your publisher or record company can't take this money if you're unrecouped or make you sign it away in a standard contract (at least not anymore).

These rights are yours, period. If someone wants you to sign these rights away, say, "No" in a loud voice and run for safety. You might feel scared, but go ahead and tell everybody what happened. Trying to take a writer's performance rights is immoral and unethical, and most people won't do business with someone who engages in this practice. Even if you assign your performance monies to someone else (which is stupid), your PRO will probably refuse to pay anyone but you, unless your publisher gives you an advance specifically on performance royalties or you temporarily assign performance rights to a bank to secure a loan.

Radio Time

Songwriters receive performance royalties when their songs are played on the radio. PROs have slightly different ways of figuring out which radio stations are playing which songs. To keep collection costs down, most PROs find out what some stations are playing during a given period of time. The PRO then counts how many times the monitored stations played your song, then estimates how many total plays you probably received and pays you based on that estimate. ASCAP does this by tuning in to lots of randomly chosen radio stations for a few hours at a time. The station can be anywhere in the country and it can be any time of day. Stations are not given notice if or when they will be monitored. BMI asks each station to fill out logs for certain weeks each year stating what songs the station played during that time.

TV and Movies

TV is big bucks for songwriters these days. The nice thing about TV performance royalties is that all commercially run stations or networks have to keep logs of all music used in their programming. That means you don't get "missed" as you might on radio.

Movies, too, are simple to track. Cinematic performance royalties in the United States can be easily calculated if you multiply the number of screens showing a movie by absolutely nothing. That's right. Due to some clever legal machinations, the movie industry avoids paying performance monies to songwriters and publishers. That's why you and your publisher should punish them as much as possible when they ask for a synch license. If the movie is screened in Europe, a lovely place where songwriters make performance royalties from movies, you'll get paid based on a percentage of the box office receipts. This can mean hundreds of thousands of dollars for you and your publisher.

ALERT!

Watch for the phrase "work for hire" in any contract you see. It means that you give up all rights to the work and never get paid for that work again. If someone wants you to compose a song or soundtrack as a work for hire, then you need to charge a whole lot more as you'll only get paid that one time.

Printing Money

No, you don't get to print money. What you do get, hopefully, is money when people print copies of your music and/or lyrics. Your publisher collects royalties on printed versions of your song and, if you're recouped, pays you based on your contract. Publishers usually collect 20 percent of the retail list price on single-song sheet music—that's eighty cents on a four-dollar copy. For some odd reason, publishers usually pay the songwriter only five or ten cents. For marching band, choir, dance, and instrumental instruction arrangements, the royalty usually drops to 10 percent.

In songbooks with multiple songs, called "folios," between 10 and 12.5 percent of the list price is set aside for royalties. The money is then divided by the number of songs in the book and paid out to the corresponding publishers. You should be able to get half of what the publisher takes in on multiple song folios. For the printing of your songs in books and magazines, the publisher usually collects a flat fee that may range from fifty dollars to several hundred dollars or more. How much of this you get depends on your contract. If you ever get a folio put out with your name and picture on the front, you might get as much as another 5 percent to fight over with your publisher. Since it's *your* face and name, you should come out okay on this one. Usually, nobody gets paid for the inclusion of lyrics in album liner notes. Hey, you're already getting a few pennies for every record—don't get greedy.

If you are ever involved in negotiating royalties for a song folio, make sure the license states that the royalties are divided by the number of songs with active copyrights. Otherwise, any public domain works in the book will eat up a share at no cost to the printer.

Subscription Services

You know you've really made it when you hear your song in an elevator. Even though you never envisioned kazoo and banjo taking turns on the vocal melody, it's just undeniably cool to hear your song this way. Subscription services provide music to businesses, like the hotel the elevator is in, for a monthly or annual fee. Recently, private use subscription services like satellite radio have begun to offer consumers access to commercial-free digital broadcasts.

A subscription service may use a version appearing on someone's album or a version, often instrumental, made for a specific purpose. If your song is licensed to a subscription service, you might hear it played in the grocery store or as hold music on the phone. Get ready for some good news. Muzak and other subscription music services are monitored by the PROs. You have another paycheck coming in addition to the licensing fee.

Jukeboxes and More

Jukebox owners have to pay a licensing fee to your publisher to use your song. PROs count jukeboxes, too. Are you starting to see how a big hit can add up? But wait, there's more! Your PRO also checks out what the live band is playing when the jukebox takes a break. This is true not only for bars, but also for performance halls, concerts, and festivals.

FACT

When they are first introduced, many public forms of entertainment go through a period during which no laws exist under which they have to pay performance royalties. Up until 1976, jukeboxes were legally considered "toys" under U.S. copyright law and were not liable for payment of performance royalties.

Synch Rights

Synchronization rights, or synch rights for short, pertain to use of your songs as an audio component in "timed synchronization" with a visual component, like a movie shown in a theater, a videotape or DVD movie for home use, or a TV show or commercial. A similar kind of rights, called "transcription rights," covers radio jingles. Publishers collect for synch and transcription rights. If your contract doesn't give them away and you're recouped, your publisher should pay you.

Here's how the money part works: Your publisher grants a license to the movie, TV, or radio people that either lasts forever (usually for theater use) or for a set amount of time (a few years for most TV uses). In return, the publisher gets anywhere from absolutely nothing to millions of dollars. Why? Well, a publisher might agree to take absolutely nothing for an unknown song that will get exposure from the use (which can translate to increased performance and mechanical royalties). More often, though, the publisher gets some money for the license, usually between $1,000 and $5,000 for a TV show and from $10,000 to $100,000 for a theatrical release. Think that's a lot of money? Sit down and take a deep breath. If your song is used for a nationally released commercial, the synch license could generate anywhere from $25,000 to over half a million dollars in a single year. The reason that these price ranges are so wide is that the fee depends on how well the song is known, how much of the song is used, whether it's in the background or prominently featured, how good your negotiating team is, and how bad the other party wants it.

New uses for music pop up all the time. One of the newest potential uses for your song is as a musical ring for a cellular phone or pager. The manufacturer or service provider pays a license fee for this use. Make sure that your next contract guarantees a share of this new income source.

Internet Royalties

While a few agreements with some of the larger companies using music on the Internet have been reached, ASCAP and other PROs are just now starting to negotiate licenses for many Internet music users. The exciting thing about Internet royalties is that it's possible for computers to automatically count the number of times your song is used, which means very accurate royalty distributions.

Mechanical Royalties

Mechanical royalties, or simply mechanicals, are the royalties your song earns from the sale of records. For those of you who don't know what a record is, it's an audio recording, like a CD or cassette tape (or, in ancient times, a black vinyl disc). The record company pays mechanicals for using a copyrighted song on a record. In the United States, the Harry Fox Agency takes care of collecting mechanicals, paying publishers, issuing the licenses, and auditing the record companies every now and then to make sure things are fair and square. For all this, they charge 4.5 percent.

Statutory Rates

In the United States, the federal government has mandated a minimum royalty rate per unit sold that must be paid to the songwriter's publisher by the record company. As of January 2002, mechanicals went up to a whopping eight cents per song for each copy sold. This may not seem like much and, frankly, it's not, but it's a little better than the original two-penny royalty rate that was in effect from 1909 to 1976. That's a long time to go without a raise. To make things worse, the writer only got a penny out of those two cents, with the publisher getting the other half. That's right. You split mechanicals with your publisher.

Mechanicals are different, or sometimes nonexistent, in other countries. Canadian mechanicals are a little lower and the agency that collects in Canada, the CMRRA, charges 5 percent for its services. As of 2002, most Chinese record companies don't pay a dime to anybody in the United States. They just pirate copies of records made by American companies and sell them. The huge differences in mechanicals from place to place will make you wish you had someone in each country to figure it all out.

FACT

Just because you don't know about the money doesn't mean it's not there. If you don't have a sub-pub in a given country, the royalty payments for your song go into a black box fund, which is eventually split up between publishers in that country.

Well, your wish has been granted: If your songs get played outside the United States, you or your publisher will need to contract with a sub-publisher, called a sub-pub in the biz, in each country where your song is getting exposure. Your sub-pubs collect mechanicals for their respective countries and, after deducting a percentage, pay your publisher. What percentage a sub-pub makes is up for negotiation.

Reduced Rates

Unfortunately, there's still a way to rip songwriters and recording artists off—the controlled composition clause. Even though the law requires a minimum royalty on songs, record companies make most recording artists sign a contract saying that they voluntarily agree to accept less than the legal minimum royalty for songs they write and record. Is this fair? No! Is it legal? Well, nobody seems to be stopping it.

Even worse, labels usually put a ceiling on mechanicals for a project that's far below the statutory rate. This means the artist has a choice of either talking you and your publisher into taking less than the legal minimum royalties for your songs or making up the difference out of his or her own royalties, which were already reduced in the first place. In some cases, the artist can actually end up owing royalties on his or her own record. This is one reason why many recording artists believe that record companies are basically evil. Record companies often push for further reduced rates for compilations, budget priced records, mail order clubs, and "greatest hits" packages. Some record companies will give you full statutory royalties if you sign a publishing deal with their publishing company, which is kind of like hiring a weasel to guard your chickens.

DART Money

DART is like mechanicals; it has to do with making copies. Unlike mechanicals, it's not about copies made and sold, but about copies yet to be made: It's a tax on the copying machine and the blanks used to make the copies.

Why would anyone pass such a law? Back in the old days, vinyl records and analog cassette tapes wore out over time. Home copies made from these recordings weren't as good as the originals and the problems got even worse if a copy was made from another copy. When digital recorders came around, people could suddenly make copies that sounded as good as the original. This means that as long as you keep making copies at home, you never have to buy another copy. This also means that you can make a great-sounding copy for your car, your summerhouse, or all your friends, neighbors, pen pals, and any strangers who happen by with five bucks to spend. The first two of these copying options (copies for your car or your other abode) are legal; the others are a violation of federal law.

To offset this copying boom and the loss of sales it caused, Congress passed the Audio Home Recording Act of 1992. Also known as the DART (Digital Audio Recorders and Tapes) Bill, this law imposes a tax on digital recorders and recording media for home use. The record companies get the lion's share. Recording artists come next, followed by publishers and professional songwriters, who collect from PROs. The musician's union and the union that covers backup vocalists get what's left.

> **When do I get paid?**
> Your publisher usually pays you royalties twice a year (if you're recouped). It may take a couple of years for the money to get from the record store to the distributor to the record company, to Harry Fox to the publisher, and finally to you. You get draw by the week or month. Most PROs pay quarterly.

In the Future

Songwriting income is probably about to undergo a major paradigm shift. Computers—capable of downloading music, burning copies, printing liner notes, playing music, and showing videos—may eventually replace home stereos, record stores, and TVs in one fell swoop. Hopefully, legislation will be in place to insure that songwriters can be adequately compensated for use of their songs.

Currently, some Internet companies, like MP3.com, pay artists for downloads or "listens" of their music. These services "source license," which means they get permission to use a song directly from the copyright holder instead of paying a PRO. If PROs can gain a foothold on the Internet, a download should gain the songwriter a mechanical royalty and a "listen" should get some sort of performance credit, since it's being broadcast from a Web site, which is a public place. This will be an interesting area to watch.

The Internet is opening up new markets for songwriters and increasing sales in niche markets. Many singer/songwriters find the Internet to be a place where they can sell their own recordings: Sean Mullin, Aimee Mann, and Creed all have had highly successful recording projects that were helped by Web activity and achieved without the interference of a record company. Songwriters are also using these resources to build peer groups, meet publishers, and even co-write with people across the globe.

Chapter 19

Moving to a Music Hub

If you want to be a surfer, Nebraska isn't the place to do it; you have to be where the waves are. To be a professional songwriter, you have to be where you can make some waves. One of the most important things you can do for your career is to move to a city with a strong presence in the music industry.

Planning Ahead

Don't just sell your house, rent a U-Haul, and go. There are things you need to do, know, and think about before you pack up and head out for Music Row, Tin Pan Alley, or Hollywood. Making a permanent move is a big deal. A little planning can make the transition a much smoother one.

Surveillance and Reconnaissance

The first thing you need to decide is which hub is right for you. While the top three hubs (Nashville, LA, and New York) have a little of everything, many of the smaller hubs specialize in one or two genres and don't offer much to songwriters outside those styles.

FACT

A songwriting organization's branch office in a given hub can be a great source of information. If you're a member of NSAI or SGA, have your local coordinator hook you up with members in various hubs and ask them about the town, the scene, and other information you should know before making a visit.

Scenes sometimes change overnight, but you can generally find the following genres (and maybe more) in the following places:

- **New York City:** pop, hip-hop, R&B, jazz, rock, alt, punk, house, show tunes, new age, classical, experimental, blues
- **Nashville:** country, pop, gospel, alt-country, Americana, Christian contemporary music singer/songwriter, alt, bluegrass, new folk, roots rock
- **Los Angeles:** pop, hip-hop, salsa, rock, country, alt, punk, new age, Christian contemporary music, classical
- **Seattle:** alt, grunge, nu-metal, hardcore
- **Austin:** country, alt-country, singer/songwriter, Western swing, blues, rock
- **Atlanta:** nu-soul, hip-hop, R&B
- **Detroit:** hip-hop
- **Dallas:** country, Western swing, jazz, blues
- **Miami:** dance, salsa

- **Bakersfield, CA:** country
- **New Orleans:** Dixieland, zydeco
- **Chicago:** blues
- **Memphis:** blues, R&B
- **Cleveland/Toledo:** polka (not a good way to get rich)

Make some trips to your prospective new home to get a feel for the place and the people. Make friends who can clue you in and help you find your way around. Most importantly, see if it's the right hub for the kind of writing you want to do.

Finding a Place

Before you move to a music hub, decide what living arrangement will suit your needs best. Do you need a house or an apartment? Will you buy, rent, or lease? How close do you want to be to the publishing district or your place of work? Ask your friends (the ones you made during your scouting trips) about things like the bad parts of town, traffic patterns, and where to get a good pizza after midnight.

ALERT!

It's good to fit in, but don't be afraid to let people know where you're from. In most hubs, there are people from all over. Odds are you can hook up with some homies, which gives you some instant friends with whom you already have a lot in common and helps when you get homesick.

Finding a Job

Just because you're making the transition to professional songwriting doesn't mean that the bills will magically pay themselves. You're going to need a job in your new hometown, probably for several years. If you have a marketable trade or a college degree, a headhunter service might help you find the right job. If not, the classifieds are a good place to look. If you can live cheaply, find something with flexible hours, so that you have time to schedule co-writing sessions and publisher meetings.

No More Money Gigs?

The job you won't find in a music hub is a decent-paying music gig. If you're used to making a living as a musician or singer, you're out of luck. The competition for gigs in these places is tough and some people will play for free or even pay to play just to be seen. It's not so bad in New York, but in Nashville, LA, or Austin it's tough to get a paying gig. Most of the musicians who play the strip in Nashville play for tips *only*. It's common to see players from the touring bands of big stars playing for tips on their time off just so that they can stay visible in the scene and maybe reunite with friends for a couple of days or weeks before hitting the road. While finding a paying gig in some hubs can be tough, hubs can be great places to learn by watching big stars and famous songwriters up close.

Digging In

When you make your move, don't waste time. Set up a routine as soon as possible. Don't kill yourself: The object is to set up a sustainable situation that moves you steadily toward your goals. Set up a writing routine. Renew contacts with people you've met and schedule co-writes. Get to know the writer's hangouts. Don't think you're going to take over the town in two weeks. This is going to take a while. You're here for the long haul; treat it that way.

You may have to make some adjustments. If you've never lived in a big city, be prepared for culture shock in places like New York and LA, where Kamikaze cabdrivers, gridlock, and crime might be new experiences for you. If you're heading down to Nashville or Atlanta, get ready for sweet tea, hot summers, and bugs you've only seen in movies. In any hub over a hundred miles from your home, people may talk, drive, and eat differently. The sooner you embrace the culture of your hub, the sooner you'll stop looking like a tourist.

Spend Some Time Networking

No matter which hub you land in, you need to meet people—and as many as possible. The music business is about relationships, and you can't have relationships with people you don't know. You need to make the acquaintance of writers, publishers, producers, musicians, artists, and potential artists—the people you need to know in order to do what you're here to do.

Hi, My Name Is . . .

Rule number one: You don't meet many people hanging around your apartment watching TV. As a matter of fact, put your TV in the closet, so that it's still in good shape when you have to pawn it for demo money. Don't worry, there will still be Seinfeld reruns when you have a mantel full of Grammies and all the time in the world to watch them. Get out there and meet some people! Where? Well, if you did your homework, you should have a list of hangouts and a couple of friends who can introduce you to their friends and friends of friends. Get to it!

FACT

Sports and other hobbies can be a great networking tool and a sanity saver. Find some friends who like what you like—fishing, opera, roller blading, whatever—and make a regular thing of it. If you don't golf, learn. Golf is the greatest networking sport in the biz and the sport of choice for many publishers.

Be Who You Are

Don't be someone you're not. It's easy to put on airs because you want to impress people and fit in. If you're a performer, you can probably patter with anyone for half an hour (or however long the breaks are in the clubs you played on the road). The difference here is that you really need to get to know these people and they need to know you. Publishers have B.S. detectors so sensitive that they can spot a politician twenty miles away. They'll see you coming. Your goal is to end up working with these people and you'll have to be yourself when you do that.

Find Your Tribe

Find people you like who like you. You're going to be here a while, maybe the rest of your life. Do you want to do business with people you don't like? Someone who sees your potential and likes you as a person may take you under his or her wing. Someone who sees your potential but doesn't like you probably won't. Spend your time with people you relate to and trust; they'll be more likely to want you to succeed. Add to that the fact that you'll be much happier this way, and that's a win/win situation.

Writer's Nights

In certain clubs and cafés, the writers rule. Most of these are "originals only" venues where a cover tune can get you laughed off the stage. When you move to a hub, writer's nights may be the center of your world for the first few years. A writer's night is the best place to make friends, network, test-market songs, and learn how things work. You don't get paid for this gig, unless opportunities are worth something to you.

What if I just can't sing?
If you absolutely can't carry a two-ounce tune in a five-gallon bucket, you have two options for the writer's nights: Either hire a singer or rely on your co-writers to do the singing. You might even book a round of your co-writers somewhere.

The host, usually a well-respected songwriter, decides who plays and when, and you'll probably have to audition. If you pass, the host will book you for a round in which you take turns playing songs with two to four other songwriters. Eventually, you may get to pick the other people for your round or even get to do a solo feature of several songs by yourself.

Being Seen

You might see anybody at a writer's night, from the other newbies to hit writers, publishers, A&R reps, and even the occasional celebrity. This means these people will see you as well. No matter what night of the week or what time it is, there could be someone important in the room or about to walk in at any moment, so be at your best, both onstage and off. Before you get tipsy and dance on the tables, tell a tasteless joke, or insult someone in public, think carefully; if you're lucky, these are the people you'll be dealing with for the rest of your life.

Being Heard

Each host may have slightly different rules; learn them. There is a code of etiquette for writer's nights. The faster you learn it, the more quickly you'll be accepted into the songwriting community. The following writer's night rules are adapted from the July 22, 2001 edition of the *Nashville Rant* e-zine. Nashville writer's night hosts Camille Schmidt, Barbara Cloyd, CJ Watson, Debbie Champion, Jack Scott, and Lee Rascone provided source material for the article.

How to Play Writer's Nights
Without Getting Shot or, Worse, Ignored

1. When you arrive (early!), check in with the host. Ask where to tune and store your instrument. Tune with an electronic tuner *before* your round. Be ready and set up quickly: If you waste three minutes getting ready, someone loses a song.
2. Spend money, bring friends, come early, and stay late. Hosts usually work on a percentage. Promoting the gig means you are market minded and motivated, which are as important as talent in this business. If you stay to hear other people, they are more likely to come hear *you*. (Remember the part about bringing friends?)
3. Talk as much as you like . . . as much as you like *others* to talk during *your* songs.
4. You were a star back home? Winning the Ox Booger, South Dakota Talent Show, and Potato Auction three years in a row doesn't count for much now. Get over it and start making a name *here*. Nobody will ever compliment you on the vastness of your ego.
5. A seven-minute song is not going to win you many friends. You just

burned up three-and-a-half minutes of someone else's time on an uncuttable song. Ax that intro where you soulfully strum 32 bars of "E." Most of us know "E" too. It doesn't impress us; get to the hook. Don't talk about the song for half an hour. If they can't tell what it's about by *listening to the song*, there's a problem.

6. Be nice to the host/sound person. This is like the rule that says not to annoy anyone who's going to touch your food. Be polite and quick during soundcheck. Don't ask for reverb in the monitor; it causes problems. If you don't like your voice, practice. Get a guitar with a pickup. If you can play, play. If you don't play, bring someone to play for you; backup tracks are for karaoke singers.

7. Be nice to the waitstaff. Most of the people working at a writer's club are songwriters and/or friends with some big writers. If they like you, they'll say nice things about you. If they don't, you will not only die of thirst, but you may die in obscurity as well. Also, you may soon *be* a waitress or bartender, so be nice, tip what you can, and remember that it takes as long to bring you a glass of water as it does to bring a quadruple shot of Wild Turkey with a flaming pink umbrella.

8. Skill with harmony or a lead instrument can be valuable assets, but ask before jumping in. Practice with friends and learn parts for each other's songs. Four drunks doing the same exact thing on acoustic guitars is not "ensemble" playing.

Laws in hub cities and among clubs vary. Ask before bringing minors to a gig. Sneaking a drink into a writer's club, even bottled water, could get it shut down. In Tennessee, a club can get busted for unlicensed dancing, and you really don't want to be known as the person who got the writer's club closed down.

Being Proactive

Fame is not going to come find you; you have to hunt it down and grab it by the throat. Many brilliant songwriters remain undiscovered because they think that writing great songs is enough. It's not; you have to get them recorded and heard and keep at it until somebody gets it. You are not a planet or a scientific theory; no one is going to discover you unless you get someone's attention. Don't "gherm" people, but you can ask questions and advice of anyone you know. You can also watch the incoming newbies and be the first person to befriend those with talent and potential.

Most importantly, keep trying. If someone is too busy for a meeting, ask if you can send a CD or call back at a better time. When you have a meeting, get as much feedback as possible. Get specifics; if someone says, "Your lyrics need work," ask if there are particular areas that need improvement. Find out which writers a publisher likes and study their songs. If a publisher says you can come back in a month or even a year, follow up on it and make sure you have some great new songs for the next meeting. If a host doesn't book you for a round after playing the open mike, ask for feedback and work harder to get in. Proving that you are focused and relentless will impress people as much as having talent.

FACT

Getting appointments with publishers is much like telemarketing. If you know someone with telemarketing experience, ask for pointers. Develop a "script" so you know what to say and practice until it's second nature. Compare notes with friends about what works and what doesn't.

Setting Goals

Time has a way of flying by when you get settled in somewhere. Set goals to make sure that you are making progress. Sometimes your ultimate goal (a #1 hit, a Grammy, or a house in the Bahamas) can seem unreachable. Setting short-term and intermediate goals can help you stay positive and focused and keep you on track as you journey toward the big ones.

Keep lists of your goals; as you accomplish a goal and cross it off your list, you can replace it with a new goal. Examine the ways in which some goals support others. Here's a simplified example of a probability goal chain, where every step builds on the goal results from the last level to reach toward the next:

1. If you put in the time and the effort, you'll learn more and write more.
2. If you learn and write enough, you'll probably come up with a great song.
3. If you write enough great songs and have enough publisher meetings, you'll probably get a single-song contract or a staff deal.
4. If you get enough single-song contracts or work hard enough at your staff-writing job, you'll probably get some holds.
5. If you get enough holds, you'll probably get a single.
6. If you get enough singles, you'll probably get a hit.
7. If you get enough hits, you'll probably get a #1 hit, a Grammy, or a house in the Bahamas.

See? It's easy. All you have to do is accomplish one set of goals to make the next set easier to reach. Of course, it still requires hard work and commitment, but focusing on your work allows you to go further and faster.

Goals aren't "one size fits all." Some goals may be bigger or smaller to you than they are to others. If you just started lessons, getting onstage with your guitar is a bigger deal than if you grew up playing it.

Keeping the Faith

The hardest thing to do is to keep on believing, but it's also the most important. Getting cuts is a sales job and belief is the foundation of sales. If you don't believe in the product (your songs), you're in the wrong business—find something else to do.

Sooner or later, and probably more than once, you will feel like giving up. Being prepared for this will help you get through it. Build a support group of people you believe in who also believe in you. Keep track of your progress and acknowledge even the little victories. Once a year, listen through your catalog to see how much you've learned. It can be hard to see how far you've come without looking back. Ⓔ

Chapter 20

Careers in Songwriting

"Number-one hit songwriter" isn't an entry-level position. Fortunately, it's not your only hope; Barry Manilow wrote jingles for big clients like McDonald's, Chris Isaak composed the theme for the *Craig Kilborn Show*, Sir Elton John scored big on *The Lion King* soundtrack, and Quincy Jones is a successful publisher. In a business where competition is the only constant, the more options you have, the better.

Staff Writing

Being a staff writer is a great job, as long as you're getting cuts. If you get too far unrecouped, you'll be let go, so you always have to be working toward your next cut. Some songwriters manage to keep a deal for twenty years or more, but the average is a lot lower.

Exceptions do occur. Harlan Howard had hits in four different decades, but many staff writers never get a single one. These people often end up living on the street, walking around, muttering to themselves, and hating songwriters, though some become publishers, A&R reps, or record company presidents who walk around, mutter to themselves, and hate songwriters.

If you ever start getting a lot of cuts, don't slow down until your "hot streak" is over. A change in popular styles could mean the end of the gravy train for you. A lot of writers who had #1 hits a few years back are broke today. Capitalize on success while you can.

Film Scoring and Movie Music

Writing songs and music for movies can be a good living. If you manage to do it without ever seeing the words "work for hire" in your contract, it can be a *great* living. The "work for hire" clause is the single biggest rip-off in the music business. It means that you not only give up any right to further payment, but also that you're not legally the author of the work. That's right. If you sign a "work for hire" contract, the company that employs you is officially the writer and you don't exist. This is just one of the many differences between writing for movies and writing for recording artists.

Scoring

Music written especially for a movie is called the "score." Though scores are mostly comprised of background music to accentuate the moods of different scenes, sometimes the theme song (which usually plays under the credits) is part of the score. Every now and then a score, or the theme from a score, will become a hit, as happened for John Williams when his theme for *Star Wars* hit the charts.

Theaters in the United States don't pay performance royalties, so scoring work pays fairly well up front to compensate. An established film composer working for a major studio may earn in excess of half a million dollars per film. A new writer working for an independent studio might make 5 percent of that, but it beats a kick in the head. Most scoring jobs for major studios pay at least $100,000.

FACT

Film scoring used to be dominated by classically trained composers with theory and composition degrees. These days, a decked-out MIDI-studio can be enough to score a movie and then, if live musicians are needed, an orchestrator writes out the parts for the musicians.

Extra cash can be made if you can orchestrate, conduct the musicians, and produce the recording, so a degree and/or practical experience in these areas still comes in handy. As a scorer, you only get mechanicals on the soundtrack record if you negotiate for them. There are lots of other deal points and tricks to watch for. If you go into scoring, find an attorney who specializes in this kind of deal.

How to Win Without Scoring

When it comes to writing a song for a particular movie, you'll usually get an up-front fee of anywhere from zilch (for those starting out) to over $50,000 (for big-name writers). Although you don't get performance royalties from U.S. theaters, you will get them from European theaters and TV use. Also, you can usually negotiate for about the same sheet music royalty you'd get from a publisher. Some studios, for obvious reasons, prefer to do a spec deal in which they pay a small fee for a demo of the song, then decide if they like it before paying more. In most cases, the main fee you are paid is a "buyout"; the movie studio owns the copyright.

Television Music

Television music isn't what it used to be. Background scoring isn't used as much as it once was for weekly series, but a few composers still make money doing background music for TV shows, especially "movie of the week" type shows. The money ceiling for TV scoring is substantially lower than for movies. The upside is in the performance royalties, which you get even for reruns. The best ways for songwriters to make money in TV (aside from jingles) are by writing the theme songs that start and end shows or by having a song that's already been cut placed in a show as featured or background music.

Competition in the theme song market is tough, because the money can be huge. Think about it: A theme song gets played at least once every time the show runs, sometimes twice. Fragments of the theme are often used when returning from a commercial. Every use means more royalties. With the right show, reruns can keep you living in style for the rest of your life. To break into the theme song market, you may need a music degree and/or connections in the TV industry. Be prepared to pay a lot of dues.

These days, an increasing number of television shows use music by up-and-coming bands. The Rembrandts, already a fairly popular band, received a major career boost when their song "I'll Be There for You" was used as the theme song for the TV show "Friends." Vonda Shepherd became famous almost instantly when the TV show "Ally McBeal" began featuring her songs. The best way to get your songs placed in TV shows is by having a publisher with connections in the TV industry or by making some connections yourself.

Commercial Jingles

Most jingle writers work for jingle studios or ad agencies and have degrees in advertising or theory and composition. Of course, if you've got a Pro-tools studio and know how to sequence, record, master, and hire out anything else you need, you can work without a degree and even bypass the ad agency.

The easiest way to break into the jingle business is on the local level. You might have to give a few away to establish yourself, but once you get some stuff on the air, you can make decent cash while working your way up to the regional and national levels.

The practice of licensing established popular songs for jingle use has become common. Hit songs can sometimes generate more money as jingles than they did from airplay. Some bands have even gone the reverse route, having a song that was licensed for jingle use become a hit due to the exposure from radio and TV.

Children's Music

Children's music is a very specialized market. You'll probably want some sort of education degree and good political skills to move up in this area, as there's a lot of competition for very few jobs. Much of the children's music market centers around television shows, so New York or LA are your hubs of choice in this field. Many of these shows hire a team of staff writers. In this situation, you may have to come up with new songs every week and you might be on the production team as well. On the movie side of the children's market, publishing affiliates of the major movie studios (Disney's Lyric Street, Dreamworks, and others) may use staff writers to come up with some of the songs for kids' movies. In any field of children's music, start by specializing in an age group and expand from there. If you're not at home with finger-painting or food fights, this job is not for you. To write convincingly for kids, you must be a kid at heart.

Religious Music

Though there is still a small market for "old time" gospel music, the Christian contemporary music (CCM) genre has exploded in the last several years with the rise of superstars like DC Talk and Michael W. Smith. The CCM genre is separate from other genres only by virtue of its subject matter: Musically, anything that would work for the pop market will work here.

Children's religious music, like for Sunday schools and vacation bible schools, is a growing market, but you'll need good networking skills with fussy church ladies. A degree in music education or religious education can be a big plus in this field. Many writers of children's religious music teach a Sunday school class to stay in touch with the market and have a test group available on which to try out new material.

ALERT!

Although the CCM market can be a potential moneymaker, be advised that it is a very political market. Denomination cliques exist within the industry and non-Protestants may have an especially tough time. Perhaps even more so than other genres, CCM is all about connections and networking.

Classical and Jazz Composers

The tough part for modern classical composers is that current recordings of classical music by well-known orchestras consist mainly of songs by established composers. Most of this material is public domain stuff, written by people who have been dead too long to collect royalties. Not that there's a lot of money in the classical market; 50,000 units is considered a big sales success and airplay is primarily on public radio, which doesn't pay much in performance royalties.

Mechanicals for classical music recordings are often even lower than for popular genres. In times past, classical composers augmented their incomes by conducting orchestras and choirs. Now, noncomposers who specialize in conducting usually fill those roles. Classical composer's main sources of income are commissioned works, grants, endowments, wealthy patrons, and some performance royalties for a lucky few.

Formal jazz composers may also receive grants, endowments, and commissions, but the successful composer of modern jazz generally survives through the formation of a playing ensemble, of which he or she is often a member, to record and perform new works. A minimum of a master's degree in music theory and composition with studies in grant writing is recommended for those with aspirations of being classical or jazz composers.

Being Your Own Publisher

Some of the money to be made in the songwriting business is on the publishing side. Think about it; half the money goes to publishers, why shouldn't you cash in on that at some point? Of course, there's more overhead on the publishing side, and a whole different set of hassles, but you can start small and build from there. The only certain drawback to starting a publishing company is that you won't be able to blame everything on your publisher anymore.

When to Start a Publishing Company

Unless you want to be a publisher instead of a songwriter, don't start your company until your songwriting career is established. Even then, the less time you have to spend working as a publisher, the more time you can devote to songwriting. The ideal times to start a publishing company are when you already have publishing income or you have too much money and need to get rid of a few million dollars in a hurry. Assuming that you're not a millionaire, start your company when you've had some cuts and get a co-publishing deal, partial ownership of the publishing on your own songs.

FACT

By the time you get a co-pub deal, you'll probably know dozens of other songwriters who have co-pub and/or own a publishing company. These friends and acquaintances can be great sources of information about the pitfalls and strategies of starting your own company.

Administration Deals

An administration deal, or "admin deal" for short, is what generally happens when you first get co-pub. At this point, you and your publisher are sharing publishing income on your songs. You need a publishing company to collect your share, but it would eat up all your profits to have an office, employees, and the other stuff that goes with a "real" company. You're in luck; your publishing company only needs to exist on paper. With an admin deal, your publisher still does the pitching, collects the money, and does most of the paperwork, then gives you your share of the net. There are a few differences between this and a staff deal; you'll owe a portion of the publisher's share on demos and have to do taxes on your company but, for the most part, it's business as usual.

PRO Affiliation

The first step is to affiliate with a PRO. Just like a songwriter, a publisher must be affiliated with a PRO. Because a publisher can only be affiliated with one PRO, if you want to be covered all ways you have to start a different publishing company to affiliate with each PRO. At first, you won't really need to do this; when the main purpose of your publishing company is to handle your co-pub, affiliate your publishing company with the same PRO that handles the songwriter's portion of the songs. If you want to handle the publishing for other people's songs or hire staff writers, then you can start another company or two.

PRO forms for publisher affiliation are pretty simple. After setting up with a PRO, you still need to incorporate your publishing company. You may have a few options here; consult with your attorney about incorporation options and how they affect tax structure and liability issues. You also need to file copyright forms reassigning any songs you own to your publishing company.

If you've never run a small business before, you're in for a major learning experience. You have a lot of different options for getting into publishing. You can test the waters, get your feet wet, or dive in headfirst. Regardless, get some professional advice from an attorney and some practical advice from people who have run publishing companies.

Office Space

At first, a desk, computer, and file cabinet in your home will probably do as an office for your publishing company. It's better if these are 100 percent dedicated to your publishing company and not the same ones you use for writing. The point at which you'll need to actually get a real office is the point at which you start hiring full-time employees. Even if you only hire one person, you don't want somebody hanging out in your house forty hours a week.

Hiring Help

It's possible (just barely) for one person to run a small publishing company by working lots of overtime and staying very focused. Of course, this means giving up all your writing time. Luckily, the person running the company doesn't have to be you. As a matter of fact, unless you're giving up being a songwriter, it *should* be someone else.

So, you need to hire someone to answer the phones, do the books, make copies, do pitches and drop-offs, and all the other things that need doing while you're staring out the window, trying to be brilliant. You need someone who believes, who's committed, who has experience—are you starting to miss your publisher yet? As a matter of fact, you might think about hiring someone from your old company, or from a publishing company you've done business with, who's ready to move up.

When to Expand

In some ways, it's easier to run a mid-sized publishing house than a small one. If the company has only one writer (you), you're paying someone to go make drop-offs for one writer. For the same money, you could drop off stuff from several writers. Your "staff of one" may be a great plugger, but lousy at doing the books or vice versa. Adding someone with the skills your staff doesn't have can free people up to do what they do best. If you're making money hand-over-fist and you know some great writers who'd work for peanuts, it might be time to move up.

Going Big, the Three-Year Plan

When it's time to expand, it's a whole new game. It's possible to make or lose tens of millions of dollars by starting a big publishing company. Even if things go well, it'll probably take three years to get your company off the ground—a year to get the songs in place, a year to get the staff up to speed and start getting holds, and a year at full steam to start getting cuts—if everything goes smoothly. It takes a year to start collecting money on cuts, so you need at least enough money to run the company for four years.

FACT

Starting a big publishing company can cost more than even a successful songwriter can afford to lose. A method of risk management commonly used in the publishing business is to acquire startup capital either from a venture capital firm, for an expected return on the investment, or from an established publisher, for a piece of the company.

Building a Catalog

The first step is to get a bunch of great songs. A publishing house is basically a song leasing and rental store that delivers. The better your selection and the higher the quality of the merchandise, the better your odds of attracting customers. You need to build up a general catalog with songs of different grooves, sub-genres, and tempos to suit a variety of artists' needs. Now you're looking at things from the publisher's perspective: If you can get a single-song contract on a great tune for no money down, get the writer to provide a killer demo, and get the exclusive right to pitch the song for the next three to five years (with copyright ownership if you get it cut), it's a good thing. Do this as often as possible. Never mind that the songwriters are calling you a greedy old tyrant, you're trying to make a living here and doing them a favor in the process!

At this point you might also hire staff writers. This means you'll want to make them write as many songs as possible for as little money as possible and try to get all their old songs for cheap or free while you're at it. After all, if you don't make a profit, they won't be able to keep their jobs.

Hiring the Team

Now you need a team that works like a well-oiled machine to get the best out of your writers and to market all the great songs in your catalog. You'll need at least one experienced plugger and people to keep track of catalog activity and make copies, handle the writers and schedule demo sessions, and a secretary to answer phones, make appointments, screen songs, make coffee and do everything else that nobody else seems to be able to do. You also need someone to make decisions in your place. You're a writer; you won't always be available. Find a creative director with a strong business background who believes in the catalog.

Hopefully, you've made a lot of contacts over the years and can draw from that pool to find employees. You can also put out the word that you're hiring. After you screen out the weirdoes, wannabes, and songwriters, who will descend on your office like a Mongol horde, you'll hopefully have a few people worth trying out. In the worst-case scenario, fill a few jobs like receptionist and copy boy with interns from music business programs. You don't have to pay them much, if anything, and you can work them to death. Interns may surprise you with their dedication and intelligence.

What is an intern?
An intern is like an apprentice. Most interns are college students who receive class credit for work that relates to their respective field of study. The major perk for an intern is the chance to make connections in the business before graduating.

Until the Money Comes

Now you have to keep everyone doing the best they can and integrate them into a working team. Here's where you find out who doesn't belong. Sometimes an otherwise competent person just doesn't fit in with the team. This is a problem; for a publishing company to work, everyone must work together, believe in the catalog, and trust each other. Do what you have to do. Keep an eye on the market and the pitch sheets and guide your writing staff (including yourself) to keep up with, or stay ahead of, what's going on.

Selling the Catalog

If, by some quirk of fate, you pull this off and end up running a big, successful publishing company, things will get easier in some ways. You can hire people to take care of the more mundane aspects of the job and start working on European markets, film, and TV. You can get caught up in making deals and earning more money than most people can imagine. You can start companies that specialize in other genres and hire big-time lawyers to figure out how to rip off your writers.

Or you can sell the whole catalog for a pile of cash and start over. One of your rights in the standard contracts your writers sign is the right to sell your ownership in their songs.

FACT

There are companies that buy "used" copyrights for large sums of money. These companies are expert at making money from established catalogs, so it might even be good for your writers.

Remember to Write

You used to be a writer, right? Ouch! Well, you have to decide at some point whether to be a big publisher who used to write or a big writer with a small to midsized publishing company. This might be the perfect time to sell the catalog, take a long vacation, and write some songs. Let the company run itself for a little while; it's easier without that big old catalog weighing everyone down. Maybe it's time to get a place in the Bahamas, or maybe the Keys. Somebody get Buffet on the phone; tell him to expect a visit!

Appendices

Appendix A

Songwriter's FAQ

Appendix B

Seeking
Professional Help

Appendix C

Glossary

Songwriter's FAQ

We asked the members of Tunesmith.net and subscribers of the *Nashville Rant* e-zine for questions they'd like to have answered on the music industry, and put them to an all-star professional panel. Here are the results.

The Panel

Don Wayne: Hall of Fame writer of timeless classics like "Saginaw Michigan" and "Country Bumpkin." Winner of Song of the Year honors from the CMA, ACM, and NSAI, as well as NSAI Songwriter of the Year. His mantel is home to three BMI awards and one ASCAP award. He has cuts with Ernest Tubb, Eddy Arnold, Lefty Frizzel, Hank Williams Jr., Cal Smith, Tex Ritter, and a host of others. Don also has one of the best country voices in Nashville.

Scott Gunter: As Creative Director at Almo-Irving Music, Scott helps shape the careers of some of the best songwriters in the world. A very abridged list of songwriters he has worked with includes Anthony Smith (Mercury recording artist and co-writer of the George Strait #1 "Run"), Annie Roboff ("This Kiss," "Unbroken"), Craig Wiseman (eleven #1 hits and counting), and Grammy nominated singer/songwriter Gillian Welch. All this and he's still one of the most humble, down-to-earth guys you'll ever meet.

Steve Fox: One of the hottest young artists in Canada, Steve struck songwriting gold in the United States with the Montgomery Gentry single "Daddy Won't Sell the Farm." Further credits include an ASCAP award, Song of the Year from SOCAN (ASCAP's neighbor to the North), and Juno award nominations including Best New Country Artist and Best Male Vocalist. Steve has written twenty Canadian Top Twenty hits and once had four songs in the Top Twenty at one time. His son, Jack Henry, will rule the world one day.

Jimmy Payne: Another "Hall O' Famer," Jimmy was originally a recording artist on Epic. His recording career was eventually overshadowed by his success as a songwriter. From pop hits "Woman, Woman, Have You Got Cheating on Your Mind," which helped the Union Gap outsell The Beatles the year following its release, to country gems like the Charley Pride hit "My Eyes Can Only See as Far as You," and cuts with Dottie West, Hank Snow, Tammy Wynette, Grandpa Jones, and countless others, he's proven to be as versatile as he is enduring. His current project, "Three Chord Heroes," is an album recorded with friends Don Wayne, Danny Dill ("The Long Black Veil," "Detroit City"), and Dick Feller ("Some Days Are Diamonds" and "Eastbound and Down"). Jimmy is also the nicest songwriting legend you'll ever meet.

Bart Herbison: Bart is Executive Director of the Nashville Songwriter's Organization International, the largest organization of its kind. A quick Internet search will turn up Bart's name all over the place, usually in connection with song-writers' rights and legislative efforts. He's also a veritable treasure trove of songwriting history. You can visit his organization online at *www.nashvillesongwriters.com.*

Q **What are the biggest mistakes inexperienced writers make?**

Jimmy: They write them too long. They demo them too long. I came up in the sixties and seventies when they said, "Why, it's already two minutes!" Radio won't play it. New writers also write things from too much of a personal perspective. It needs to be more general.

Don: It's inevitable that a new writer is going to make mistakes. A lot is trial and error. Write something and sing it and see how people respond. Don't worry about making mistakes if you're new in the game. I would sure advise songwriters to stay away from drugs and drinking. I've seen a lot of talent go to waste, not taking care of business, home, and families. It's sad to see brilliant people with it all laid out there waiting for them just for the taking. . . .

Steve: You know, speaking strictly lyrically, the most common thing that I find is complicated ideas. When I see really inexperienced writing I see a thread . . . lofty concepts that you need several listens to get. Clarity is really a mandate

in the country market. Also, too many verses, too long a song.

Scott: Editing themselves, not putting what they feel on paper. And for another thing, I don't like people to sell me on what they do. I just want to hear the song. Let that speak for itself.

Bart: Amateur songwriters that want to come here and do it? I get a lot of [complaints of] problems about co-writing. When you start to write a song with someone else, there's a tacit 50 percent agreement when you do that. The other person owns half the song. Then that other person has the right, even if it was your idea, if they don't like the way it happened, to take the song to someone else and rewrite it again. Then you're a third owner on your song that they turned into something different. You need to know these basic elements before you get too far down the road.

Q **Do you feel that your PRO does a good job of getting you royalties and protecting your rights?**

Jimmy: I think BMI has done a wonderful job. I like their method of collecting and how they come to certain figures from actual logs of song played. I favor BMI.

Don: I'm with BMI. I think they are definitely trying to do all that.

Steve: Yes. I'm with SOCAN in Canada and ASCAP in the States. They sure have taken care of me. I'm guilty of not knowing a lot of the nuances of bills passed in government but, on a personal level, I've needed back up and they've come through for me. They've made me a believer.

Scott: They all do the same job. ASCAP has sent more writers to me than BMI, so that's my experience with it. ASCAP and BMI have two radically different personalities. We have writers at both of them. You have to walk in the building and see which one works for you. One thing I do love about ASCAP is that songwriters run it.

Q Are you politically active about songwriters' issues like piracy and copyright extension?

Jimmy: I'm behind it, but I don't keep up with it right now.

Don: Back in the seventies when I was working with NSAI on the new copyright bill [which we got in 1976], we worked with the NY songwriter's guild. I recently went with NSAI to Washington to represent songwriters.

Steve: No, but I'm embarrassed to say it.

Scott: I'm not but I need to be. First, you just try to pay the bills. You have to get a little farther along, make a little more money to have the time and resources to invest in that part of your protection. Hit songwriters are the most active in this because they have the most to protect.

Q How important do you think the Internet will be in the future of the music business?

Jimmy: It's already playing a big part. It works

both ways, though. It's easy to download illegally, but on the other hand it's much easier to communicate overseas and cross-country.

Don: That's a gimmie. I think it'll get ironed out, and the good will outweigh the bad.

Steve: This is stating the obvious, but we're in the Dark Ages in terms of the Internet. Nobody really knows what's going on in terms of how it's all going to play out. But I think we know that songwriters are not being paid what they should and too much music is going out there for free. Everybody out there knows that we can't rely on people dropping twenty dollars on a CD anymore. The Internet is here to stay. It's the primary way to sell anything.

Scott: Radically important. It'll be that we'll have to find other ways to make money from copyrights outside of sales . . . sync licenses, airplay, computer games . . . any way you can make money outside of sales.

Q How many songs do you write in a year?

Jimmy: Truthfully, last year I just wrote one. In my busiest time though I wrote about a song a week and maybe started another one. Some nights me and Glaser would start two or three songs. We wrote on Tuesday nights. We'd go play pinball at what was the Burger Boy on 19th and Broadway 'til we got loosened up. It was nothing to see Kristofferson or Waylon over there playing pinball.

Don: I used to write forty to fifty songs a year, but not all any good. If you're writing seriously, a song a week is a good thing to shoot for particularly if you co-write. I don't write so many now. Those were the years of my "Not So Magnificent Obsession" (grins). Now I write ten to twelve songs a year.

Steve: I've had a couple of years where I've written a hundred songs. I'd say that on average, sixty to a hundred. I don't know how many are any good . . . history will say.

Scott: I don't think there is a blueprint, but the writers that seem to do the best write more songs. It's a numbers game. As productive as you can be, the better you'll be. It can be the worst song you wrote that got cut. Don Schlitz says he writes [a] lot of songs because he only feels like he's great 10 percent of the time.

Q Do you [or did you] have a support group of people to bounce new songs off of and get feedback? Do you think that's an important thing for a songwriter to have?

Jimmy: I really do think that's important. I don't have that right now like I'd like to. It's tricky to bounce an idea off of another writer that I don't write with. They can subconsciously remember an idea and even use it before they realize it. You have to be careful.

Don: I think it's extremely important. Especially starting out. Even for any of us. That's one of the good things about picking parties.

Steve: I do now. Songwriting can be altogether way too insular. You can gain so much by having the right person listen. Often it's a spouse or someone who is not in the business. My wife is such a good listener. She's listening while she's doing all the things that your listeners do . . . washing the dishes, preparing dinner, living life. I also have a song plugger who gives great input. If there are local songwriting groups in a town, that is great too. Songwriting is about emotionally affecting other people. I don't know how people can do that without feedback at some point.

Scott: It's good to get feedback. Writing is such an insecure art that you need support. Writing support and emotional support. It's good to have someone to talk to who is coming from where you are coming from.

Q Do you play an instrument?

Jimmy: I play harmonica and guitar.

Don: I play *at* an instrument. I try. I used to saw on the fiddle, but now it's just guitar.

Steve: I play guitar, piano a bit, and bass. I write mostly on guitar, about 95 percent of the time.

Scott: Nope, I was a singer.

Q Where do you find ideas for songs?

Jimmy: Everywhere. . . . In people's conversations. You tune into when something's said different. Good phrases trigger your imagination. People tell you stuff if you listen. Writers talk in song titles. They give themselves away. Once you say it, it's public domain.

Don: Just anywhere and everywhere . . . reading, driving (but don't get to seeing too many images and drive off the road), listening, meditating, and thinking.

Steve: I love writing from a title. It's old-fashioned, but it's a great way to start. A title can give you options. Some of the most enjoyable co-writing I've done is spending half a day talking about what a song is. A song of mine is "Where was I?" It can mean different things depending on the emphasis. It can be "Where was I before you came along?" Or it can be, "Where was I before I was so rudely interrupted?" Lot of times I'll start with a guitar chord riff or melody, but less often. The title ends up being the absolute essence of a great song, even a story song.

Scott: Hit songwriters find ideas in movies, books—everywhere.

Q What's the secret of longevity in the music business?

Jimmy: Be talented and lucky at the same time.

Don: I wish I knew for sure. I haven't had it, at least not consistently. Some are consistent for twenty-five or thirty years, like Bob McDill. He's been writing hits since around 1971. He hasn't missed a year in a thirty-year run of having a song do well.

Steve: Some degree of success. If you're making a living at it, that's success. Some years it's not much of a living, but to be doing it has kept me going. Since I was twenty years old I've carved out some living in the music business. Wow, my bills are paid and all because I make music! Also, talent and perseverance. Clichés are clichés because they are true.

Scott: Hard work and persistence.

Q What advice do you have for a writer who's just starting out?

Jimmy: Obviously, let somebody that has a background in the music business hear your songs. There are a lot of people that will tell you whether you're on the right track without getting into a big producer's office.

Don: Regardless of where a writer is living, he's probably fairly close to a chapter of the NSAI. They provide a priceless service to new writers. The camaraderie is worth something. You might find a co-writer. Definitely look for a support group.

Steve: Keep writing . . . try to keep your antennae and your energy up. Sometimes it's when I'm doing something else that I have ideas for great songs. Keep your mind on it, whatever your doing. *Don't* focus on how hard it is. Focus on writing good songs.

Scott: Work hard in every aspect—network, pay attention business-wise. You better move to Nashville if you're not already here. Even songwriters on staff do better when they're in town. When a songwriter is in the building more I see their face and I have more opportunities to ask them for ideas and give them input. I keep lists and lists of people and songs but somebody walking through the door will spark an idea of a song to pitch. I even ask songwriters about pitching ideas. If they aren't here I can't ask them.

Bart: Do your business homework is my first piece of advice. I recently had a fella standing in the lobby and he was beaming. He was in his sixties and he was just so contagious with his glee. I said, "What is up with you?" . . . and he said, "I've just recorded my first CD" and to hear him talk about it, I thought he's gotten a record deal. Somebody had charged him $36,000 to do six demos. They just raped him. Now, this guy was smart, ran a business. He would never have purchased a car, bought a house, or even a magazine subscription without knowing all the details but, because he was trying to pursue a dream and buy into that dream, he came up here and made the idiot's mistake of not making two or three phone calls.

Q On average, how much editing and rewriting would you say you do? What about when you were starting out?

Jimmy: Quite a bit now. It depends on who I'm writing with. When I first started calling myself a songwriter I did not do a lot of editing, but the more I learned about writing, the longer it took.

Don: I edit and rewrite as much now as when I started out. I do quite a bit. When you write slow, you have less to do. If you try to knock it out in a day's time, then you'll need to revisit it.

Steve: They are two different things to me. I'm a big editor. I often think we don't need this or that. If a song is over three and a half minutes, I think it's problematic. Rewriting is more rewriting of

what is already there. I am usually excited to move on to the next song. That's why I write so many.

Scott: Different writers work different ways. Anthony does so much editing in his head before he plays it. That's why he works slow. It's harder for him to rewrite because he's already thought through a lot of options already. Craig [Wiseman] is the opposite. He writes a song in a day, then goes back and revisits it. I do hear songs that I don't think are really finished, but some of them are hit songs. There's really not a right or wrong. There's just making money or not making money.

Q Anything else?

Bart: How bad do you want it? There's a guy from my hometown named "George" who may be the best basketball player I ever saw in my life. He's Jordanesque. Now, why is George not playing in the NBA? He didn't want it bad enough! He wasn't disciplined enough to play on the high school team and go to practice and get a college scholarship and do what it took to get in the NBA. Same thing with songwriting; to be in that handful that are multiple hit songwriters, the odds are about the same as (being in the starting lineup) in the NBA. How bad do you want it? You have to ask yourself that question and be willing to make the sacrifices that you'd make in any other occupation.

Steve: It's not impossible. Don't tell yourself it can't happen.

Seeking Professional Help

Both CEOs and athletes often train at the collegiate level and receive guidance from professionals. Successful songwriters have usually had the benefit of professional help on the way to the top of the charts. Here's a list some of the resources available for songwriters today and how to find them.

Songwriting Schools

Berklee Songwriting Degree Program

Chaired by Jack Perricone, a successful producer/songwriter who has worked with Michael Jackson and Lou Rawls and has film and jingle experience as well. Spring break features a trip to Nashville to meet professional songwriters.

> Berklee College of Music
> 1140 Boylston St.
> Boston, MA 02215
> ✆ 800-421-0084
> ✍ *www.berklee.edu*
> ✍ *summer@berklee.edu*

The Music School on Music Row (MSMR)

The songwriting workshop with hit songwriters Pete and Pat Luboff is highly recommended. Pete and Pat have had hits with Snoop Dogg and Patti LaBelle and are authors of many acclaimed books on songwriting. Other cool classes at the MSMR include publishing, music business, notation, advanced production, and various instrumental/vocal performance classes.

> The Music School on Music Row
> 1520 Demonbreun St.
> Nashville, TN 37203
> ✆ 615-321-6096
> ✍ *www.themusicschoolonmusicrow.com*

Songwriting Clubs and Organizations

Nashville Songwriter's Association International

As a beginning songwriter, or one moving to a hub, an NSAI membership is about the best $100 you can spend. Membership gets you admittance to the monthly regional workshop near you. Every six weeks, you can send in a song for critique, and there are lots of other perks, too. NSAI members wrote hits like Rock Song of the Year "Blue on Black" (Kenny Wayne Shepherd) and Grammy winner "Change the World" (Eric Clapton). Visit NSAI online at ✍ *www.nashvillesongwriters.com.*

Songwriters Guild of America

Like NSAI, SGA has cool seminars and is politically active on songwriter's rights issues, but there are enough differences between the two that you might consider joining both groups. SGA's contract evaluation service alone is worth the price of membership. Visit SGA online at ✍ *www.songwriters.org.*

Songwriting Organization Finder

Here's a list of songwriting organizations around the United States and a few other places. If you hit a dead end on one of these, try a Web search.

ALABAMA
Birmingham NSAI Workshop, ✆ 256-892-0600
Florence Muscle Shoals SW, ✆ 256-760-0218
Garden City Alabama SW Guild, ✆ 256-352-4873
Mobile NSAI Workshop, ✆ 334-666-2097
Opp NSAI Workshop, ✆ 334-222-8216

ARKANSAS
Bono/Jonesboro NSAI Workshop, ✆ 870-935-5857
Little Rock Arkansas SW Assn, ✆ 501-565-8889

ARIZONA
Phoenix Arizona SW Assn, ✆ 602-973-1988

CALIFORNIA
Fresno/Hanford NSAI Workshop,
 ✆ 209-585-0718
Los Angeles/Santa Monica NSAI Workshop,
 ✆ 323-255-8765
Newport Beach Newport SW Assn, ✆ 714-669-5409

Orange County/ Irvine NSAI Workshop,
 ✆ 949-733-2717
Sacramento NSAI Workshop, ✆ 916-489-1688
San Carlos Northern CA SW Assn, ✆ 800-FOR-SONG
San Diego NSAI Workshop, ✆ 858-481-5650
San Diego San Diego SW Guild, ✆ 619-225-2131

COLORADO
Denver NSAI Workshop, ✆ 303-695-8628
Colorado Springs NSAI Workshop, ✆ 719-268-9880
Durango NSAI Workshop, ✆ 970-385-3936
Ft. Collins Colorado Christian SW, ✆ 303-778-6182

CONNECTICUT
Fairfield NSAI Workshop, ✆ 203-595-8123
Glastonbury Connecticut SW Assn, ✆ 860-659-8992
Westport Songshops Co-op, ✆ 203-845-9545,
 ✍ *www.songshopscoop.com*
Connecticut Songwriters Assn,
 ✍ *www.ctsongs.com/index.htm*

DISTRICT OF COLUMBIA
Washington Folk Alliance, ✆ 202-835-3655
Washington NSAI Workshop, ✆ 301-428-3498
Washington SW Assn of Washington,
 ✆ 301-654-8434
Washington Washington Area Music Assn,
 ✆ 202-338-1134

DELAWARE
Wilmington NSAI Workshop, ✆ 302-239-4610

FLORIDA
Daytona Beach Casements SW Workshop,
 ✆ 904-252-8714

Daytona Beach NSAI Workshop, ☎ 904-252-8714

Ft Lauderdale NSAI Workshop, ☎ 305-264-0094

Hollywood SW in the Round, ☎ 954-929-0982

Jacksonville N Florida Christian Music Writers, ☎ 904-786-2372

Jacksonville NSAI Workshop, ☎ 904-259-5758

Kissimmee NSAI Workshop, ☎ 407-846-7893

Miami NSAI Workshop, ☎ 305-567-0246

N Ft Myers NSAI Workshop, ☎ 941-433-2099

Tallahassee NSAI Workshop, ☎ 850-216-1025

Tampa NSAI Workshop, ☎ 813-677-8149

GEORGIA

Athens NSAI Workshop, ☎ 706-583-8519

Atlanta Georgia Music Industry Assn, ☎ 404-266-2666

Atlanta NSAI Workshop, ☎ 770-593-6032

Carrolton NSAI Workshop, ☎ 770-854-7010

Savannah NSAI Workshop, ☎ 912-897-7623

Valdosta NSAI Workshop, ☎ 912-324-2827

HAWAII

Hawaii Songwriter's Association, ✍ *http://members.aol.com/hsasong/hsa.html*

Pacific Songwriter's Organization, ✍ *http://home1.gte.net/jazcraft/songwriters.htm*

IOWA

Cedar Rapids NSAI Workshop, ☎ 319-377-7208

IDAHO

Snake River NSAI Workshop, ☎ 208-528-8572

ILLINOIS

Chicago Songwriter's Collective, ✍ *www.chicagosongwriters.com*

Chicago NSAI Workshop, ☎ 630-887-0125

Marion NSAI Workshop, ☎ 618-964-1840

Moline NSAI Workshop, ☎ 309-762-9821

INDIANA

Bedford NSAI Workshop, ☎ 812-279-8460

Evansville NSAI Workshop, ☎ 812-985-9322

Indianapolis Indianapolis SW Assn, ☎ 317-271-6523

Indianapolis Songwriter's Association, ✍ *www.listen.to/indysongwriters*

Indianapolis NSAI Workshop, ☎ 317-273-0156

Liberty Whitewater Valley SW, ☎ 765-458-6152

Portage NSAI Workshop, ☎ 219-762-3318

Songwriters Association of Northern Indiana, ✍ *www.laidbak.com/fpm*

KANSAS

Wichita Wichita SW Group, ☎ 316-729-0022

KENTUCKY

Buffalo Heartland SW Assn of KY, ☎ 270-325-3958

Louisville NSAI Workshop, ☎ 502-452-1996

Owensboro NSAI Workshop, ☎ 812-985-9322

LOUISIANA

Baton Rouge Louisiana SW Assn, ☎ 504-925-8771

Baton Rouge NSAI Workshop, ☎ 255-766-6367

New Orleans Louisiana SW Assn, ☎ 504-924-0804 or ✍ *www.lasongwriters.org*

New Orleans NSAI Workshop, ☎ 504-488-7435

Shreveport Southern Songwriters Guild, ☎ 318-797-1122

MASSACHUSETTS

Abington MA Country Music Awards Assoc,
    ✆ 781-878-0271
Boston/Arlington NSAI Workshop, ✆ 508-895-9033
Burlington Boston SW Workshop, ✆ 617-499-6932

MARYLAND

Baltimore SW Assn, 410-455-3822 or ✍ *http://
    research.umbc.edu/~iwancio*
Annapolis/Baltimore NSAI Workshop,
    ✆ 410-647-6048
Cambridge NSAI Workshop, ✆ 410-288-6377

MICHIGAN

Battle Creek NSAI Workshop, ✆ 616-789-2874
Flint Area NSAI Workshop, ✆ 810-239-0992
Fraser Michigan Songwriter Assn, ✆ 810-498-7673
    or ✍ *www.mdsa.com*
Kalamazoo NSAI Workshop, ✆ 616-344-4428

MINNESOTA

Minnesota Assn of Christian SW, ✆ 612-544-7615
    or ✍ *www.citilink.com/~foxyfilm/macs*
Minneapolis NSAI Workshop, ✆ 612-881-4365
Minneapolis Minnesota Assn of SW, ✆ 612-770-
    2564 or ✍ *www.isc.net/mas*

MISSOURI

Columbia NSAI Workshop, ✆ 573-815-0397
Fenton Missouri SW Assn, ✆ 636-343-4765
Joplin NSAI Workshop, ✆ 417-623-0271
Kansas City NSAI Workshop, ✆ 816-763-1633
Springfield Ozark SW Assn, ✆ 417-883-3385
St Louis NSAI Workshop, ✆ 314-846-3330

MISSISSIPPI

Gulfport NSAI Workshop, ✆ 228-832-6042
Jackson NSAI Workshop, ✆ 601-483-7694

MONTANA

Missoula NSAI Workshop, ✆ 406-543-3290

NORTH CAROLINA

Hickory NSAI Workshop, ✆ 828-465-5919
Charlotte NSAI Workshop, ✆ 704-896-7234
Greensboro NSAI Workshop, ✆ 336-578-5433
Knightdale Central Carolina SW Assn, ✆ 919-266-
    5791 or ✍ *www.ncneighbors.com/147*
Chapel Hill/Raleigh/Durham NSAI Workshop,
    ✆ 919-469-5876
Roxboro NSAI Workshop, ✆ 336-599-7688
Shelby NSAI Workshop, ✆ 704-481-1086
Winston-Salem NSAI Workshop, ✆ 336-454-8694
North Carolina Songwriters Co-op, ✍ *http://
    triangle.citysearch.com/E/G/RDUNC/0000/
    17/50/cs1.html*

NEW JERSEY

Clinton Princeton Songwriters, ✆ 908-638-0239 or
    ✍ *http://community.nj.com/cc/princetonsong
writers*

NEW MEXICO

Albuquerque/Santa Fe NSAI Workshop,
    ✆ 505-466-1031

NEVADA

Las Vegas Las Vegas SW Assn, ✆ 702-223-7255
Reno NSAI Workshop, ✆ 775-626-2172

NEW YORK

Brooklyn SW & Lyricist Club, ☎ 718-855-5057

Long Island NSAI Workshop, ☎ 631-757-9141

New York American Composers Alliance, ☎ 212-362-8900

New York NSAI Workshop, ☎ 516-822-7942

Rochester NSAI Workshop, ☎ 716-681-1024

OHIO

Cleveland NSAI Workshop, ☎ 330-887-5328

Columbus NSAI Workshop, ☎ 614-523-1989

Columbus Songwriters & Poets Critique, ☎ 614-253-1125

Cincinnati/Dayton NSAI Workshop, ☎ 937-847-0023

Toledo NSAI Workshop, ☎ 419-661-0404

OKLAHOMA

Oklahoma City NSAI Workshop, ☎ 405-794-9659

Oklahoma City SW & Composers, ☎ 405-478-2346 or ✍ www.oksongwriters.org

Tulsa SW Assn, ☎ 918-227-0108

OREGON

Portland SW Assn, ☎ 503-727-9072 or ✍ www.PdxSongwriters.org

Redmond NSAI Workshop, ☎ 541-548-3072

Central Oregon Songwriters Association, ✍ http://members.tripod.com/~COSA4U

PENNSYLVANIA

Philadelphia NSAI Workshop, ☎ 610-375-1727

Philadelphia Songwriter's Association, ✍ http://members.aol.com/philasong

Pittsburgh NSAI Workshop, ☎ 412-367-3766

Philadelphia Area Songwriters Alliance, ✍ www.voicenet.com~jhammer/pasa.html

Bucks County Folk Song Society, ✍ www.bucksfolk.org

RHODE ISLAND

Rhode Island Songwriter's Association, ✍ risa@chowda.com

SOUTH CAROLINA

Charleston NSAI Workshop, ☎ 843-763-1250

Rock Hill Carolina Assn of Songwriters, ☎ 803-327-7691 or ✍ www.caos.org

SOUTH DAKOTA

Midwestern Songwriters Alliance, ✍ www.midwestsongwriter.org

TENNESSEE

Chattanooga NSAI Workshop, ☎ 423-756-7508

Hendersonville Tennessee SW Assn Int'l, ☎ 615-969-5967 or ✍ clubnashville.com/tsai.htm

Hermitage Nat'l Assn of Christian SW, ☎ 800-796-2227

Johnson City NSAI Workshop, ☎ 540-944-5484

Knoxville Songwriters Assn, ☎ 423-581-5154 or ✍ http://personal.lig.bellsouth.net/lig/t/r/trshel

Knoxville NSAI Workshop, ☎ 423-971-4626

Memphis SW Assn, ☎ 901-577-0906 or ✍ www.memphissongwriters.com

Memphis Nat'l Assn of Christian SW, ☎ 901-324-6473

Memphis NSAI Workshop, ☎ 901-272-2729

Nashville NSAI, ☎ 615-256-3354

TEXAS

Austin SW Group, ✆ 512-442-TUNE or
✎ *www.austinsongwriter.org*
Austin NSAI Workshop, 830-905-2119
Beaumont Area NSAI Workshop, ✆ 409-751-3929
Dallas SW Assn, ✆ 214-750-0916 or
✎ *www.dallassongwriters.org*
Dallas/Ft Worth NSAI Workshop, ✆ 972-491-1153
Fort Bend Songwriter's Assn, ✎ *www.fbsa.org*
Fort Worth Songwriter's Assn, ✎ *www.fwsa.com*
Houston NSAI Workshop, ✆ 832-722-3753
Houston/Fort Bend SW Assn, ✆ 281-497-5958
Pickton Texas SW Assn, ✆ 903-866-3002

UTAH

Provo NSAI Workshop, ✆ 435-623-0688

VIRGINIA

Charlottesville Area Songwriters Assn,
✎ *www.esinet.net/cabg/a+e/casa.html*
Tysons Corner NSAI Workshop, ✆ 301-428-3498
Hampton NSAI Workshop, ✆ 757-723-6549
Petersburg SW Group, ✆ 804-733-5908
Roanoke NSAI Workshop, ✆ 540-864-7043
Salem Southwest Virginia SW, ✆ 703-389-1525 or
✎ *kirasong@aol.com*

WASHINGTON

Seattle NSAI Workshop, ✆ 253-474-6349
Seattle Pacific NW Songwriters, ✆ 206-824-1568
Songwriter's Association of Washington,
✎ *www.saw.org*
Olympic Peninsula Songwriters Assn (OPSA),
✎ *sousasong@tenforward.com*
Songwriters of the Northwest Guild,
✎ *www.songnw.com*

WISCONSIN

Green Bay NSAI Workshop, ✆ 715-854-2215
Songwriters of Wisconsin,
✎ *http://geocities.com/Nashville/Rodeo/2907/page8.htm*
Hubertus NSAI Workshop, ✆ 262-628-0934

WEST VIRGINIA

Charleston NSAI Workshop, ✆ 304-697-2739

WYOMING

Jackson Hole NSAI Workshop, ✆ 307-734-1281

AUSTRALIA

Songwriters, Composers and Lyricists
Association, Inc. (SCALA),
✎ *www.senet.com.au/~scala/homepage.htm*
Songwriting Association of Australia,
✎ *www.ozemail.com.au/~songsoc*

BERMUDA

Bermuda Songwriters Assn, ✎ *studiob@ibl.bm*

CANADA

Stouffville Ontario NSAI Workshop, ✆ 905-642-3645
Surrey Vancouver NSAI Workshop, ✆ 604-581-8360
Winnipeg NSAI Workshop, ✆ 204-358-2355
Toronto NSAI Workshop, ✆ 905-453-6104
Thunder Bay NSAI Workshop, ✆ 807-622-2526
Songwriters Association of Nova Scotia,
✎ *www.sans.ns.ca*
Songwriters' Association of Canada,
✎ *www.songwriters.ca*

Sheffield NSAI Workshop, ✆ 01144-1142452705
British Academy of Composers and Songwriters,
    ✍ *www.britishacademy.com/splash.htm*

Edinburgh Songwriters Showcase,
    ✍ *www.met.ed.ac.uk/~mwm/song*

Auckland NSAI Workshop, ✆ 011-64-7-849-4365
Songwriters Association,
    ✍ *www.musicnz.co.nz/sanzsa.html*

Seminars and Workshops

The Tunesmith Songwriting Seminar

Biannual, four-day seminar with hit writers, publishers, musicians, pluggers, and entertainment attorneys. Features include classes, a song contest, publisher critiques, a showcase, and a guitar pull. Entrants receive two written critiques. For more information, go to ✍ *www.tunesmith.net*.

NSAI Songcamp

A three- to four-day writing intensive program with big time pros like Hugh Prestwood, Angela Kaset, Skip Ewing, and Chuck Cannon in group and one-on-one settings. Visit their Web site at ✍ *www.nashvillesongwriter.com*.

Barbara Cloyd's Songwriting Workshop

Traveling workshop limited to fifteen participants per event, picked by CD submissions, usually two or three really big publishers there to listen and give advice, run by hit writer Barbara Cloyd; three-day event, cost around $180; the publisher time alone is worth it. Barbara Cloyd's Songwriting Workshop, PO Box 121497, Nashville, TN 37212. ✆ 615-383-5616, *www.barbaracloyd.com*.

Berklee Summer Songwriting Workshop

1140 Boylston St., Box 34
Boston, MA 02215
✆ 800-421-0084
✍ *www.berklee.edu*
✍ *summer@berklee.edu*

NashCamp

PO Box 210396
Nashville, TN 37221
✆ 888-798-5012
✍ *http://nashcamp.tripod.com*
✍ *nashcamp@nashcamp.com*

PRO Sponsored Workshops

Your PRO probably sponsors great workshops and seminars, some of which may be free. Contact them to find out more. Also, some PROs have started opening up regional offices in places like Miami and Chicago, find out if there's one near you.

    ASCAP
    ✍ *www.ascap.com*
    Los Angeles ✆ (213) 883-1000
    Nashville ✆ (615) 742-5000
    New York ✆ (212) 621-6000

BMI
✏ *www.bmi.com*
Los Angeles ✆ (310) 659-9109
Nashville ✆ (615) 291-6700
New York ✆ (212) 586-2000

SESAC
✏ *www.sesac.com*
New York ✆ (212) 586-3450
Nashville, ✆ (615) 320-0055

Free Songwriter Web Sites

These days, you can learn a lot from the comfort of your own home. You can get song critiques, meet co-writers, learn song craft, read songwriting e-zines, buy songwriting books, and find all sorts of other stuff on the Internet.

Tunesmith.net

Based in Nashville, Tennessee, Tunesmith.net is a free Web site for aspiring professional songwriters. Members can post MP3s on the free server space provided and get critiques from other members and the site admins. Q&A forums are run by industry professionals and cover topics like recording, vocal technique, and the music biz. Once a month, site admins choose a "featured" for the front page. Several of these writers now have publishing deals and/or cuts. Tunesmith.net has a dedicated chat room on a digichat server and hosts live chat critiques with publishers and profession songwriters. ✏ *www.tunesmith.net*

Muse's Muse

Canadian-based Muse's Muse is a fun site with tons of great articles on songwriting and related matters by industry pros and a critique board for lyrics. The site is well organized and aesthetically pleasing. The atmosphere is less brutal than Tunesmith and the focus is more on exploring creative boundaries than making a living. Get in touch with your muse at ✏ *www.musesmuse.com.*

Just Plain Folks

Just Plain Folks (JPF) is a good place for novices to get their feet wet. JPF has loosely organized chapters in several cities in the United States and Canada and has a traveling rally, where members can get together in person. The critiques here are gentle and encouraging for those new to songwriting. ✏ *www.justplainfolks.org*

Copyright Resources

United States Copyright Office, ✏ *http://lcweb.loc.gov/*

Guide to Music Copyright, ✏ *www.musiclibrary assoc.org/Copyright/faqcomp.htm*

line Magazines

ter (classical and jazz list
s), ✐ *www.amc.net*

American Songwriter Magazine,
✐ *www.americansongwriter.com*

ASCAP PLAYBACK, free e-zine,
✐ *www.ascap.com/playback/newsletter*

Billboard, ✐ *www.billboard.com*

BMI Music World, free e-zine,
✐ *www.bmi.com/musicworld/index.asp*

Christian Songwriters,
✐ *www.christiansongwriting.org*

Echo (e-zine), ✐ *www.humnet.ucla.edu/echo/*

Electronic Musician, ✐ *www.emusician.com*

Film Music Network, ✐ *www.filmmusic.net*

Gig Magazine, ✐ *www.gigmag.com*

Music Books Plus, ✐ *www.musicbooksplus.com*

Music Dish (news online magazine),
✐ *www.musicdish.com*

Music Industry News Network, ✐ *www.mi2n.com*

Music Row magazine, ✐ *www.musicrow.com*

Music Theory Online Magazine,
✐ *http//:smt.ucsb.edu/mto/*

National Academy of Songwriters Songtalk
magazine, ✐ *www.nassong.org*

New Age Voice, ✐ *www.newagevoice.com*

Oasis Salsero! (Latin, Salsa, Afro-Cuban, and
more), ✐ *www.oasissalsero.com*

Performing Songwriter Magazine,
✐ *www.performingsongwriter.com*

Professional Composers of America (film and
TV), ✐ *www.procomposers.org*

Radio and Records,
✐ *www.radioandrecords.com*

Roughstock, ✐ *www.roughstock.com*

Other Music Resources

WriteExpress Online Rhyming Dictionary,
✐ *www.rhymer.com*

Free guitar tablature and links to more,
✐ *www.tabalorium.com*

Ultimate Band List, ✐ *www.ubl.com*

Independent Songwriter,
✐ *www.independentsongwriter.com*

Jason Blume (pro critiques),
✐ *www.jasonblume.com*

Barbara Cloyd (pro critiques),
✐ *www.barbaracloyd.com*

Songcatalog.com, online catalog used by
writer/publishers feedback, legal support,
reasonable rates, and track record.
✐ *www.songcatalog.com*

Songlink, monthly tip sheet, "Genie in a Bottle"
was cut through this resource, also cuts with
Sheena Easton, Diana Ross, Tina Turner,

subscribers include publishers from Acuff to Zomba, $285 for a year. ✍ *www.songlink.com*

Forwarding Services

TAXI, $300 per year membership and $5 per song submission fee: ✍ *www.taxi.com*

TONOS, $11.95 per month or $99.95 per year for pro membership: ✍ *www.tonos.com*

Contests and Competitions

The John Lennon Songwriting Contest, pretty good as contests go, at least one winner (Lisa Carver, 2001) has a deal now. ✍ *www.jlsc.com*

International Songwriting Competition, ✍ *www.songwritingcompetition.com*

The USA songwriting competition, ✍ *www.songwriting.net*

Recommended Reading

Songwriter's Market (published annually by Writers Digest Books)

All You Need to Know about the Music Business (Don Passman; Simon & Schuster, 2000)

The Craft of Lyric Writing (Sheila Davis; Writers Digest Books, 1985)

88 Songwriting Wrongs and How to Right Them (Pete and Pat Luboff; Writers Digest Books, 1994)

Your First Cut (Jerry Vandiver, Gracie Hollombe; 11/22 Publishing, LLC, 2002)

Writing Music for Hit Songs (Jai Josefs; Music Sales Corp., 2000)

The Essential Songwriter's Contract Handbook (NSAI, 1994)

Soul of a Writer (Susan Tucker; Journey Publishing Co., 1996)

Guitar Pull (Phillip Self; Cypress Moon Press, 2002)

Songwriters on Songwriting (Paul Zollo; DeCapo Press, 1997)

Songs in the Rough (Stephen Bishop; St. Martin's Press, 1996)

How to Make Money: Scoring Soundtracks and Jingles (Jeffrey P. Fisher; MixBooks, 1997)

Appendix C

Glossary

Almost any major industry has a set of words and phrases with meanings that are unique to that field. Each different artistic medium also has its own patois. Songwriting, being a combination of industry and art form, has enough terms for its own dictionary. Until that book comes out, here's an abbreviated list of terms songwriters should know.

A&R: "Artists and Repertoire," department at a record company in charge of signing artists and advising them in matters like choosing a producer and songs.

administration deal: Arrangement whereby one of the parties involved in joint ownership of a copyright agrees to collect, distribute, and account for the monies generated by publishing income for that copyright.

alliteration: Literary device wherein two or more words in a line or couplet start with the same sound.

ASCAP: American Society of Composers, Authors, and Publishers; see **PRO.**

assonant rhyme: A rhyme of final vowels followed by nonrhyming consonants.

Berne Convention: An international treaty, signed by the United States and most of Europe, covering copyright and intellectual property laws.

black box money: Unclaimed money collected by performance rights organizations.

blanket license: A license by which a music user may use all of the compositions represented by a particular entity (usually a PRO).

BMI: Broadcast Music Incorporated; see **PRO.**

build: See **lift.**

catalog: A songwriter's or publisher's collection of copyright holdings.

catalog building: Unscrupulous business practice in which a publisher obtains copyrights, then does not demo or pitch the songs.

channel: See **lift.**

co-pub (co-publishing): Two or more parties sharing publishing rights on a song.

co-write: To write a song with another songwriter; a song written by multiple persons.

compulsory license: A license to record a copyrighted work that has already been commercially recorded, automatically granted at statutory mechanical rate.

controlled composition clause: The clause in a contract stating that you agree to the record company breaking the federal statutory mechanical royalty rate law and paying you less than what they owe you.

copyright: Set of exclusive, assignable rights of the creator of an artistic work.

creative director: Decision-maker for creative matters at a publishing company, in charge of the writing staff and personal managers.

cross-collateralization: A situation where recoupment from draw or advances may come from an income source not directly related to the debt.

cut: To commercially record a song; a commercially recorded song.

DART (digital audio recorders and tapes) Bill: A law imposing a tax on digital recorders and recording media meant to partially compensate record companies, artists, publishers, and songwriters for revenues lost due to digital copying.

demo: A demonstration recording of a song, designed to clearly communicate the song for the purpose of securing a commercially released recording.

depth cut: A song not intended to be a single but rather one put on an album for purely artistic purposes, to give the album relevance, depth, or balance.

donut: Also known as a "wraparound," it's when a song's first line is also the song's last line.

draw: Monies regularly advanced by a publisher to a songwriter against future mechanical royalties, print royalties, and licensing fees.

engineer: Person who operates the recording equipment in a studio or live setting.

fair use: Uses of copyrighted material allowable without permission or license.

gherm: Soliciting favors from or attempting to befriend important people for reasons of personal advancement; a phony, a sycophant, an undesirable.

hook: The main or key line of the song, usually the title.

hook reinforcement: The craft device of making parts of the song feed into, accentuate, point to, or otherwise reinforce the hook or central statement of a song.

hub: A city with a major music industry presence.

infringement: Violation of a copyright or intellectual property law.

internal rhyme: A rhyme that occurs within a line, rather than at the end.

lift: Also known as ramp, build, pre-chorus, and channel, a lift is a short (usually two lines) section that acts as a dynamic liaison between sections.

loop: A long sample that repeats to establish a groove.

mechanical royalty: Monies collected for use of copyrighted material that are pursuant to the actual sales of mechanical reproductions (recordings) of the work.

melodic hook: Catchy, short, repeated vocal or instrumental melodic figure.

MIDI (Musical Instrument Digital Interface): A cable-based system that allows electronic instruments and computers to share musical information.

minus one: Mix of a song with the lead vocal removed.

modulate: To change keys during the course of a song.

music hub: See **hub.**

Nashville Number system: The system by which songwriters and studio musicians communicate musical ideas and make charts for recording.

near rhyme: A rhyme that is not perfect but is close enough to please the ear.

NSAI: Nashville Songwriter's Association International.

Performance Rights Organization: See **PRO.**

performance royalty: Fee for use of copyrights in live or recorded performances.

personal manager: Person at a publishing company whose job it is to guide the careers and output of songwriters.

pitch: To actively market a song to a publisher, producer, artist, or other outlet for the purpose of getting the song commercially recorded and released.

pitch to own: See **spec pitch.**

plugger: Also known as pitcher or pitch man, a plugger is a person who pitches songs professionally.

PRO: Performance rights organization, a company that collects performance royalties from copyright users and distributes them to songwriters and publishers.

producer: Decision-maker regarding the production (arrangement, instrumentation, recording, mixing, and sometimes song selection) of a project.

prosody: State wherein the musical component of a work is complementary to the lyrical component on a representational level.

ramp: See **lift.**

recoup: To collect money owed from advances by the withholding of income.

reversion clause: A contractual point setting terms and conditions for the return of a copyright to the original owner.

right of first recording: An exclusive right of the copyright holder to grant or withhold permission for the first commercial recording of a work.

rhyme palette: Collection of rhymes for a word or words to be used in a song.

rhyme scheme: The arrangement of rhymes within a section of a song.

round: Performance setting in which three to five writers take turns playing.

royalty: Fee paid for use of a copyrighted work.

screener: First person in the "listening chain" at a publishing company who checks incoming songs for length, listenability, genre appropriateness, and other basic qualities before throwing them away or passing them on to the next level.

SESAC: The Society of European Stage Authors and Composers. See **PRO.**

shark: An unscrupulous person in the music business, especially one who charges fees that are inflated and/or in conflict of interest.

single: Song released and endorsed to radio stations to promote sales.

single-song contract: A contract assigning copyright, or options on the copyright, for an individual song.

spec pitch: A pitch agreement, usually without written contract, whereby a party's ownership of all or part of a copyright is contingent upon getting a cut.

staff deal: Contract by which a publisher retains a songwriter exclusively.

staff writer: A songwriter working exclusively for one publisher.

standard contract: An imaginary creature that exists in the minds of the gullible—there is no such thing as a standard contract.

statutory rate: The minimum sales royalty set by federal law, which record companies routinely ignore.

sub-pub (sub-publisher): A publisher who represents the interests of a copyright holder in a foreign country, collecting royalties for a percentage.

synch rights: Rights involving the use of songs in television or movies.

synch license: License a TV station or movie studio must obtain from the copyright owner before using a copyrighted work.

tempo: Speed of a song, usually expressed in beats per minute.

tessitura: Where, within the melodic range of a song or section of a song, the melody generally resides.

turnaround: A short thematic reprise often used to end a section of a song.

vocal up: Mix of a song with the lead vocal raised in volume.

word palette: A list of complementary words for a subject, idea, hook, or title.

work for hire: A phrase meaning that a work was created solely for a predetermined payment and that the creator relinquishes all rights to the work, including the right to be credited with its creation.

writer's rep: PRO representative who advises member writers.

Index